Philosophy of Education in the Era of Globalization

Routledge International Studies in the Philosophy of Education

1. Education and Work in Great Britain, Germany and Italy
Edited by A. Jobert, C. Marry,
L. Tanguy and H. Rainbird

2. Education, Autonomy and Democratic Citizenship
Philosophy in a Changing World
Edited by David Bridges

3. The Philosophy of Human Learning
Christopher Winch

4. Education, Knowledge and Truth
Beyond the Postmodern Impasse
Edited by David Carr

5. Virtue Ethics and Moral Education
Edited by David Carr and Jan Steutel

6. Durkheim and Modern Education
Edited by Geoffrey Walford and
W. S. F. Pickering

7. The Aims of Education
Edited by Roger Marples

8. Education in Morality
J. Mark Halstead and
Terence H. McLaughlin

9. Lyotard: Just Education
Edited by Pradeep A Dhillon and
Paul Standish

10. Derrida & Education
Edited by Gert J. J. Biesta and
Denise Egéa-Kuehne

11. Education, Work and Social Capital
Towards a New Conception of
Vocational Education
Christopher Winch

12. Philosophical Discussion in Moral Education
The Community of Ethical Inquiry
Tim Sprod

13. Methods in the Philosophy of Education
Frieda Heyting, Dieter Lenzen and
John White

14. Life, Work and Learning
Practice in Postmoderniity
David Beckett and Paul Hager

15. Education, Autonomy and Critical Thinking
Christopher Winch

16. Anarchism and Education
A Philosophical Perspective
Judith Suissa

17. Cultural Diversity, Liberal Pluralism and Schools
Isaiah Berlin and Education
Neil Burtonwood

18. Levinas and Education
At the Intersection of Faith and Reason
Edited by Denise Egéa-Kuehne

**19. Moral Responsibility,
Authenticity, and Education**
Ishtiyaque Haji and Stefaan E. Cuypers

20. Education, Science and Truth
Rasoul Nejadmehr

**21. Philosophy of Education in the
Era of Globalization**
Edited by Yvonne Raley and
Gerhard Preyer

Philosophy of Education in the Era of Globalization

Edited by Yvonne Raley
and Gerhard Preyer

Routledge
Taylor & Francis Group
New York   London

KH

First published 2010
by Routledge
270 Madison Ave, New York, NY 10016

Simultaneously published in the UK
by Routledge
2 Park Square, Milton Park, Abingdon, Oxon OX14 4RN

Routledge is an imprint of the Taylor & Francis Group, an informa business

Library of Congress Cataloging-in-Publication Data
Philosophy of education in the era of globalization / edited by Yvonne Raley and
   Gerhard Preyer.
      p. cm. — (Routledge international studies in the philosophy of education)
   Includes bibliographical references and index.
   1. Education—Philosophy.   2. Education and globalization.   I. Raley, Yvonne.
II. Preyer, Gerhard.
   LB14.7.P545 2009
   370.1—dc22
   2009009743

ISBN10: 0-415-99606-6 (hbk)
ISBN10: 0-203-87111-1 (ebk)

ISBN13: 978-0-415-99606-8 (hbk)
ISBN13: 978-0-203-87111-9 (ebk)

12/1/10

Contents

Introduction   1

PART I
Education in a Globalized Society

1   How Should We Educate Students Whose Cultures
    Frown upon Rational Disputation? Cultural Difference and
    the Role of Reason in Multicultural Democratic Education   7
    HARVEY SIEGEL

2   Can Liberals Take Their Own Side in an Argument?   15
    ROBERT TALISSE

3   Literacy and Citizenship: Tradition, Reason, and Critique in
    Democratic Education   30
    HANAN ALEXANDER

4   After All, How Small is the World? Global Citizenship as an
    Educational Ideal   51
    DORET DE RUYTER

5   Education for Global Citizenship and Survival   67
    RANDALL CURREN

PART II
New Pedagogical Approaches

6   Why They Hate Us: A Pedagogical Proposal   91
    IRFAN KHAWAJA

7   Global Aspirations for Gender Equality in Education:
    What Kind of Pedagogy?   110
    ELAINE UNTERHALTER AND AMY NORTH

8   'Let Us Now Praise . . .': Rethinking Role Models and Heroes in
    an Egalitarian Age   129
    MEIRA LEVINSON

PART III
Moral and Religious Education

9   Privilege, Well-being, and Participation in Higher Education   165
    HARRY BRIGHOUSE AND PAULA MCAVOY

10 In Defense of Multiculturalism   181
    MARK HALSTEAD

11 Children's Autonomy and Symbolic Clothing in Schools:
    Help or Hindrance?   198
    DIANNE GERELUK

12 Global Religious Education   212
    PETER SIMPSON

Contributors   227
Author Index   231
Subject Index   237

Introduction

One of us recently had the following experience. She had written a short case study on the suffering of women in some parts of the Islamic world. The case study was intended as a discussion basis for the topic of gender equality in a forthcoming ethics text. During the review process, one reviewer recommended—with an obvious air of sarcasm—that the author turn the case into a marketing campaign for the book. The reviewer suggested that the author condemn the Prophet Mohammed so that radical Muslims could condemn us to death in turn. The ethics text would make headline news, the reviewer went on to say. The author, he thought, had a good chance of getting herself killed, but the publisher would make a nice profit.

While this may have been intended to be amusing, the aim of these comments was to show clearly that the issues this case study was bringing up could be considered too politically sensitive for the classroom. What is more, the reviewer's comments prompted the editor to consider removing the case from the book. After some discussion about academic freedom and the value of a liberal education, the case stayed in the text. But a lesson was learned: Something has changed. The classroom is no longer as insulated from politics as it once was. It is no longer a place where sensitive issues can be discussed without concerns about repercussions. The makeup of the students is also different from what it has been in previous decades, and educators find themselves facing an unprecedented variety of educational, ethnic, and religious backgrounds in their students. Last, today's students are facing an entirely new set of problems compared to the world of as little as ten years ago.

These changes cannot be ignored. Indeed, as educators we would not be doing well by our students if we did ignore them. Terrorism, ethnocentrism, religious tension, competition over limited resources, and war are just a few of the issues that educators must find ways to engage in with their students. But we must also consider *how* the issues are best addressed. After all, higher education is supposed to help students prepare for citizenship in this new and much more globalized world.

As educators, we must ask ourselves some fundamental questions: What is an ideal global citizen, and how should global citizenry be fostered? What kind of skills and abilities are needed in democratic decision making? How do we deal with cultures in which democratic decision making and argumentation are not considered to be important values? How should education address the problems of cultural clashes that globalization brings with it? By and large, Western societies endorse rational discourse, as well as religious and value pluralism. Against that background, how can educators even begin to explain terrorism and religious fundamentalism to their students? And how do we instill religious tolerance in a time when fundamentalism has become inextricably tied with terrorism? To what degree should religious tolerance be promoted in the first place? Furthermore, how do we promote economic growth in the face of overpopulation and its depletion of resources? How should we address the gender inequalities that still exist in the world? And last but not least: Do institutions of higher learning have an obligation to improve their students' character, so that they might feel obligated to promote change? Should education, in other words, be value neutral or value laden?

This volume of new essays in the philosophy of education tries to grapple with the questions just raised. The book has been divided into three parts. Part I: Education in a Globalized Society contains several introductory essays that address fundamental questions. Harvey Siegel, in his essay "How Should We Educate Students Whose Cultures Frown upon Rational Disputation? Cultural Difference and the Role of Reason in Multicultural Democratic Education," suggests that the skill of rational argumentation is crucial to full participation in democratic decision making. While some cultures may reject the democratic ideal of reasoned discourse, Siegel argues that this ideal takes precedence—at least in societies that aspire to having a democratic system in the first place.

Robert Talisse's essay "Can Liberals Take their own Side in an Argument?" addresses a tension within liberal democracy itself: that because of the value pluralism that liberalism is built on, it cannot find a rational basis for one of the very principles that is fundamental to it, the principle of toleration. In this era of globalization, and the culture clashes it has brought with it, this problem has become even more pressing. As Talisse puts it, "there are no argumentative resources available to the liberal when making a principled case for core liberal values." Talisse then tries to find a way to allay these tensions, both in education and in society in general.

Hanan Alexander's essay "Literacy and Citizenship: Tradition, Reason, and Critique in Democratic Education" concerns itself with a dilemma involved in the idea of democratic literacy: Because democratic literacy entails 'initiation' into particular modes of expression, it can end up excluding particular groups—groups that express themselves differently—from what the author calls 'the language of political power.' Alexander's essay promotes one particular account of democratic literacy that he views as resolving this dilemma.

Doret de Ruyter, in "After All, How Small is the World? Global Citizenship as an Educational Ideal," sets out to develop and defend a particular conception of global citizenship. In her view, a world citizen has the moral and political duty to respect the rights of others to live their lives as they see fit. Second, a world citizen should be committed to promoting human flourishing. Randall Curren is also concerned with what kind of global citizenship education should foster. His essay "Education for Global Citizenship and Survival" starts with the important assumption that our current ways of life—especially in Western society—are actually materially unsustainable. Therefore, for Curren, any conception of global citizenship, and consequently the education that prepares for it, must take into account the challenges of sustainability and survivability in light of resource depletion, overpopulation, and climate change.

Part II: New Pedagogical Approaches offers a variety of pedagogical suggestions that attempt to respond to the changed circumstances of the last decade. Irfan Khawaja, in his essay "Why They Hate Us: A Pedagogical Proposal," advocates that the explanation of terrorism needs to be explicitly taught on the undergraduate level. While Khawaja thinks that adequately doing so would require students to develop an understanding of the complexities of philosophical action theory, he nevertheless considers the explanation of terrorism to be something any undergraduate student must confront during his or her studies. The essay by Elaine Unterhalter and Amy North, "Global Aspirations for Gender Equality in Education: What Kind of Pedagogy?" evaluates the efficacy of three different approaches to pedagogy that the Millenium Goals for global gender equality and education entail. Last, Meira Levinson's essay, "'Let Us Now Praise . . .': Rethinking Role Models and Heroes in an Egalitarian Age," examines the educational value of role models in contemporary democracies. In her view, a more thoughtful approach to the use of heroes and role models in education is as a desirable tool for both self-improvement and civic engagement.

Finally, Part III: Moral and Religious Education deals with the controversy over whether, and to what degree, education for global citizenry should have a moral and religious dimension. The opening essay, "Privilege, Well-being, and Participation in Higher Education," by Harry Brighouse and Paula McAvoy, takes the stance that higher education ought not merely improve students' job opportunities and earning potential. It should also contribute to turning them into well-rounded individuals, individuals capable of being responsible citizens. The advantages they receive as a result of their education, Brighouse and McAvoy argue, bring with them the obligation to use this education not only for personal benefit, but also for the benefit of others.

Mark Halstead, in "In Defense of Multiculturalism," distinguishes three different degrees of multiculturalism, ranging from a full acceptance of cultural difference to a very minimal multiculturalism, which makes only minimal allowances for cultural difference. Halstead advocates a stronger form of multiculturalism and then explores its implications for education: To what degree, he asks, should education promote the values that a stronger multiculturalism brings with it?

In "Children's Autonomy and Symbolic Clothing in Schools: Help or Hindrance?" by Dianne Gereluk, the degree to which multiculturalism should be respected in schools is concretized. In particular, Gereluk focuses on the question of whether or not symbolic clothing should be banned in schools. Using Rawls' theory of justice, she argues that banning symbolic clothing is contrary to the liberal aims of education. In the final essay of this volume, "Global Religious Education," Peter Simpson argues that the moral teachings he thinks all religions have to offer ought to be part of education everywhere. As Simpson sees it, this would increase virtue and promote happiness.

The collected essays show that educators have to continuously reflect on the way globalization affects the classroom situation and make changes on a continuous basis.[1]

This book was planned together with the journal and research project *Protosociology*. We wish to express our thanks to our authors for their contributions. We also thank our Routledge editor Benjamin Holtzman for his continuous encouragement.

Yvonne Raley, Felician College, Lodi, USA
Gerhard Preyer, Goethe-University Frankfurt am Main, Frankfurt a. M., Germany

NOTES

1. On contemporary researches about globalization see G. Preyer, M. Bös, eds., *Borderlines in a Globalized Word: New Perspectives in a Sociology of the Word-System*, Social Indicators Research Series Vol. 9 (Kluwer Academic Publishers: Dordrecht, 2002). On consensus and controversies about globalization see J. Nederveen Pieterse, *Globalization and Culture: Global Mélange* (Rowman and Littlefield: Lanham, 2004), 7–21. On the dimensions of globalization see G. Preyer, *Soziologische Theorie der Gegenwartsgesellschaft: Mitgliedschaftstheoretische Untersuchungen* (VS Verlag Sozialwissenschaften: Wiesbaden, 2006), 181–215; *Soziologische Theorie der Gegenwartsgesellschaft III: Mitgliedschaft und Evolution* (VS Verlag Sozialwissenschaften: Wiesbaden, 2008), V 1–3. Further publications of the globalization-project of Protosociology, see www.protosociology.de.

Part I
Education in a Globalized Society

1 How Should We Educate Students Whose Cultures Frown upon Rational Disputation?
Cultural Difference and the Role of Reason in Multicultural Democratic Education

Harvey Siegel

DEMOCRATIC PUBLIC EDUCATION AND CULTURAL DIFFERENCE: THE PROBLEM

How should public education in democratic states deal with cultural differences among citizens?

This question gains point and practical relevance from the increasingly diverse cultural constituencies that collectively constitute the citizenry of contemporary democratic states. However, to shed light on it, it is helpful to step back and consider the question first without reference to culture. So: What should public education in democratic states be like (irrespective of the cultural make-up of its citizens)? At what should it aim?

One common answer, which I endorse, is that it should aim at fostering in students the skills and abilities, attitudes and dispositions needed to fully and successfully participate in democratic decision-making and, more generally, in democratic life. This may not be the only aim of public education in democratic states, but it is clearly a central one. Fostering these skills, abilities, attitudes and dispositions amounts to helping students become critical thinkers; that is, helping them to become rational or reasonable persons. Public education in democratic states should aim, that is, at the cultivation of reason in its students (Siegel 1988, 1997, 2003; Bailin and Siegel 2003).[1]

Why should this be thought of as a central aim of public education in democratic states? There are two sets of reasons, the first having to do with education per se, and the second with the nature of democracy. First: Education must, for moral reasons, treat students in ways that treat them with respect as persons and that further their own interests (as opposed to those of the school or the state, where the latter might conflict with the former). The Kantian principle of respect for persons is one that has relevance far beyond the bounds of education, but is as applicable there, governing the treatment of students, as it is everywhere else. Moreover, education has to

prepare students for adulthood, where this is conceived not as preparation for a predetermined slot in the preexisting social/economic matrix—
that slot being determined by the state—but rather as enabling students to
determine for themselves, to the greatest extent possible, the character of
their lives and their place in the social order in which they find themselves.
Further, education must endeavor to provide students with a suitable introduction to, and understanding of, the many intellectual traditions developed during the long course of human history. In all these, the 'cultivation
of reason'—or, less prosaically, the fostering of rationality, reasonableness,
and the abilities and dispositions of critical thinking—is central (Siegel
1988, chap. 3; Siegel 2003).

The second set of reasons for thinking that public education in democratic states should aim at fostering rationality, or critical thinking abilities
and dispositions, in its students relates directly to the nature of democracy
itself. It is a commonplace that democracy requires an educated citizenry.
But what sort of 'educated citizenry' is required? What is needed, I sub-
mit, is a *critical* citizenry: that is, citizens who are able to and disposed to
settle matters of public policy and concern by appeal to relevant reasons.
For democratic states to flourish, their citizens must be able to conceive,
consider, and properly evaluate reasons for and against alternative policies and practices concerning the many varied matters that require public
deliberation and decision. Citizens must be able to imaginatively construct
arguments, and to assess their own arguments and those of others in accordance with the epistemic principles governing the assessment of reasons
and arguments, in order to wisely determine the course of social policies
and institutions. Without a critical citizenry, the state itself is threatened.

Worse, in my view, than the situation of a democratic state peopled by
an uncritical citizenry is the situation of the uncritical citizen herself in a
democratic state. Such a citizen has no adequate way to contribute to public
discussion, to voice her concerns, to protect her own and her community's
interests, or to work for constructive political change. She is marginalized,
left on the outside, unable to participate meaningfully in democratic life.
Her lack of critical abilities and dispositions renders her unable to enjoy the
fruits of that life. Insofar as we value democracy and think it a good thing
that states are democratic, we must deplore both an uncritical citizenry in
such states in general, and the fate of the marginalized uncritical citizen
in them in particular. In valuing democracy, we recognize the crucially
important place of the critical citizen in democratic states, and the central-
ity of democratic public education's task of cultivating the reason of its
students.[2]

With this view of democracy and the place of reason in it established,
we are in position to pursue our initial question. How, then, should public
education in democratic states be conceived, in light of significant cultural
differences among citizens? It is worth noting that the question is not of
merely theoretical interest. Virtually all so-called 'First World' democratic

states have large and growing numbers of immigrants, from a range of cultural groups. Around the globe, and perhaps especially in contemporary North America and Western Europe, the question is of pressing political moment. While the practical relevance of the matter is clear, in what follows I abstract away from such practical considerations and offer an answer to the question that depends rather on particular aspects of cultural difference and the demands of democratic education themselves.

THE SOLUTION?

A quick answer is: Cultural difference doesn't matter. The conception of democratic public education rehearsed above, as involving the fostering of the abilities and dispositions of reason/critical thinking, is the correct one for democratic states, whether or not citizens in those states are members of different cultures. In fact, it might be plausibly argued that the more culturally diverse citizens are, the more important it is that they be able to engage in rational, democratic decision-making. If cultural differences cannot be managed rationally and democratically, those differences might well render impossible peaceful and just social existence. (The recent and current state of various cultural conflicts around the globe seems to provide some evidence for this claim: where democratic institutions are in place and functioning, there appears to be at least a chance of peaceful and just resolution of conflict; where not, not.)

While this 'quick' answer is plausible, it obviously does not resolve the most fundamental form of the problem because it does not acknowledge two different sorts of cultural conflict. First, there can be conflict between cultures, both (or all) of which—despite their conflict—embrace democratic ideals, principles, and a commitment to endeavor to resolve their conflict through participation in reasoned discourse and in democratic institutions and procedures. The quick answer might well suffice for this sort of cultural conflict.

But a second, more difficult sort of cultural conflict involves cultures, some (or all) of which reject democratic ideals, principles, and practices, including those involving reasoned argumentation. In such a circumstance, it is difficult to see how the quick answer can succeed. For how can such conflicts be resolved when (at least some of) the parties to the conflict explicitly reject the value or worth of the sort of argumentation and reasoned deliberation required for democratic decision-making?[3]

This problem can seem particularly pressing in situations in which large numbers of recent immigrants originate in nondemocratic states and so have no experience of, and/or lack cultural respect for, the reasoned deliberation characteristic of democratic decision-making at its best. There are, of course, many different sorts of nondemocratic states and/or cultures. A short list would include those characterized by forms of patriarchy in which women are denied access to the existing education system and are systematically excluded from participation in public life; overtly racist ones in which certain groups are systematically excluded from meaningful participation in political life on the basis of race; those in which policy is determined not by citizens or their elected representatives, but by nondemocratically selected monarchs or oligarchs; and those governed by religious leaders according to religious precept. There are also those that are democratic but are nevertheless characterized by an antipathy toward the rough-and-tumble of open democratic deliberation and debate. As Alvin Goldman rather circumspectly puts the point:

> In almost every culture, and especially in certain cultures, there are norms that deter critical argumentation. It is widely said that in Japanese and other Asian cultures people are encouraged to conduct their discourse so as to preserve harmony. The expression of conflict, including verbally explicit disagreement, is said to be discouraged . . . [S]tudies definitely reveal contrasts between different cultures in their toleration of critical discourse. (Goldman 1999, 147)

In such cases, the quick answer won't do. Or will it? There are actually two distinct possibilities here.

In the first possible scenario, members of cultures that reject the value or worth of reasoned deliberation in the context of democratic decision-making simply reject democratic values as incompatible with their culture or way of life. Here, democracy itself is rejected. In this case, the political/educational task is to persuade them—rationally, of course—of the value of democratic institutions and practices in the actual multicultural social context in which they find themselves. We may well fail in this task. If we cannot succeed, our question appears to be irresolvable: Public education for democratic citizenship is itself, in such circumstances, impossible. Such citizens do not actually want to live in a democratic state.[4]

Alternatively, they might recognize the conflict between democratic values and institutions and their own undemocratic cultural values, but nevertheless value living in a democratic state. In such a case there seems to be no alternative to the compromising of their cultural values—i.e., their rejection of reasoned deliberation, etc.—insofar as such compromise is necessary for democracy to flourish or, less ambitiously, for them to participate in their state's democratic life.

So: When democratic and non- or antidemocratic cultural values conflict, it is essential (a) to respect and allow cultural difference to flourish as much as possible, because this sort of respect is morally required (Siegel 1997, 1999). But it is also necessary that (b) in such cases of conflict, *democracy trumps cultural difference*. That is, when members of anti- or nondemocratic cultures become citizens of democratic states, the requirements of democratic participation must take precedence over their non-democratic cultural values. When cultural values and attitudes and the requirements of democratic education conflict, the latter must prevail. Why must the requirements of democratic participation, and education for it, take precedence over conflicting nondemocratic cultural values? Because if it does not, educating for democratic citizenship—and so, the commitment to democracy itself—is abandoned.

BEGGING THE QUESTION?

But doesn't the argument just given beg the question against those who value their culture more highly than they do democratic citizenship? This is an important objection; I conclude by responding to it.

First, no question has been begged. The argument merely points out that its conclusion—'democracy trumps non- or antidemocratic cultural values'—is required in cases of such conflict for education of a democratic citizenship to be possible. Rejecting the conclusion in such cases amounts to rejecting that sort of education, and so democracy itself. But since the question being addressed is that of the character of precisely that sort of education—i.e., education for democratic citizenship in democratic states in multicultural contexts—such rejection seems clearly enough to amount to throwing the baby out with the bath water.

Second, the problem at hand is that of understanding how to maximize respect for and toleration of cultural difference, while at the same time educating new citizens for full participation in democratic life. A citizen who is unwilling to so participate not only in effect rejects democracy. She also marginalizes herself, by rendering herself unable to fully participate in the life of the democratic state in which she finds herself. This inability must be discouraged by education for democratic citizenship, since any such education aims at preparation for precisely such participation. But the benefit of such education comes at a price, for it inevitably encourages the 'relaxing' of her relationship to her original culture. This price might be judged by many to be too high a price to pay, although so judging amounts, as we have seen, to valuing that relationship more highly than democracy itself.

Moreover, such 'relaxing' is not necessarily a bad thing, because cultures—in the contemporary world, at any rate—are not monolithic, but rather are fluid and changing. As Seyla Benhabib (2002, ix, 4, 24–6, and *passim*) has characterized them—compellingly, in my view—cultures are best conceived not as monolithic and static, but rather as hybrid, multi-faceted, fluid, porous, polyvocal, interdependent, and mutually influential. Relatedly, Pradeep Dhillon and J. Mark Halstead have effectively criticized "the assumption that cultures are hermetically sealed" (2003, 157). If this is correct—that is, if cultures are indeed fluid and changing rather than monolithic—then even members of cultures who are most concerned to cling to those cultures have no alternative to negotiating such changes and the 'outside' influences that bring about those changes. Closing off oneself and one's culture from the rest of the world is simply not a realistic option. If so, the kind of education called for above seems suitable even for such members. Preserving a citizen's relationship to her culture, whatever state that culture happens to be in at the time in question, and conceiving of that state as fixed, is thus both to erroneously conceive of that culture as fixed and static, and is moreover obviously not a good thing from the point of view of education. Enabling her to be open to positive cultural change, or even to judge stasis to be preferable to such change on the basis of relevant reasons and evidence, requires just the sort of education being called for.

In any case—and this is perhaps the most important point of all—democracy is a substantive matter with substantive values. There is no reason to think that all cultures—especially those with antidemocratic values—can thrive in a democratic state. Opting for democracy amounts to opting for its substantive values—including those animating its education—thus opting against incompatible cultural values. If, for example, a person values decision by religious leader or military dictator rather than decision by democratic institution, or if she disvalues reasoning, deliberation, argumentation, public discussion, defense and critique of proposed policies and practices—for example, as disrespectful or disharmonious—she has yet to fully embrace democracy and its substantive values.[5]

If the foregoing considerations are correct, our problem is solved. Democracy requires democratic public education; such education must take precedence over respect for cultural traditions that reject it. It is, of course, crucially important to respect cultural differences. But when non- or antidemocratic cultural traditions conflict with democratic public education, the latter must prevail. If it does not, democracy itself is given up. If it is not to be given up, then in actual cases of such conflict, culture must yield to its demands—including, especially, those of its public education.[6]

ACKNOWLEDGMENTS

An ancestor of this chapter was presented in November 2001 at the conference on "Citizenship Education, Political Theory, and Their Reflection in Language" in Bled, Slovenia, and also appeared in *The School Field* 13, no. 6 (2002): 33–39. I am indebted to the conference participants for their helpful comments and criticisms, and to Michael Slote and Jennifer Uleman for excellent suggestions on an earlier draft. The current version also borrows a bit from Siegel (2007).

NOTES

1. By 'reason' I do not mean to refer to the cultivation of some metaphysically mysterious entity. Rather, as articulated in the works just cited, I mean to refer simply to the abilities and dispositions involved in constructing, evaluating,

and being appropriately guided by reasons (on this point see Scheffler 1989, 3). It is obvious that this is an individualist, 'Enlightenment' value/commitment; I defend this orientation in the works just cited.

2. It might be further suggested that in some circumstances the appropriate course is to relax our commitment to democracy in the name of tolerance and respect. However, such a course fails to respect, for it leaves such citizens marginalized in the ways just characterized. Thanks here to conversation with Michael Slote.

3. Here make the idealizing assumption that cultures can be monolithically anti-reason in order to sharply focus the problem being discussed. In fact, I doubt that there are any such cultures. As with individuals, being pro- or anti-reason (like being reasonable or unreasonable) is best seen as a matter of degree, and particular cultures are best seen as occupying some particular interval along that continuum. Thanks here to conversation with Jennifer Uleman.

4. Public education for democratic citizenship could of course be imposed on such citizens. But this would clearly enough be contrary to the obligation to respect such cultures and their members, and contrary to the spirit of democratic citizenship as well. Thanks here to Michael Slote.

5. It is important to note that multicultural concerns may well, and rightly, impact the ways in which we put democratic ideals into practice. For example, in cases where disenfranchised and/or marginalized citizens are relatively unable or unwilling to advocate for themselves in public forums, such forums may well have to be redesigned in order to allow such citizens to participate fully, fairly, and effectively. Thanks here to Jennifer Uleman.

6. My discussion is obviously a 'bare bones' one, without either real-world examples, exploration of related issues (e.g., how democratic principles are best put into practice in culturally diverse democracies), or references to relevant philosophical discussion. My intention has been to avoid these, in order to more clearly focus the basic issue. A more thorough, adequate discussion would need to include them all, and in particular, references to and consideration of the important work on these matters of Amy Gutmann, Will Kymlicka, Iris Marion Young, and many other contemporary authors, as well as the agenda-setting work of John Dewey and other major historical figures.

BIBLIOGRAPHY

Bailin, S. and H. Siegel. "Critical Thinking." In *The Blackwell Guide to the Philosophy of Education*, eds. N. Blake, P. Smeyers, R. Smith, and P. Standish, 181–193. Oxford: Blackwell Publishing, 2003.

Benhabib, S. *The Claims of Culture: Equality and Diversity in the Global Era.* Princeton, NJ: Princeton University Press, 2002.

Dhillon, P. A., and J. M. Halstead. "Multicultural Education." In *The Blackwell Guide to the Philosophy of Education*, eds. N. Blake, P. Smeyers, R. Smith, and P. Standish, 146–161. Oxford: Blackwell Publishing, 2003.

Goldman, A. I. *Knowledge in a Social World.* Oxford: Oxford University Press, 1999.

Scheffler, I. *Reason and Teaching.* Indianapolis: Hackett Publishing, 1989. First published 1973 by Routledge & Kegan Paul.

Siegel, H. *Educating Reason: Rationality, Critical Thinking, and Education.* London: Routledge, 1988.

———. *Rationality Redeemed? Further Dialogues on an Educational Ideal.* New York: Routledge, 1997.

————. "Multiculturalism and the Possibility of Transcultural Educational and Philosophical Ideals." *Philosophy*, no. 74 (1999): 387–409.

————. "Cultivating Reason." In *A Companion to the Philosophy of Education*, ed. R. Curren, 305–317. Oxford: Blackwell Publishing, 2003.

————. "Multiculturalism and Rationality." *Theory and Research in Education 5*, no. 2 (2007): 203–223.

2　Can Liberals Take Their Own Side in an Argument?

Robert Talisse

Liberal democracy is the dominant framework for politics in the modern world, both in theory and in practice. Yet charges that liberal democracy is in crisis, or even decline, are increasingly common. Typically, such charges derive from concerns regarding globalization and the immanent 'clash of civilizations' that globalization brings. At the same time, liberal democracies are rife with political conflict in the form of an ongoing 'culture war' that has divided the US at least into opposed 'red' and 'blue' regions. There is a long story to tell about how the clash of civilizations story and the phenomenon of culture war are intertwined manifestations of the same political tensions arising out of the theoretical features of liberal democracy itself, but I will not attempt this here. Instead, I want to call attention to those tensions and suggest, even if briefly, a way we might allay them. Although the discussion will tend to hover at a high and abstract altitude, a crucial feature of the analysis will turn on an examination of the case of *Mozert v. Hawkins*, which raises the question of the extent to which a liberal society can officially embrace core liberal values and seek to cultivate the same among students in its public schools.

I　THE PROBLEM OF LIBERALISM AND TOLERATION

Robert Frost is often credited with the quip that a liberal is someone who cannot take his own side in an argument. As with many a bon mot, the kernel of insight in his observation is difficult to explain. Here's an attempt: Liberalism is a family of views concerning the nature and limits of political authority. Despite important differences among varieties of liberalism, all are united in the conviction that there is a considerably broad sphere of activity within which individuals are not accountable to anyone other than themselves. In fact, most liberal theories identify this sphere with liberty itself, maintaining that liberty consists in the ability to pursue "our own good in our own way, so long as we do not attempt to deprive others of theirs, or impede their efforts to obtain it" (Mill 1991, 17).

Liberals divide over precisely what should count as an attempt to deprive others of their good and what social conditions, if any, must be in place in order to enable individuals to pursue their own good in their own way. Some liberals (otherwise known as libertarians) contend that taxation is an unbearable obstruction of liberty. Welfarist liberals argue that muscular systems of economic redistribution are required in order to establish and maintain the social institutions necessary for individuals to exercise their liberty. To be sure, debates between various forms of libertarianism and welfarism have dominated the philosophical literature for the past several decades. But ultimately these skirmishes are possible only because of the common ground shared among the contenders, which, stated more broadly now, comes to this: The state—indeed, political association generally—exists solely for the purpose of securing and protecting individual liberty from intrusion by other individuals and other states. Any state that fails at this task, either by adopting more robust ambitions or by proving unable to provide the necessary protections is illegitimate ipso facto and, morally speaking, should be dissolved. This is to say that *power* stands in need of justification, not liberty. Liberty is the *default*.

Consequently, liberalism tends to go hand-in-hand with democracy. Because according to liberalism political power must be justifiable to those over whom it is exercised, the political institutions that wield such power must be accountable to the individuals within its jurisdiction. Democracy, understood as self-government constrained by the demands of individual liberty, ensures this accountability by subjecting government officials and policy to periodical review and revision under conditions of transparency, freedom of information, protected dissent, and so on.

Such is the theoretical core of liberalism. A quick examination of a practical implication of liberalism will help us to unpack Frost's witticism. The liberty to pursue our own good in our own way entails the liberty to adopt, devise, and revise our own *conceptions* of our good. Just as individuals are free to pursue what they judge to be good (within the usual constraints), they are also free to decide for themselves what is most worthy of pursuit, what makes a life good. According to liberalism, it is not the state's job to prescribe or officially endorse any particular vision of the good life, secular or religious. This is not to say that the liberal state must adopt a morally relativist or skeptical view concerning the good life; rather, the liberal state simply does not pronounce on deep moral questions at all, it adopts an official stance of neutrality.

Accordingly, in a liberal society a wide variety of distinct moral doctrines, religious faiths, ethnic traditions, and, in general, 'ways of life' will arise and flourish.[1] As they are *distinct* ways of life, they will often conflict. Such conflicts can manifest in at least two ways: *divergence* and *opposition*. When two ways of life diverge, they prescribe different actions, pursuits, ideals, and dispositions. When two ways of life stand in opposition, each requires a negative estimation, or explicit *rejection*, of the other. For example, the Catholic must evaluate the Protestant as practicing a religion that is not merely different from her own, but is, to some degree at least, *incorrect, incomplete*, or *misguided*. In extreme cases, the one must see the other as not practicing a *religion* at all, but only a deformed and wicked surrogate of religion.[2] The same goes for many of the more familiar non-theological conceptions of the good. Kantians and utilitarians, for example, see one another not only as offering a different and opposed conception of morality, but also often accuse each other of having missed the point of morality altogether.

It is important to note that this state of affairs is endemic to liberalism and not an accident; as John Rawls keenly insisted, the very liberties secured by a liberal political order give rise to a pluralism of ways of life (2005, 36). Hence we see the importance of *toleration* to a liberal society. If liberal democracy is to endure and be stable, citizens must adopt an attitude of toleration toward ways of life that they must regard as unwholesome, seriously in error, and even morally and spiritually dangerous. Of course, citizens of a liberal democracy need not tolerate *every* way of life. Nazis and similar extremists are not tolerated, even though those who wish to "play at" being Nazis are (Macedo 1990, 257).[3] Antiliberal extremists are tolerated only insofar as they operate within liberal constraints; in other words, Nazis are tolerated in the liberal state only if they are willing to be *tolerant* Nazis. *Intolerant* Nazis are not accommodated but opposed and, when necessary, fought.

So the liberal state requires this much of their citizens: They must be tolerant. To be sure, the requisite toleration is *morally thin*. Toleration implies no degree of endorsement or appreciation or approval of that which is tolerated, but only nonobstruction, what Chandran Kukathas calls 'indifference' (1998, 2003). Yet toleration even in this thin construal is a requirement for membership in good standing in a liberal society. Moreover, it does impose constraints on individuals, and, as Macedo notes, in some cases respecting these constraints will not be easy (1990, 257). Hence toleration stands in need of justification.

And here is the rub. The liberal must make a case for toleration that can be accepted by citizens who are otherwise deeply divided, perhaps opposed, at the level of their fundamental moral commitments. In other words, the liberal state must justify toleration in a way that is consistent with its official neutrality on controversial matters of the good. Consequently, the strategy of proposing a *moral* argument for the value of toleration must fail. Any such argument will inevitably employ premises that presuppose or favor a particular moral conception, which some citizens must feel morally obligated to reject. The case for toleration must be acceptable to all citizens, thus a moral argument for toleration is self-undermining.

But what other kind of argument could there be? To propose an argumentum ad baculum ('be tolerant or else!') is to forfeit the very idea that political power stands in need of justification. To appeal to the need for a modus vivendi truce at best provides a thinly prudential and unstable case for toleration, for it proposes toleration as only a strategic device, useful only for as long as one is not powerful enough to dominate one's opponents (Rawls 2005, 147). Hence Frost's claim comes to this: There are no argumentative resources available to the liberal when making a principled case for core liberal values. Is he correct?

II POLITICIZING LIBERALISM

Thus far the discussion has been mostly academic, perhaps some would say anemic. Maybe this is to be expected. Seldom do we confront 'gung ho' Nazis these days. Domestically, groups and individuals who are *extremely* illiberal—that is, intolerant in even the minimal sense we identified above— are relatively rare and, for the most part, effectively contained. Such are the benefits of liberalism. To be sure, matters are different on the global scene. Yet international organizations, such as the United Nations, have accomplished a great deal toward securing lasting peace on liberal terms.

However, if we turn away from the cases involving the extremities of genocide and the hatred of others and toward more modest versions of nonliberal ways of life, we will find more familiar versions of these serious tensions. The combination of pluralism and neutrality provides fertile ground for conflicts between individual liberty (especially liberty of conscience) and political authority. As we have said, liberalism recognizes that the core of individual liberty is the liberty to choose and pursue one's own way of life. But some ways of life include very specific prescriptions not only about how one is to live and how one is to regard those who live differently, but also about how one is to understand the relation between one's deepest moral convictions and one's political and legal obligations. Such cases are common coin in the vast literature on multiculturalism. Sikhs are morally obligated to carry a ceremonial dagger at all times, yet in the United States and elsewhere it is illegal to carry a knife on a plane. Muslim women are morally obligated to cover their heads in public, yet French law prohibits the display of religious symbols, such as headscarves, in certain public contexts, including public schools and courts. Some are religiously obligated to wear a turban, and thus cannot wear the kind of protective helmet that is legally required in some jurisdictions on construction sites and while riding a motorcycle. In these cases, the neutralist stance of the liberal state appears to impose especially heavy burdens on some citizens, who must violate their conscience if they are to engage in normal activities (such as riding a motorcycle) or even participate in crucial activities of citizenship (serving as a juror, attending public school).

A similar kind of difficulty arises at the intersection of liberalism and democracy. The liberal state aspires to neutrality and so must avoid legislating on the basis of principles that presuppose or favor any particular way of life. But the laws and policies of the liberal state are at least in *some* sense the products of the collective will of its citizens, and this collective will is at least in *some* sense the product of the wills of the individuals who comprise the citizenry. Hence the constraints associated with moral neutrality trickle down to individuals in their roles as citizens. This means, for example, that jurors must *not* decide cases on the basis of their sectarian moral convictions, even though many are forced by conscience to regard those very convictions as the foundation of justice itself.[4]

In the more ambitious participatory and deliberative conceptions of democracy that are presently in currency among liberals, this trickle-down effect is even more pronounced, as it affects citizens' behavior as voters. For example, Rawls argues that citizens have a "duty of civility" to appeal to nonsectarian "public" reasons when deciding how to vote and when advocating in public for their preferred option (2005, 217). To be sure, Rawls stipulates that these constraints apply only when "constitutional essentials" and "questions of basic justice" are at stake (ibid., 214). In later work, he clarified the position (some would say that he *revised* it) by adding that citizens may vote and advocate on the basis of sectarian reasons, provided they are willing "in due course" to provide public reasons for their position (ibid., 462).[5] Nonetheless, critics have argued, rather forcefully in some cases, that any norm that seeks to contain citizens' internal and collective deliberations concerning their political behavior within the limitations of public reasons is unfair, anti-democratic, and illiberal.[6]

All of these cases are frighteningly difficult, and I will not attempt an analysis of them here. The point is that Frost seems correct at least to this extent: The central commitments of liberalism give rise to very hard cases, even in contexts far removed from Nazis and other forms of extreme anti-liberalism. In fact, we might say that the multiculturalism and religion cases are much more difficult than cases involving those with ambitions that are genocidal and aggressive. There is broad support for regarding even play Nazis as a kind of necessary evil in a liberal society: it is for the sake of keeping open the channels of toleration for less extreme, but perhaps still objectionable, ways of life that we must tolerate the play Nazis. However, in the multiculturalism and religion cases, unlike the Nazi case, allowing the ways of life in question to have their way will not result immediately in mass murder and violence. To be sure, in all such cases there are distinctive public goods at stake, such as public safety in the case of helmet laws in the US, and civic unity in the case of the headscarves in France. But there are significant costs to individual liberty, too. Some liberals have argued for "maximum feasible accommodation" (Galston 2002, 119) in such cases. Others adamantly reject this, insisting that equal treatment trumps all (Barry 2001, 17).

What can be done? As I mentioned earlier, a substantively *moral* argument for prioritizing public safety or civic unity over duties of conscience cannot succeed. Must we then resort to either ad baculum or modus vivendi appeals, both of which confirm Frost's claim?

The dominant answer among contemporary liberals is no. Following Rawls (2005), many liberals countenance a middle ground between substantive moral argument and purely prudential argument. This middle ground is called 'political' argument, and the liberalism based on such argument is called, naturally enough, 'political liberalism.' A *political* case for toleration does not invoke a substantive moral theory yet still appeals to the moral, rather than simply prudential, value of toleration. It does this by construing toleration as a *civic* value, a moral good whose goodness derives from no substantive moral conception of the good life in particular, but rather from the most fundamental values implicit in the very idea of a liberal society. The requirement of toleration follows from the core liberal commitments to free and equal citizenship and to viewing political society as a cooperative system (Rawls 2005, 15ff.). The argument runs that if we are to collectively enjoy as free and equal citizens the important goods that a liberal political order manifests and secures, we must adopt a norm of toleration toward those who live in ways we find morally disagreeable or worse, provided that they respect the usual liberal constraints and adopt the same norm of toleration. Notice that the claim is not that being tolerant is a necessary constituent of a good life, or that being tolerant makes one happy or a better person; rather, toleration is posed as a virtue for liberal citizens, or for persons in their role as liberal citizens. Thus to reject this ideal of *civic* toleration is to reject the very idea of liberal politics. Those who reject liberal politics in this way are regarded not as wrong or wicked, but as unreasonable, simply unfit for citizenship in a liberal political order.

This politicizing strategy promises to forge a unique path between the merely prudential and the substantively moral. If it succeeds, citizens will have a moral reason to uphold the norm of toleration—now understood as a civic value—deriving from their own moral reasons for pursuing a liberal political order, yet the liberal state will not have violated neutrality. Consider: With those already committed to pursuing a society of free and equal persons, liberals can appeal to civic versions of core liberal values; with those not so committed, neutrality is not a requirement, and so liberals may employ their substantive moral reasons. Politicization enables liberals to take their own side in an argument. Frost is mistaken.

III   PROBLEMS WITH POLITICIZED LIBERALISM

Yet the scent of the illicit lingers. Can the tensions we have been discussing really be dispelled by simply placing the word 'civic' before the concepts that seemed to be causing the trouble? In order to assess this, we will need to examine an actual application of politicization. Let us consider the oft-discussed case of *Mozert v. Hawkins*.

First it should be noted that Eamonn Callan (1997, 157) is correct to observe that the *Mozert* case is complicated in part because the plaintiff's complaint "confounded reasons of extremely uneven merit." I do not intend, therefore, to engage in an extended discussion of the details of the case. Rather, I want to examine Macedo's (1995, 2000) view about the decision in *Mozert*, which represents the 'political' strategy we identified above. To this end, I will follow Macedo's own account of the relevant details of the case.[7]

In *Mozert*, several born-again Christian families brought the complaint against the public school board of Hawkins County in Tennessee that the primary grade reading curriculum violated the families' free exercise of religion. The textbooks used in that curriculum exposed their children to stories told from a wide variety of religious points of view, including Buddhist, Native American, Islamic, New Age, and Christian. One of the plaintiffs, Vicki Frost (no relation to Robert Frost, I presume), objected to the even-handedness with which the non-Christian views were presented; she claimed that a proper Christian must refuse to see other religions as "equal" to Christianity (Macedo 2000, 168); as Macedo indicates, according to Vicki Frost, the "exposure to diversity" of religious worldviews itself constitutes a violation of the free exercise of her religion, which commands her to raise her children to be Christian, and which in turn requires her to teach her children that there are no other religions in the proper sense (1995, 471).

What makes the *Mozert* case compelling from the point of view of liberalism is that the parents were not attempting to have the reading curriculum abolished or the textbooks in question replaced. Rather, the parents sought an *exemption* for their children from the classes that employed the textbooks. The parents agreed that their children needed reading instruction, and proposed that their children would be taught to read at home and would sit for the same standard reading examinations as the other students in the class. That is, the *Mozert* parents did not attempt to impose their own religious convictions on other students, they simply claimed their right to control the kinds of worldviews to which their children were exposed.

The Hawkins County school board initially allowed the proposed exemption, but quickly reversed its decision and declared participation in the reading curriculum mandatory for all students, vowing to suspend any student who refused. Although many of the concerned parents withdrew their children from the public school system, others brought a case against the school board. A federal court dismissed the case, but a higher court, which decided to uphold the parents' complaint, reversed this dismissal. However, this decision was eventually reversed by a federal appeals court, which found in favor of the Hawkins County School Board.

Macedo frames the philosophical issues well:

Can respectful exposure to diversity interfere with the free exercise of religious beliefs? And if so, do state officials—operating on the basis of their democratic mandate—have the authority to condition a benefit such as public schooling on the willingness of parents to have their children exposed to diversity, or does doing so violate fundamental rights or run afoul of some other principled limit on public authority? (Macedo 2000, 161)

Furthermore, Macedo gives what seems to me to be the right response. Macedo concedes that the reading program interferes with the *Mozert* parents' ability to "teach their children their particular religious views," but he denies that this constitutes a violation of the parents' moral or constitutional rights (2000, 162). Macedo writes,

> While it is true enough that out liberal Constitution protects freedom to proclaim that the religious doctrines of others are heretical, a more complex dynamic is at work here. A liberal democratic polity cannot endure without citizens willing to support its fundamental institutions and principles and to take part in defining those principles. . . . Liberal citizenship carries with it not only privileges but also obligations, including the obligation to respect the equal rights of fellow citizens, whatever their faiths. . . . Our constitutional order must shape citizens, and not only establish political institutions. Citizens, not courts or legislatures, are the ultimate custodians of our public morality. We have every reason to take seriously the political project of educating future citizens with an eye to their responsibilities as critical interpreters of our shared political traditions—that is, as participants in a democratic project of reason giving and reason demanding. (Macedo 2000, 164–165)

Macedo sees the democratic project he describes as part of his broader "civic liberalism" (2000, 169), a species of political liberalism that "includes an account of the political institutions and social structures that help promote a publicly reasonable liberal community" (ibid.). Macedo claims that his civic liberalism "focuses our attention on shared political values without requiring or expecting agreement on ultimate ends or a comprehensive set of philosophical values" (ibid., 170). Accordingly, Macedo contends that his civil liberalism can "avoid directly confronting or denying the *Mozert* families' contention that the Bible's authority should be accepted uncritically" (ibid., 174). Instead, civic liberalism recommends that we proceed by "simply leaving aside the religious question as such"; this "leaves the school door open to reasonable fundamentalists—that is, to those willing to acknowledge *for civic purposes* the authority of public reasonableness" (ibid., 175).

According to Macedo, then, the fact that the Hawkins County public school reading curriculum promotes attitudes of toleration toward other religions and worldviews does *not* constitute a violation of the *Mozert* parents' free exercise; this is because the toleration that is promoted is strictly civil rather than substantive (2000, 175). In other words, Macedo holds that public schools are warranted to—in fact, are obligated to—engage in a "reasonable attempt to inculcate core liberal values" such as "toleration and other basic civil virtues" (ibid., 201) because such values are necessary for citizenship in a modern democratic society. Macedo contends that these values can be inculcated without taking a stand on larger questions of the good life or salvation; they are, again, the civic virtues appropriate to our role as citizens, not as persons as such. Thus Macedo's civic liberalism is based in the claim that "the lives of liberal citizens are in a sense properly divided: we have a public and a private side, and the public (or political) side is guided by imperatives designed to make our shared life together civilized and respectful" (ibid., 164).

Macedo recognizes that the civic virtues will inevitably "spill over into other spheres of life," and that these virtues are "far from neutral with respect to the forms of life that are likely to prosper and gain adherents" in a society governed by them (2000, 179). But this failure of neutrality of effect is of no concern, for Macedo contends that the relevant sense of neutrality is that of justification (ibid.). As we've seen, Macedo holds that the values and virtues associated with his civic liberalism can be justified "independently of religious and other comprehensive claims" (ibid.). Macedo holds that the justification for his civil liberalism derives from the "widespread (though not perfect) consensus on the sorts of basic guarantees that constitute the core of a political morality" that Americans enjoy; he holds that, despite deep disagreement, "there is nevertheless a reasonable consensus on certain shared matters of urgent political concern, a consensus that is freestanding in the sense that we do not need to agree on any one comprehensive religious or philosophical grounding" (2000, 173).

But here is where the limits of the politicization strategy come to the fore. The *Mozert* case demonstrates that the reasonable consensus Macedo describes is not as widespread as he seems to think. More importantly, it could be the case that the *Mozert* parents indeed recognize the high value of the "basic guarantees" which constitute the "core of a political morality" that Macedo describes. This is suggested by the fact that the *Mozert* parents did not press an objection to the idea of secular education as such.[8] On a plausible reading of the case, part of what they objected to is the idea that this core political morality should take priority over the aims and values of their religious or substantive morality. What reason could Macedo give that is consistent with his justificatory neutralism for prioritizing political morality over substantive morality in cases of direct conflict? His response to this kind of challenge is telling; in considering that certain religious believers may object to the very idea of partitioning their 'private' and 'political' morality in the way civic liberalism requires, Macedo writes,

> At this point, there may be nothing more to say to such people, except to point out that their religious beliefs are, unfortunately, inconsistent with the demands of good citizenship in a religiously pluralistic society. (Macedo 2000, 186)

This is an awkward reply because the aptness of Macedo's conception of the demands of good citizenship in a religiously pluralistic society is precisely what is in question. Elsewhere, he concedes that "civic education is bound to have the effect of favoring some ways of life or religious conviction over others"; but instead of offering a justification for his conception of civic education in light of this effect, he simply declares, "So be it" (2005, 202). But this is not a justification of any sort, and, in any case, it is an odd stance given Macedo's commitment to the idea that "public institutions should operate based on mutually accessible reasons" (2000, 184).

The problem is that in order to avoid appealing to controversial moral claims in his justification of his civic liberalism, Macedo must appeal to "shared political values" (2000, 185). But *Mozert* shows that even if there were a suitably robust collection of such values, there would still be a question of how they are to be prioritized in cases of conflict. To declare simply that the political values override religious ones is to betray the very justificatory ideal that Macedo claims is central to his liberalism; however, to give a moral argument for the priority of the political to the religious is necessarily to invoke the kind of controversy Macedo most wants to avoid. Perhaps Robert Frost was right after all.

IV   SOCIAL EPISTEMIC LIBERALISM

In this concluding section, I want to sketch a different kind of approach to these issues, an approach I call 'social epistemic liberalism.'[9] The main idea of social epistemic liberalism is that despite deep differences over fundamental moral, religious, and metaphysical commitments, there is a cluster of *epistemic* norms and values that we hold in common; these norms are substantive enough to provide the basis for powerful argument for core liberal commitments, yet epistemic and so able to sustain moral neutrality.

To explain: Each of us is epistemically dependent upon others for many of our factual and normative beliefs (Buchanan 2004, 102). This dependency consists not only in the fact that many of our beliefs ultimately have their source in the testimony, experience, research, and expertise of others, but also in that our epistemic habits are socially derived. Our epistemic habits include not only the ways in which we form, revise, and maintain our beliefs, but also how we select those to whom we show epistemic deference and the extent of that deference. Insofar as such habits are truth-conducive, they are epistemically virtuous; insofar as they are not, they are epistemically vicious.

Epistemic dependence is unavoidable because every individual has limited cognitive resources. However, this dependence in itself is not a bad thing; great stores of knowledge and information that could not be produced by a single person are available to us precisely because of the division of epistemic labor that epistemic dependence necessitates. Nonetheless, epistemic dependence is risky, because one may defer to the wrong persons to the wrong extent and so become vulnerable to developing beliefs and epistemic habits that engender and sustain falsehood. The risks associated with having false beliefs are both prudential and moral: They are prudential insofar as false beliefs frustrate one's deliberations about means; they are moral insofar as they can lead one to adopt immoral ends.

In light of the risks associated with unavoidable epistemic dependence and our strong interest in getting moral matters right and avoiding moral error, we should agree that those social institutions are best which tend to minimize the risks of dependence while maximizing the benefits of the epistemic division of labor. The social epistemic case for core liberal commitments follows naturally: The extent to which a society manifests core liberal values is roughly the extent to which that society satisfies these desiderata. Liberal societies satisfy these desiderata because they (1) recognize individual liberties of thought, conscience, and association that enable information to be freely shared and disagreements to be rationally engaged; (2) feature a meritocratic system of identifying experts that encourages proper epistemic deference and discourages improper deference; and (3) encourage a broad culture of moral egalitarianism that enables citizens to confidently address, question, and criticize each other and socially identified experts. As Buchanan concludes, anyone "who takes seriously the moral and prudential risks of social epistemic dependence ought to support liberal institutions" (2004, 100), no matter what her substantive theory of the good life may be.

To state the argument succinctly, despite the ways in which reasonable comprehensive moral doctrines are otherwise deeply divided, all should countenance the fact of epistemic dependence, and all should recognize that a well-functioning system of social epistemic risk reduction is necessary for proper moral judgment, whatever one takes that to consist in. Liberal institutions are the most effective of the available options at managing epistemic risk. Thus, despite deep disagreement at the level of moral fundamentals, all reasonable persons have a reason to support liberal society. The most important feature of the social epistemic argument for liberalism is that it proposes epistemic reasons for core liberal values and institutions rather than moral reasons, substantive or politicized. Accordingly, social epistemic liberals can with great vehemence take their own side in a debate, for their claim is that liberal norms must be in place in order for an informed and responsible debate to occur.

We can think of the social epistemic approach, then, as following the political liberal in resisting appeals to substantive moral norms in making a case for liberal values. However, whereas the political liberal offers politicized versions of core liberal values, the social epistemic liberal offers an epistemologized view of toleration, equality, liberty, and the like. According to social epistemic liberals, these values must be manifest in our politics if we are to effectively manage the epistemic risks to which we are all subject.

In other words, we must uphold norms of toleration, egalitarianism, and liberty if we are to benefit from the free and open exchange of information and reasons. And we should seek these benefits because, on any plausible theory of the good life, responsible moral agency requires moral delibera-tion, which in turn requires access to reliable sources of moral and factual information. Of course, social epistemic liberals need not claim that these values are exhaustively epistemic, and social epistemic liberals need not deny the decidedly moral components of these values. The point is rather that one may appeal to the epistemological dimension of these values in conflicts concerning their moral dimensions.

But where does this leave the parents in *Mozert*? What does the social epistemic liberal say to Vicki Frost, who claims that "the word of God as found in the Christian Bible is the totality of my beliefs" (Macedo 2000, 158)? Presumably Vicki Frost sees no need for moral deliberation, and thus no need for toleration.

The social epistemic liberal could begin by pointing out that it cannot possibly be true that the word of God is the totality of Vicki Frost's beliefs because the Bible does not contain the sentence, 'The word of God as found in the Christian Bible is the totality of Vicki Frost's beliefs.' Thus, by her own admission, Vicki Frost has beliefs that are not contained in the Bible, and therefore she is committed to the idea that there are some truths that are not found there. The next move would be to present her with the vast Christian literature devoted to biblical interpretation, laying bare all of the internal controversies among Christian scholars concerning the Bible's core moral teachings. The aim would be to follow Michael Perry in urging that

> [w]idespread transdenominational disagreement among Christians over whether the Bible teaches about morality what some claim that it teaches is not a new phenomenon. In the past, there was such disagree-ment over, for example, whether the Bible teaches that slavery can be morally permissible. Precisely because such disagreement is not a new thing, and because the historical experience of Christians discloses that Christians can be radically mistaken about whether in fact the Bible teaches about morality what some claim that it teaches, such dis-agreement—increasingly widespread disagreement among Christians, disagreement that is not interdenominational but transdenomination-al—should be an occasion for Christians to subject the traditional be-lief to careful, critical scrutiny. (Perry 2003, 63)

According to Perry, such "careful, critical scrutiny" will often require "dia-logue with the other" (2003, 76) because such dialogue is frequently what is needed if we are to uncover the tacit assumptions and intuitions driving our own thinking. Now, it may seem that the injunction to engage in critical dia-logue for the sake of testing one's religious commitments *itself* constitutes a violation of one's religious commitments, since it seems to call for some kind of skepticism or a willingness to doubt one's religious beliefs. However, Perry correctly emphasizes that the kind of scrutiny he calls for does *not* require religious believers to deny or doubt core commitments of their faith. The recognition that the Bible has in the past been wrongly interpreted, and thus that any proposed interpretation must be examined carefully, does not conflict with a commitment to the Bible's infallibility; it requires only an admission of one's own fallibility in interpreting the Bible, an admission that is perfectly fitting for Christians in light of their view of "the fallenness, the brokenness" of human beings as such (Perry 2003, 79).

Perry's point is crucial and obviously quite in line with social epistemic liberalism. No matter what their moral comprehensive doctrines happen to be, citizens have, from their own epistemic perspective, compelling reasons to engage each other in critical, reasoned dialogue. But in order for that dialogue to be epistemically responsible in light of the risks of epistemic dependency, it must be conducted against the background of a well-functioning social epistemic system that provides access to reliable sources of moral and factual information.

Consequently, the social epistemic liberal supports Macedo's position that the *Mozert* parents should not be accommodated on the grounds that "We have every reason to take seriously the political project of educating future citizens with an eye to their responsibilities . . . as participants in a democratic project of reason giving and reason demanding" (2000, 165). But whereas Macedo's justification of this position necessarily invokes the kind of moral controversy he correctly aspires to avoid, social epistemic liberalism justifies this position on the grounds that Vicki Frost's positive epistemic commitments must support critical engagement with opposing doctrines for the sake of upholding the epistemic norms that enable her and her children to better satisfy the demands of their own moral doctrine. Again, the argument does not appeal to a supposedly "widespread consensus" on a shared "political morality" (Macedo 2000, 173), but rather draws from the epistemic commitments we already endorse in light of the facts that we are all subject to social epistemic risk, and we are interested in getting morality right.

I have here provided only a sketch of social epistemic liberalism. There is much more to be said, of course. But from what has been said, this much can be said by way of conclusion: We are living in the midst of a rapid and surprising transformation of the global order. Economic, technological, political, and social changes (some would call them advances) force liberal societies to confront, both domestically and abroad, persons, groups, and populations who endorse ways of life that, while not radically antiliberal, are nonliberal to a degree sufficient to call into question central liberal norms. Liberals are bound by their own doctrine to providing justifications for their commitments. If the academic literature is any indication, there is a palpable sense that liberalism is at present working through a legitimation crisis brought on by challenges deriving from sources as diverse as multiculturalism, feminism, communitarianism, and religious traditionalism. In many cases, these challenges come in domestic and global varieties, and often there is great variation in the character of the challenge posed.[10] It will not do for liberals to simply trot out their favorite accounts of the substantive good of autonomy, liberty, equality, or individuality; such accounts beg the question. Nor will it do for them to import a simple distinction between 'civic' and substantively 'moral' virtues and obligations; for these too beg the question, only less directly. The social epistemic approach, however, holds the promise of being able to provide philosophical reasons to uphold liberal principles without thereby begging the very moral questions over which people are divided. For those who take themselves to be offering criticisms of liberal norms, or who allege that liberalism cannot take seriously the ways in which we disagree, or who insist that political power must justify itself, the social epistemic approach should be sufficient to provide a liberal basis from which further argument could proceed.

NOTES

1. Throughout, I shall use the term 'way of life' to refer to what Rawls calls a "comprehensive doctrine" (2005, 12n). Others refer to 'conceptions of the good' to the same effect.
2. See, for example, Joseph Ratzinger's *Dominus Iesus*, which declares that some Protestant churches are "not churches in the proper sense" and all suffer from "defects" (2000, 17). Official condemnations of Catholicism from Protestant sects are easy to find. Those who see the Protestant/Catholic conflict as more a case of divergence rather than opposition may change the example to Catholicism (or Protestantism) and, say, Wiccanism or Scientology.
3. The passage should be quoted in full: "The liberal polity requires that the Nazis be law-abiding Nazis and that is not easy. They cannot be 'gung ho' Nazis, in fact they cannot *be* Nazis at all but only play at it" (Macedo 1990, 257). This is not to suggest, however, that play Nazis do not pose serious problems for liberal politics.
4. In 2003, a judge in Colorado overturned the death sentence of a convicted rapist and murderer after discovering that the jurors collectively consulted the Bible during their deliberations. The Judge's ruling was upheld in 2005 by the Colorado Supreme Court. See *People v. Harlan*, Colorado Supreme Court Case no. 03SA173.
5. It should be noted that Rawls first proposed his public reason doctrine in the 1993 edition of *Political Liberalism*. He later revised and further clarified that view along the lines suggested above in his 1997 paper on "The Idea of Public Reason Revisited." This 1997 paper now appears in the 2005 expanded edition of *Political Liberalism*.
6. Nicholas Wolterstorff makes the point nicely: "It belongs to the *religious convictions* of a good many religious people in our society that *they ought to base* their decisions concerning fundamental issues of justice *on* their religious convictions. They do not view it as an option whether or not to do so. . . . Their religion is not, for them, about *something other* than their social and political existence; it is *also* about their social and political existence. Accordingly to

require of them that they not base their decisions and discussions concerning political issues on their religion is to infringe, incquitably, on the free exercise of their religion" (1997, 105). See also Eberle 2002.

7. See Bates 1993 for a comprehensive account of *Mozert*.
8. As John Tomasi (2001, 92) notes, some of the parents objected not to the mere exposure of their children to the non-Christian stories, but to the fact that Christianity was not given equal representation in the readers.
9. Much of what follows draws heavily from Buchanan 2002 and 2004. For further elaboration, see Talisse 2000 and forthcoming. Goldman 1999 provides a comprehensive and original survey of the field of social epistemology.
10. See, for example, the critical responses to Susan Okin's essay "Is Multiculturalism Bad for Women?" collected along with Okin's reply in Okin 1999.

BIBLIOGRAPHY

Barry, B. *Culture and Equality*. Cambridge, MA: Harvard University Press, 2001.

Bates, S. *Battleground*. New York: Poseidon Books, 1993.

Buchanan, A. "Social Moral Epistemology." *Social Philosophy and Policy*, 19, 2002: 126–52.

———. "Political Liberalism and Social Epistemology." *Philosophy & Public Affairs* 32, no. 2 (2004): 95–130.

Callan, Eamonn. 1997. *Creating Citizens*. New York: Oxford University Press.

Eberle, C. *Religious Conviction in Liberal Politics*. Cambridge: Cambridge University Press, 2002.

Galston, W. *Liberal Pluralism*. Cambridge: Cambridge University Press, 2002.

Goldman, A. *Knowledge in a Social World*. New York: Oxford University Press, 1999.

Kukathas, C. "Liberalism and Multiculturalism: The Politics of Indifference." *Political Theory*, 26, no. 5 (1998): 686–699.

———. *The Liberal Archipelago*. New York: Oxford University Press, 2003.

Macedo, S. *Liberal Virtues*. New York: Oxford University Press, 1990.

———. "Liberal Civic Education and Religious Fundamentalism: The Case of God vs. John Rawls?" *Ethics* 105, 1995: 468–496.

———. "In Defense of Liberal Public Reason: Are Slavery and Abortion Hard Cases?" In *Natural Law and Public Reason*, eds. R. George and C. Wolfe. Washington, DC: Georgetown University Press, 2000.

Mill, J. S. *On Liberty and Other Essays*. New York: Oxford University Press, 1991.

Okin, S. *Is Multiculturalism Bad for Women?* Princeton, NJ: Princeton University Press, 1999.

Perry, M. *Under God?* Cambridge: Cambridge University Press, 2003.

Ratzinger, J. *Dominus Iesus*. Vatican: Vatican City, 2000. http://www.vatican.va/roman_curiacongregations/cfaith/documents/rc_con_cfaith_doc_20000806_dominus-iesus_en.html (accessed 16 June 2008).

Rawls, J. *Political Liberalism*. Exp. ed. New York: Columbia University Press, 2005.

Talisse, R. B. "Toward a Social Epistemic Comprehensive Liberalism." *Episteme* 5, no. 1 (2008): 106–128.

———. *Democracy and Moral Conflict*. Cambridge: Cambridge University Press, forthcoming.

Tomasi, 2001. *Liberalism Beyond Justice*. Princeton, NJ: Princeton University Press.

Wolsterstorff, Nicholas. 1997. "The Role of Religion in Decision and Discussion of Political Issues," in *Religion in the Public Square*, Robert Audi and Nicholas Wolsterstorff. (Lanham, MD: Rowman and Littlefield)

3 Literacy and Citizenship
Tradition, Reason, and Critique in Democratic Education[1]

Hanan Alexander

In this chapter I assess the role of literacy in three standard accounts of democratic education: republican, liberal, and (for lack of a better term) radical, with special attention to the education of Jewish and Arab (or Palestinian) citizens of Israel as illustrative of liberal republics more generally. I argue that each account is problematic—the republican because it tends to emphasize one particular community to the exclusion of others, and the liberal and radical because each promotes distinct but equally universal ideals at the expense of the particular idioms literacy and democracy require. To conclude, I suggest an alternative grounded in what John Gray, in keeping with Isaiah Berlin and Michael Oakeshott, has called 'value-pluralism.' Yael Tamir refers to the political theory associated with this view as 'liberal nationalism,' the educational consequences of which I dub the 'pedagogy of difference.'

It is commonly accepted that citizens of democratic societies should be literate. To vote, deliberate matters of public concern, or protect one's interests or those of one's family, community, culture, class, race, ethnicity, gender, or sexual orientation, requires some ability to decipher language, interpret social cues, understand cultural practices, or grasp—even apply—ethical, political, aesthetic, or other sorts of values. But what does it mean to be literate under circumstances such as these? On John Searle's account, language constitutes the so-called 'ontological substance of civilization,' the very stuff of which human societies are made (Searle 1997, 59–78). To acquire the ability to use language, on this view, is to learn to express one's purposes or intentions in the context of particular societies, cultures, or traditions. To become literate, then, is to be initiated into a particular community that expresses itself in certain ways and not others; and to inquire about the sort of literacy required of democratic citizens is to ask about the varieties of purposes and intentions with which citizens in democratic societies should be concerned.

Democratic literacy then appears to involve a dilemma. On the one hand it entails initiation into cannons of expression that in the nature of the case will be used by particular communities for the purposes of articulating their customs, beliefs, and practices—in short, their ways of life or concepts of the good. On the other hand, to limit these cannons to a particular group excludes from the language of political power others who are not members of that group. Enfranchising all members of society requires that citizens be provided with skills to articulate their own purposes, intentions, interests, and desires; yet requiring people to adopt a particular way of talking in order to be invited into the corridors of power can deny legitimacy to other modes of expression that may not be favored by purveyors of the current dominant discourse. This is so even if that discourse promotes common cannons of communication, since what counts as 'common' will itself vary from one community of discourse to another.

This is no abstract problem. Consider Israel, which was conceived as a Jewish and democratic state to provide for the cultural and political aspirations of an ancient people presumably without denying the parallel desires of others. Approximately 80 percent of Israel's citizens are secular and religious Jews, while around 20 percent are Arabs of Muslim, Christian, and Druze dissent, many of whom identify culturally and politically as Palestinians. The language of political discourse into which Jewish Israeli youngsters are initiated in school is grounded in the modern Hebrew culture created by the founders of Zionism in the first half of the twentieth century. Yet, even though the language of primary education for Palestinian youngsters who are citizens of Israel is Arabic, which is also an official language of the country, Jewish and Zionist history and culture play an important role in the curriculum of Arab Israeli schools, and the language in which Palestinian youngsters must matriculate and pursue higher education is Hebrew. It is entirely unclear what ought to count as the sort of literacy necessary for participation in Israeli democracy for these two groups of citizens. On the view that Israel should be a Jewish state, Palestinian Arab language and culture would seem to be excluded from the corridors of power, which could raise questions about Israel's democratic character. However, the claim that democracy requires granting cultural rights to all, which challenges the privilege afforded Hebrew culture, may preclude a nation-state from grounding its political culture in the traditions of a particular people, which as we have seen could in turn undermine the possibility of literacy and hence democracy altogether. Nor is Israel alone in facing this problem; most democratic societies around the world were founded as expressions of particular national cultures, yet they face the difficulties of educating significant minority populations whose history, heritage, and language may be different than that of the majority the state was founded to promote, but who aspire nonetheless to equal rights as citizens (Tamir 1995, 124–130).

Philosophers have long been concerned with dilemmas of this sort. How, they ask, is one thing possible, supposing certain other conflicting or contradictory things? How is it possible for us to have free will, supposing that all actions are causally determined, or for evil to be possible, given the existence of an omnipotent, omniscient good God? (Nozick 1981, 8) Addressing these sorts of questions requires what Robert Nozick has called a 'philosophical explanation,' which articulates deeper principles that can remove the apparent conflict and put one's beliefs in alignment. The search for such an explanation, Nozick points out, is often conducted as much to assuage the internal affairs department of one's own belief system as it is to convince others. What follows then is an attempt to put my own beliefs in alignment by asking how an account of literacy suitable to political education in democratic societies is possible that is sufficiently grounded in particular traditions or cultures for the term 'literacy' to be meaningful, yet which also takes into account relevant concerns for the enfranchisement of all citizens.

In this chapter I will address this question by assessing the role of literacy in three standard accounts of democratic education: republican, liberal, and (for lack of a better term) radical, in light of what John Gray (2002) has called the 'pluralistic face of liberal toleration.' Drawing on the political theories of Isaiah Berlin (1953, 1990) and Michael Oakeshott (1991), I will argue that each of these standard accounts of democratic literacy are problematic: the republican because it tends to emphasize one particular community to the exclusion of others, and the liberal and radical because each promotes distinct but equally universal ideals at the expense of the particular idioms literacy and hence democracy requires. To conclude, I will suggest an alternative grounded in a liberal communitarian view that Yael Tamir (1995) calls 'liberal nationalism.' I have referred to the educational consequences of this political theory as the 'pedagogy of difference' (Alexander 2004, 2007).

RIVAL CONCEPTIONS OF LITERACY
IN DEMOCRATIC EDUCATION

Three traditions of thought dominate the literature of political education in democratic societies, each of which approaches the literacy of citizens differently: republican, liberal, and radical. By political education I mean very broadly the intentional initiation of members in a society into the concepts, ideals, and practices that are used to govern; and by democracy I mean again very loosely a society that, as Lincoln put it so well, conceives itself as being "of the people, by the people, and for the people," although there is considerable disagreement among the three traditions in question as to who is to be counted as one *of* the people and what it means for government to be *by* and *for* them.

According to the republican tradition—from Aristotle (1981), Marcus Tullius Cicero (2009), and Niccolo Machiavelli (1984) to J. G. Herder (Berlin 2001, 168–242) and G. W. F. Hegel (1967) and perhaps contemporary communitarians such as Alistair MacIntyre (1981, 1989) and Michael Sandel (1998)—being a citizen entails membership in a particular group. This might be determined by virtue of lineage or heritage, which is sometimes called ethnic or national republicanism. It may also be a result of having been taught or chosen a particular way of life or concept of the Good, which can be referred to as ethical or ideological republicanism. For government to be by and for the people on this account means that it uses the powers of the state to support and sustain this group or way of life; and to be a literate citizen is to be initiated into the customs, beliefs, and practices of that ethnicity, nationality, culture, or tradition.

When Israeli high school matriculation requires exams in modern Hebrew language and literature or Zionist history for both Jewish and Arab students; or when A- and O-level exams in the UK demand proficiency in English language and literature or British history from all students regardless of background, and the state allocates funds for teacher preparation, curriculum construction, and classroom instruction in those subjects; or when universities do not hold classes on Jewish holidays in Israel or Christian holidays in France, Germany, or Denmark or Muslim holidays in Pakistan or Indonesia, these subjects and customs are granted special privilege on republican grounds. To function effectively as a citizen in a national or ideological republic one must speak its language, know something of its history or collective story, and respect its religious and cultural heritage. In McLaughlin's (1992) terms, this is likely to yield a more 'maximal,' or as Walzer (1994) would call it a 'thicker' conception of literacy for democratic citizenship, grounded in local culture, language, history, and custom.

According to the liberal account, on the other hand—from Immanuel Kant (1989, 1997) and John Locke (1988) to John Stuart Mill (1998) and John Rawls (2005a)—democratic citizenship is a legal status that requires, among other qualifications, a significant degree of personal autonomy; and for a government to be by and for its citizens entails protecting their fundamental rights to follow a life-path of their own choosing, provided of course that one's choices do not infringe on the preferences of others (Alexander 2007). According to Eamonn Callan (1988, 25–55) this entails the capacity to assess one's genuine interests realistically according to relevant criteria of rational truthfulness. By 'interests' in this context Callan has in mind one's most deeply held convictions and desires, something akin to what Charles Taylor (1985) called 'strong values,' not units of utility, benefit, or gain. Additionally, to be an autonomous person in Callan's view, one must possess the independence of mind to pursue these interests even in the face of significant obstacles. Whatever else it may mean, then, to be a literate citizen in this view entails a common conception of critical rationality among groups with alternative visions of the good life, upon which individuals can base realistic and independent choices. This view is likely to result in what McLaughlin would call a more minimal, or Walzer a thinner, account of literacy for democracy because it will seek a common and neutral discourse in which to assess personal preferences and deliberate public policies.

In small liberal republics this would constitute a strong basis for common schools in which children of different religions, nationalities, and races, both majorities and minorities, would be educated together. In the Israeli case, for instance, this would suggest that Palestinian and Jewish citizens of Israel be educated together in common schools (they are currently schooled separately) that would teach various aspects of Arab and Hebrew culture to both communities—perhaps with different emphasis for each, but with a common intellectual ethos that emphasizes enabling students to cultivate their own interests and arrive at independent choices about fundamental life choices. In large, diverse democracies such as the US, it would mitigate against state-supported separate schools for groups with differing religious or cultural orientations, and for limiting parental rights to religious education. Harry Brighouse (2005), for example, argues against the rights of Amish parents to limit the secondary schooling of their children in order to support their particular faith, on the grounds that it would infringe on the autonomy of their children, and Callan (1985) has challenged the rights of parents to bring their children up in a religious tradition altogether.

Finally, according to the radical tradition—from Plato (2008) to Karl Marx (1970) and the Frankfort school (Horkheimer and Adorno 2002) to the critical pedagogues (Freire 2000), postcolonialists (Said 1979), and poststructuralists (Foucault 2001)—all human societies are grounded in fundamental, and possibly insurmountable, conflicts over power. The people, on this account, refers to all members of society—whether or not they are recognized legally as duly constituted citizens or have more and less power—and for government to be by and for them, it must seek to equalize the distribution of resources among them by taking power from those who have it and allocating it equitably to everyone. At the heart of literacy for democracy, according to this position, is the recognition of false consciousness or wrongheaded ideology that allows those in power to deny equal distribution of resources to all.

Ilan Gur-Ze'ev (2008) argues, for instance, that Israeli education should abandon the colonial idea that in establishing a state of their own Jews are coming home or that they have achieved a utopian or messianic ideal. The Zionists were mistaken. There is no utopia, no home, no ultimate teleological end or messianic time. With George Steiner (1998), Gur-Ze'ev holds instead that we all exist in a spiritual Diaspora in which there is no Archimedean point and no view from which to base life's meaning and purpose. This holds no less true for Jews and Palestinians in the land that one calls Israel and the other Palestine than it does for those who reside abroad. Instead of educating Jewish children in Israel toward a false utopia, or Palestinian children in the nostalgic belief that the clock can be turned back to a better time (for them) when there was no Jewish state, both should be engaged in a counter-education that acknowledges the suffering each people has endured in order create a new dialogue of coexistence for the future. Following critical pedagogue Paulo Freire (2000), this can be accomplished by posing common problems on which teachers and students can collaborate, instead of treating children like banks into which instructors deposit accepted ideologies that reflect current unequal power relations.

Limitations of space do not allow a fully nuanced account that does justice to the rich diversity of opinion within each of these traditions or the deliberations and debates that transpire amongst them. However, I have tried to capture in broad strokes what the various alternatives within each orientation share in common that I take to be problematic. The difficulties I have in mind can be made plain, I think, by reference to what political philosopher John Gray (2002) has called the 'pluralistic face of liberal toleration,' though it can be applied to republican and radical political theory as well. "Liberalism has always had two faces," writes Gray:

> From one side, toleration is the pursuit of an ideal form of life. From the other, it is the search for terms of peace among different ways of life. In the former view, liberal institutions are seen as applications of universal principles. In the latter, they are means to peaceful coexistence. In the first, liberalism is the prescription for a universal regime. In the second, it is a project of coexistence that can be pursued in many regimes. The philosophies of John Locke and Immanuel Kant exemplify the liberal project of a universal regime, while those of Thomas Hobbes and David Hume express the liberalism of peaceful coexistence. In more recent times, John Rawls and F.A. Hayek have defended the first liberal philosophy, while Isaiah Berlin and Michael Oakeshott are exemplars of the second. (Gray 2002, 2)

Gray calls the politics exemplified by Kant and Locke universal (some say comprehensive) liberalism, and that exemplified by Berlin and Oakeshott a theory of modus vivendi, which he writes, "is liberal toleration adapted to the historical fact of pluralism" (Gray 2002, 6). The ethical theory that underpins the search for coexistence among alternative ways of life is called 'value pluralism.' It entails the idea that "there are many conflicting kinds of human flourishing, some of which cannot be compared in value" (ibid.). Simply put, my problem with each of these theories of literacy in democratic education is that they do not take sufficient account of the historical fact of pluralism, because they tend to embrace overly rigid approaches to what Berlin dubbed 'positive liberty' and what Oakeshott called 'rational technique'. Berlin (1953, 1990) makes the case for pluralism, I think, while

Oakeshott (1991) shows how respect for difference can be combined with commitment to particular traditions

HEDGEHOGS, FOXES, AND CONCEPTS OF FREEDOM

Following an obscure fragment from the ancient Greek poet Archilochus, Berlin (1953) marked what has become a famous distinction between two sorts of intellectual types: 'hedgehogs,' who know one big thing; and 'foxes,' who know many things.

> A great chasm exists between those, on one side, who relate every-thing to a single central vision, one system less or more coherent or articulate, in terms of which they understand, think and feel—a single, universal, organizing principle in terms of which alone all that they are and say has significance—and, on the other side, those who pursue many ends, often unrelated and even contradictory, connected, if at all, only in some *de facto* way, for some psychological or physiological cause, related by no moral or aesthetic principle. These last lead lives, perform acts, and entertain ideas that are centrifugal rather than cen-tripetal, their thought is scattered or diffused, moving on many levels, seizing upon the essence of a vast variety of experiences and objects for what they are in themselves, without consciously or unconsciously, seeking to fit them into, or exclude them from, any one unchanging, all-embracing, sometimes self-contradictory and incomplete, at times fanatical, unitary inner vision. The first kind of intellectual and artis-tic personality belongs to the hedgehogs, the second to the foxes; and without insisting on a rigid classification, we may, without too much fear of contradiction, say that, in this sense, Dante belongs to the first category, Shakespeare to the second; Plato, Lucretius, Pascal, Hegel, Dostoevsky, Nietzsche, Ibsen, Proust are, in varying degrees, hedge-hogs; Herodotus, Aristotle, Montaigne, Erasmus, Molière, Goethe, Puschkin, Balzac, Joyce are foxes. (Berlin 1953, 3)

Societies conceived by foxes encourage citizens to choose among compet-ing paths to human fulfillment provided they respect the choices of oth-ers, whereas hedgehogs assign privilege to those who follow one particular path. Foxes are drawn to Berlin's (1990) negative concept of freedom, the absence of constraints on, or interference with, a person's actions; hedge-hogs are attracted to positive liberty, the idea of self-mastery, or self-defini-tion, or control of one's destiny.

Berlin had deep reservations about the latter because of the tendency among those who advance positive accounts of freedom to distinguish between one's actual self that acts in the day-to-day world and some occult entity referred to alternatively as a 'true' or 'real' or 'higher' self of which a person might not be fully aware. Thus, it is argued that although one's empirical self may indeed feel free, one's true self may actually be enslaved. As Berlin put it so aptly, "Once I take this view, I am in a position to ignore the actual wishes of men or societies, to bully, oppress; torture them in the name, and on behalf, of their 'real' selves, in the secure knowledge that whatever is the true goal of man (happiness, performance of duty, wisdom, a just society, self-fulfillment) must be identical with his freedom—the free choice of his 'true', albeit often submerged and inarticulate, self" (1990, 133). It is not surprising, then, that Berlin (1997, 1–24) leveled this critique against the potential authoritarianism inherent in the strong 'counter-Enlightenment' romanticism associated with the likes of Hegel (1967) and his right- and left-leaning intellectual descendents, who were in many important respects heirs to the ethical republicanism of Aristotle and Cicero and the dialectical idealism of Plato, and the progenitors of the more contemporary republican and radical traditions mentioned above.

Berlin was well aware of the complexities of the many different critical traditions grounded in various forms of dialectical reasoning and conflict analysis, at least as they emerged during his lifetime. He even held that Tolstoy "was by nature a fox, but believed in being a hedgehog" (1953, 5), and he might well have said the same of the likes of Antonio Gramsci (2008), Max Horkheimer, and Theodor Adorno (Horkheimer and Adorno 2002). This said, he had harsher things to say about the intellectual descendents of Plato, Hegel, and Marx than about those of Aristotle, Cicero, and Machiavelli—in part, I think, because he believed that the latter set the stage for the sort of pluralism he embraced in ways that the former did not. We will see below how Oakeshott critiques the lack of pluralism in critical social theory on the basis of a universal application of dialectical logic. Berlin, however, had a slightly different concern in mind, that all too often the ultimate end of conflict analysis is the obliteration of difference altogether. There are, to be sure, social distinctions that ought to be dissolved because they entail an unjust abuse of power—such as those aspects of class, race, gender, ethnicity, religion, sexual orientation, and the like—on the basis of which benefits, resources, and opportunities are withheld or verbal, emotional, or physical abuse inflicted. But the exercise of power is not always evil, and its equal distribution not necessarily just. There are many instances where we want and need to rely on the state to use power wisely (in battling corruption, for example, or protecting the weak or innocent); and some tasks deserve higher reward than others, although well-intended people may differ as to what those tasks might be and how large a differential in reward is warranted. Yet, without any 'objective' standard of what is to count as justice, wisdom, corruption, or innocence, we have nothing on which to rely but political tradition in order to distinguish between the just and unjust application of power or distribution of wealth. Berlin was therefore more sympathetic to republicans such as Machiavelli (1984) and Herder (Berlin 2001, 168–242) than to radicals like Marx and Engels (1998) because he

believed that, tempered with a strong dose of negative freedom, republicanism might yield a respect for difference that could facilitate ways for deeply
distinctive peoples to coexist that are absent from the sort of critical social
theories that strive to deconstruct difference altogether.

It may be more surprising, however, to learn that Berlin's reservations
concerning the excesses of positive liberty were addressed no less to the
monist moral and political theories of Kant and Locke than to the republicans and the radicals. If he viewed Machiavelli and Herder as nascent
foxes, he saw these Enlightenment liberals as hedgehogs, headstrong about
the capacity of reason to negotiate competing ways of life. Liberalism is
normally associated with pluralism, grounded in the right of citizens to
choose a concept of the Good over any particular goods they may prefer. This assumes that they can pick freely based on relevant reasons (Raz
1988; Brighouse 2005) and engage in reasonable deliberation to adjudicate
disagreements (Gutmann and Thompson 1998; Rawls 2005b). However,
Berlin followed Hegel in holding that our choices are not always as free
nor our deliberations as reasonable as they might appear, since the very
idea of rational evaluation is historically situated; and though preferring
negative freedom, he recognized it too as an historical achievement that
tends toward its positive counterpart when transformed into a doctrine
that strives for comprehensive influence over the lives of citizens. Thus, he
counted as a fairly extreme version of positive liberty the concept of rational autonomy and the pursuit of liberal toleration as a universal ideal found
in Kant and Locke.

Berlin parted company with Hegel, however, and especially his left-
leaning followers when they argued that selections can only be genuinely free when power is distributed equally by liberating the weak and
oppressed from the ideas and material conditions that render them fee-
ble (Freire 2000; McLaren 2006; Young 2002). The ultimate source of
human power, he argued, lies not in its uniform distribution, but in the
presumption that people can step outside of their current circumstances
to choose a new path, despite all of the influences upon them or the forces
stacked against them. This is so precisely because our circumstances are
not given and even though our choices cannot be based on one view or
another of universal reason (Gray 1996). Berlin's views were thus closer
to communitarians, such as Alastair MacIntyre (1989) and Charles Taylor (1985), who held that there is no way to assess rational evaluation
other than by appeal to the very rational standards in question, and that
without a satisfactory justification of rationality, preferences may be
reduced to expressions of mere personal feeling. This confuses freedom
with caprice and isolates citizens from one another as they increasingly
center on themselves. Meaningful assessment must, therefore, be based
on values that emanate from beyond the self, linked to historically contingent communities or traditions in which citizens are embedded (Sandel 1998; Taylor 1991).

Some liberals, such as Rawls, respond to these objections by pointing out that the weak and oppressed would themselves choose the principle of distributive justice from behind a veil of ignorance (Rawls 2001) and that procedural justice is a neutral mechanism for defending personal choices grounded in affiliation—not a comprehensive doctrine in its own right (Rawls 2005b); and although others take issue with this sort of political minimalism by suggesting that liberal values should influence the private as well as the public domain (Callan 2001, Gutmann 1987, Tomasi 2001), most agree that liberal states should protect, not preclude, strong affiliations and situated identities (Feinberg 2000). But these rejoinders fail to address the full weight of Berlin's embrace of the Hegelian assault on Kant and Locke, which questions not only the capacity of reason to adjudicate difference without prejudice, but also the very rational grounds of liberalism altogether. Of course, many of the alternatives offered by radical and republican critics of liberalism are not free of difficulties associated with extreme concepts of positive liberty; liberation from false consciousness can lead to new forms of oppression, and traditionalism, if too rigid, may leave little room for those who seek fulfillment outside of prescribed frameworks. This may be why many of them return to some form of liberal justice even after they have criticized it (Macedo 1991). With all of its limitations, it appears that only some sort of liberal democracy seems to secure the basic rights and liberties, such as free expression, that make criticism possible. But if reason can serve neither as a basis for liberal values nor as a neutral arena for public deliberation, on what grounds can this reengagement with liberalism, however modified, be sustained? This brings us back to John Gray's (2002) pluralistic liberalism that assumes numerous incompatible forms of human life and pursues a modus vivendi for peaceful coexistence among them.

Eamonn Callan (1988) challenges Berlin's critique of universal (he might call it comprehensive) liberalism by questioning whether the distinction between positive and negative liberty can withstand close scrutiny, at least as Berlin has traced it in the history of Western political thought. The difficulty with Berlin's position, writes Callan,

is that if one looks hard enough at any particular instance of positive or negative liberty, it normally turns out to be describable in terms of the other sort of liberty. One might say that Berlin's putative adherents of positive freedom want the activity of collective self-determination to be free from interference of forces outside the society and disruptive elements within it, while adherents of negative liberty want the individual to be free to determine her life as she pleases within the area of self-regarding conduct. Thus, the dominant interest of Berlin's so-called proponents of positive freedom, given a different but perfectly accurate description of their position, appears to be negative; and the overriding concern of their political adversaries turns out to be with positive

freedom, given a similar descriptive change. That is not say that no significant difference exists between the two schools of political thought
which Berlin differentiates—there obviously is—but it is a difference to
which the ordinary distinction between positive and negative liberty is
wholly irrelevant. (Callan 1988, 10)

But, on Callan's view, what is the difference between the two schools of
thought that Berlin delineates? One prioritizes collective goods over individual rights, while the other prefers the right of individuals to choose a
concept of the collective Good over any goods they may choose. The former is a common way of conceiving republicanism and the latter a central
tenet of universal liberalism. However, this interpretation of Berlin misses
the essential point that even the society that promotes individual self-rule,
when left untempered by something like Mill's familiar caveat having to do
with impinging on the liberties of others, is no less oppressive in its own
way than the sorts of extreme right- and left-leaning collectivism to which
Callan, along with Berlin, objects. But the desires and aspirations of others
only acquire independent moral standing when we recognize the historical
contingency, and hence fundamental diversity, of the very sort of rationality
(Callan calls it 'truthfulness' or 'realism') upon which personal autonomy
rests. For if standards to assess ways of life were the same for all—independent of the vicissitudes of history, language, culture, and tradition—then
the very idea of self-rule would be meaningless, since universal reason, not
personal choice, would in fact govern one's will, the results of which would
turn out the same for everyone. Under these conditions, in principle, there
would be no need for a separate consideration of the Other, since everyone's
choices would turn out to be the same. In short, it would appear that in this
interpretation of Berlin's distinction between positive and negative liberty,
Callan—like many universal liberals before him—reveals himself to be a
bit of a hedgehog rather than a fox, falling prey to what Oakeshott calls the
'fallacy of rationalism' in politics.

RATIONALISM IN POLITICS AND TRADITIONS OF PRACTICE

Oakeshott's (1991) critique of rationalism shows that he too was a pluralist,
although Gray thought that he was overly committed to a single tradition.
Oakeshott's mistake, Gray contends, was to replace principle with tradition as a basis for liberalism, as if any late modern society contained only
one tradition. "If contemporary societies contain several traditions, with
many people belonging to more than one, politics cannot be conducted by
following any one tradition. It must try to reconcile the intimations of rival
traditions" (Gray 2002, 32–33). In this assessment, Gray (like other liberal
philosophers) confuses Oakeshott's concern for the political tradition of a
single society with the idea that traditions are necessarily closed and rigid,

while it is Oakeshott's critique of closed and rigid traditions that in fact points the way to understanding how people who adhere to opposing traditions can coexist and even learn from one another (Alexander 2008).

Oakeshott's position is grounded in a distinction between two sorts of knowledge, one technical the other practical. Technical knowledge entails a mastery of the techniques required to properly engage in such human activities as natural science, the fine arts, or the governance of a good society. These can be formulated in propositions—rules, principles, directions, and maxims—that are found in manuals for cooking, driving, or scientific research. Practical knowledge, on the other hand, exists only in use, and is shared or becomes common not by means of formulated doctrines, but through traditions of practice. Technical knowledge can be learned from a book, wrote Oakeshott. Much of it can be learned by heart, repeated by rote, and applied mechanically. It can, in short, be both taught and learned in the simplest meanings of these words. Practical knowledge, on the other hand, "can be neither taught or learned, but only imparted and acquired. It exists only in practice, and the only way to acquire it is by apprenticeship to a master—not because a master can teach it (he cannot), but because it can be acquired only by continuous contact with one who is perpetually practicing it" (Oakeshott 1991, 10–11).

The problem with rationalism, claims Oakeshott, is that it denies that practical knowledge should be counted as knowledge altogether, since there is no knowledge that is not technical knowledge. For the rationalist, he writes, "the sovereignty of 'reason' . . . means the sovereignty of technique" (ibid., 11). The heart of the matter, he continues, "is the pre-occupation of the Rationalist with certainty" (ibid., 12). The superiority of technical knowledge lay in the appearance that it springs from pure ignorance and ends in complete knowledge. But this is an illusion. Technical knowledge is never self-complete; it relies on presuppositions grounded in experience, without which the techniques of a particular field of inquiry make no sense. Oakeshott traces this preoccupation with certainty born of technique to Bacon's *Novum Organum* (Bacon 2000) and Descartes' *Discourse on Method* (Descartes 2000). These texts influenced John Locke's *Second Treatise of Civil Government*, which Oakeshott described as among the most popular and long-lived of political cribs (Locke 1988). On this account, Jefferson's Declaration, and similar documents of the French Revolution, merely summarized an ideology that Locke had distilled from the English political tradition, on the mistaken assumption that these principles were not the product of civilization, but "discovered in the nature of human reason" (Locke 1988, 28). However, this passion for logical technique misconceived the relation between reason and tradition by confusing genuine knowledge of political affairs with partial truths torn not only from general experience of the world, which is certainly a more reliable guide than the maxims that might be recorded in a book, but also from the traditions of a society, which can take two or three generations to acquire.

The difficulty with universal liberalism, on this view, is that it succumbs to this rationalist infatuation with uniformity and regularity. The consequence for literacy in democratic education is a strong tendency toward what historian David Tyack (2007) has called a "one best system," according to which all accounts of how and why children are taught to communicate must conform to a universal, rational standard. Rawls (2005a), for example, calls for citizens in liberal democracies to accept 'burdens of judgment' as a common basis for deliberating public goods. Among their other demands, these burdens require that public policies be defended only on grounds accepted by all, without appeal to particular value traditions. A Catholic, in this view, should not make a public case against the legality of abortion on the grounds that human life begins at conception, since this view is limited to particular traditions not held in common by all citizens. However, as Meira Levinson (1999, 17) points out, accepting this approach requires embracing an account of how pluralism is to be negotiated in the public domain that itself violates pluralism, because among other reasons it requires that our most substantive differences be left at the deliberation room door. Suggestions that Israel abandon its distinctive Jewish cultural character in order to address injustices done to Palestinians fall prey to this same fallacy of uniform technique. It presupposes a common culture to be transmitted to the young citizens of this state that is based on one form or another of universal reason divorced from a particular language or tradition; no such culture is possible, since even Enlightenment rationality is embedded in the history of a particular people who have lived at a specific time and place.

Radical social theorists also succumb to this rationalist fallacy, although they differ with liberals over the technique to which we ought to subscribe. Kant and Locke embraced an empirical–deductive logic with roots going back to Aristotle, whereas Hegel and Marx employed rival versions of dialectical reasoning that began with Plato. "No other technique has so imposed itself upon the world as if it were concrete knowledge," wrote Oakeshott (referring to the Marx and Engels 1998), "none has created so vast an intellectual proletariat, with nothing but its technique to lose" (Oakeshott 1991, 26). And nowhere is this tendency to reduce complex social relations to abstract and uniform techniques more apparent than in concepts relating to conflict and power associated with critical social theory. Consider the postcolonial claim that Zionism constitutes a form of colonialism, which draws what may be apt parallels between the exercise of Israeli and European power in the Middle East while denying the deep historic ties of Jews to the land of Israel. To be sure, power relations between Jews and Arabs in Israel and the Middle East have been troubled for centuries, and Zionism most certainly has more than its fair share of abuses to account for, as do all of the other actors in the region; but to reduce these relations to so one-sided a model as colonialism, in which Jews are the intruders and Palestinians the natives, is to misconceive in the extreme the complexity of the interactions between these peoples.[2] It is highly unlikely that a concept of literacy for democratic education based on such an analysis could contribute to a reduction of the many tensions between them for, among many reasons, it would necessitate a call for the nostalgic return to Muslim-dominated Ottoman rule, which predated the arrival of the British in 1917 and the establishment of Israel in 1948—hardly a democratic or pluralistic outcome. This is not to diminish the attention to power relations brought out by radical social criticism or to suggest that it always or necessarily lacks nuance. Rather, the point is that in a legitimate effort to deconstruct irrelevant differences among people that lead to abuses of authority and inequitable distribution of resources, critical theories too often delegitimize distinctions in culture and tradition that are essential to the moral bite of their opposition to oppression in the first place since, as Oakeshott would insist, the ethical evaluation of social conflict is itself historically contingent; or as Foucault has taught since, even dialectical reasoning is a product of power relations and so unavailable as a basis for resisting injustice.

Oakeshott's analysis extends, then, not only to how we understand rational technique, but also to the nature of political traditions. Rationalists, he claims, attribute to those traditions "the rigidity and fixity of character" that in fact belongs to the ideological principles born of "arid technique" (Oakeshott 1991, 31). However, traditions of practice are not limited by one or another conception of rational rules. They are manners of preserving, recalling, and transmitting across the generations knowledge particular peoples have accumulated from the concrete experience of living together as a community (ibid., 123). Knowledge of this sort is practical, not technical; it cannot be fully captured by any set of rules, principles, or procedures; or abridged into an abstract political or religious ideology, which although useful can easily distort or mislead; rather, it is preserved in the intricacies and details of shared lives that are communicated in the sundry institutions, rituals, manners, customs, stories, and oddities of which a collective existence is comprised. A tradition of practice, then, is not an inflexible manner of doing things. (ibid.,126) "It is neither fixed, nor finished; it has no changeless centre to which understanding can anchor itself . . . no model to be copied or idea to be realized . . . Some parts of it may change more slowly than others, but none is immune from change. Everything is temporary" (ibid.,128). Nevertheless, though dynamic and emergent, traditions are not totally fluid or without identity, since all of their parts do not change at the same time. What accounts for the identity of a tradition is the diffusion of authority between past, present, and future, in which nothing that ever belonged is completely lost. Change within a tradition of practice, then, is normal, though it emerges gradually and not abruptly by means of undirected evolution and not preplanned revolution (ibid., 126).

Unfortunately, all too often the tendency among critics of republicanism is to adopt a dogmatic as opposed to dynamic account of political traditions, closed off from valuable dialogue and debate with alternative views. One example of this is what Sigal Ben-Porath (2006) calls the 'belligerent concept of citizenship,' which emerges when national and personal security are threatened, such as in times of war. It entails a narrowing of three key components of citizenship: (1) civic participation, which is normally voluntary but becomes mandated toward the war effort; (2) patriotism, which normally reflects pride in democratic ideals but is transformed into unity and solidarity in the face of a common enemy; and (3) public deliberation, which is normally open and wide ranging but becomes attenuated, focused on security issues with limited acceptable opinions (Ben-Porath 2006, 11–14). These unfortunate tendencies arise under the pressures of war, Ben-Porath argues, because citizenship education is too often viewed as a form of initiation into national identity, which seeks to contain rather than preserve diversity because it supposes that identification with the nation-state trumps all other identities we may have. Instead, Ben-Porath proposes what she calls "expansive education," which conceives citizenship as shared fate that may entail shared cultural or ethnic identity, but can also be based on other features, such as institutional and material linkages (ibid., 23–27).

This alternative seems unobjectionable as far as it goes, but Ben-Porath's complaints about education in national identity appear to be grounded in the very dogmatic conception of tradition that Oakeshott attributes to the rationalists, which too often does not need the threat of war in order to become belligerent. Oakeshott was wrong if he supposed that no traditions of practice function in this way. Some religious and political orientations undoubtedly have a dogmatic tendency to fear the other, and one of the important contributions of critical social theory is to call them to account when they become overly narrow or oppressive. He was correct, however, to point out that many if not most traditions of practice are dynamic, not stagnant; and that given the right conditions and left to their own devices, they will evolve and adapt to threats of all kinds quite effectively, precisely because they are open to learning from alternative perspectives and from the world in which they are situated. We require, then, not merely an account of citizenship that enables people from diverse backgrounds, such as Jewish and Palestinian Israelis, to view themselves as part of a common enterprise, but also an understanding of the traditions that inform those backgrounds that allows such a dialogue across difference to take place.

LIBERAL NATIONALISM AND THE PEDAGOGY OF DIFFERENCE

Yael Tamir (1995), a student of Berlin's, outlines a potential basis for such an understanding in her defense of liberal nationalism, in which she uses the term 'culture' to refer to something very close to what Oakeshott means by a 'tradition of practice.' With many communitarian critics of comprehensive liberalism, she conceives the citizen and her choices as embedded in shared languages, histories, and customs, not governed solely by disengaged or hypothetical rationality. However, unlike the perfectionism of some communitarianism, she adopts an open and reflective rather than a perfectionist account of culture, which assumes that individuals can shape the cultures in which they choose to live and not only base life choices on the cultures they have chosen. Hence, she distinguishes between self-determination and self-rule; the former referring to the right of individuals to public cultural expression, and the latter to the right of cultural groups or nations to secure self-determination for their members by means of the state, although state power is not the only way to achieve cultural expression. National privileges are thus intrinsic not instrumental values—basic rights owed to every individual, not means to redress collective suffering or promote cultural survival. Concern for the others outside of the immediate circle of national membership is grounded in something akin to what Nel Noddings (1984) calls 'concentric circles of care:' "Individuals care most about those in the circle closest to the centre, but are not indifferent to the welfare of those who occupy farther positions" (109).

Finally, in her Preface to the 1995 paperback edition of *Liberal Nationalism*, Tamir distinguishes between national and civic education.

> In a nationally diversified political system, be it a town, a state, a federation, a regional organization, or a global society, it is especially important that all children learn to respect others who have different lifestyles, values, and traditions and view them—qua members of the political system—as equals. Beyond this thin layer each national group should foster among its young knowledge that is relevant to its own particular community, its history, language, and traditions. Separating civic from national education is thus the key for continued peaceful existence of multinational societies . . . National groups—minorities and majorities alike—should thus be given the freedom to have their own educational system (whether in the form of separate schools or, preferably, . . . special hours or days) alongside the civic one. Civic education should attempt to create civic friendship among all, but it should attempt to do so not by assimilating all into one culture, but by respecting cultural diversity. (Tamir 1995, xxix)

In addition to initiation into their own cultural heritage, "all children should thus acquire some knowledge of the culture, history, and tradition of all national groups that share their political system, and be taught to respect them" (ibid.).

Like Meira Levinson's 'weak perfectionism' (1999, 21–24), Tamir's liberal nationalism goes some distance toward managing the tension between the individual rights that democratic citizenship demands and the literacy in particular cultures needed to understand and exercise those rights—or in Berlin's terms, toward finding a proper balance between positive and negative liberty.

But one wonders whether Tamir, like Levinson, has not leaned too far in the direction of the individual to the detriment of cultural integrity and continuity, perhaps because she follows the rationalists in misconceiving traditions as rigid and dogmatic. She rejects the idea of culture 'authenticity' being dependent on roles ascribed by some "Council of Elders," since deviating from those roles might be interpreted as 'false consciousness' or hiding from one's 'true self,' both indicators of positive freedom gone awry, and argues instead that "the only authentic and genuine way of life is that freely chosen by each individual for himself" (Tamir 1995, 51). There is, then, "no Archimedean point from which we can evaluate the authenticity of cultures" (52).

> The debate about the nature of authenticity is closely related to the debate about the 'thinness' or 'thickness' of modern nations. The idea that a nation has undergone a slow and organic process of development is more authentic than one that has developed in a less stable and less continuous way—or that a society that exhibits a more contiguous set of values and beliefs is therefore more authentic than one that is new, pluralistic, and therefore heterogeneous—should then be viewed with suspicion. The assumption that individuals can exercise choice regarding both their communal affiliations and their moral identity entails respect for dynamic and pluralistic views of culture. It views with favor the fact that, at any given point in time, different cultural interpretations compete for recognition within each nation. Membership in the cultural community would then be expressed by participating in the debate, rather than by following one specific interpretation (51).

Thus Tamir appears to suppose that, with no Archimedean point to evaluate the authenticity of cultures, personal feeling is the only basis on which to make constitutive choices about the person we aspire to be. But it does it not follow from the fact that our preferences are historically contingent, determined by neither dogmatic tradition nor universal reason, that the only available option is what Taylor (1985) would call 'weak evaluation,' based on mere feeling alone. For constitutive choices to be embedded in culture as Tamir asserts requires what Taylor calls 'strong evaluation,' based on norms that emanate from beyond the self. This in turn necessitates a thicker concept of culture or tradition than Tamir appears to allow, which grows in response to dialogue with opposing views and current events, but which is not within the total control of the individual to shape at the whim of his momentary or personal desires. Traditions that develop organically in response to their environments need not be homogeneous or monolithic. Indeed, the very priority Tamir places on pluralism and heterogeneity is itself the product of such a tradition of practice.

Moreover, without a neutral standpoint, what ought to be the substance of 'civic' as distinguished from 'national' education, in what language should it be taught, or on what cultural values can it be based? In passage cited above Tamir appears to endorse state support for education in minority cultures and faiths, which might suggest a multinational approach to civic education. Yet, later on she equivocates: "Even if social resources are fairly distributed, minority groups will be more limited in their ability to practice their national culture," she writes. "Therefore, due to no fault of society, national minorities may feel culturally deprived and continue to wish that they lived in a community in which they constitute the majority" (Tamir 1995, 56). From this it might appear that the common civic education should be based, as in the US, on a version of the majority culture that is sufficiently thin so as not to offend minorities. In either case, if this culture is not sufficiently robust to override individual preferences when they run counter to such essential values as respect for difference, it is unlikely that it can promote the sort of peaceful coexistence to which Tamir aspires. This necessitates neither a total separation of national from civic education nor a thin culture of mere personal choice. Instead, multinational coexistence requires an education in tradition that is open to dialogue with opposing views within the political system, but that also seeks common ground upon which to build a joint civic education. This may include Ben-Porath's common fate, institutions, and material relations, but it should also involve common historical, religious, and ideological connections. Jewish, Muslim, and Christian religions, for example, all share connections to the narrative of Abraham and Sarah, though the stories they tell about these seminal figures may differ, but all of these stories share connections with modern European Enlightenment culture that gave birth to liberal democracy. Exploring these connections in Jewish and Arab schools in Israel, along with elements of a shared fate including institution and material ties, could be the beginning of a common civic curriculum.

For this to be possible, however, each group requires a robust education in their own tradition, viewed as open and dynamic rather than closed and dogmatic, along with exposure to the traditions of the other. In addition to awareness of the historical contingency of a student's own traditions, cultural initiation also requires a critical aspect that addresses power relations both within that tradition, and between it and other traditions. In short, we need a hermeneutic of dialogue not of suspicion à la Freire (2000), but à la Buber (1970) and Noddings (1994) that acknowledges and confirms rather than accuses the other. Education in Jewish and Zionist traditions requires a self-examination concerning how Jews have related to one another, for example, across divides of politics, religion, ethnicity, gender, and sexual orientation. But such an education also demands examination of how Jews have exercised power over, in addition to suffering at the hands of, others. Similarly, Arab students of Muslim and Christian origin should be educated in their own customs and beliefs, but taught also to critically examine the cultures and societies from which they have emerged. They should explore historic power relations between Christians and Muslims and, of course, between both communities and the Jews. The civic education that should emerge from this approach cannot be entirely separated from national education; it needs to seek roots within each national culture separately, conceived dialogically and developmentally.

The antidote to rampant rationalism and universal liberalism or egalitarianism, as I have argued elsewhere (Alexander 2007), is neither a weak and personalized culture nor a dogmatic and oppressive tradition, but an emergent and dynamic heritage grounded in what Jonathan Sacks (2003) calls the 'dignity of difference' that admits multiple compelling approximations of the truth and many acceptable visions of how to live. Given that one can never stand outside of the life one leads, one can acquire the capacity to make independent choices by learning to be different and to respect the difference of others. This requires a critical understand of the tradition into which I was born or with which I choose to affiliate, along with an acknowledgement and confirmation of others who are different from me, recognizing that it is they, not I, who should assume responsibility for their future. Following Sacks, and in contrast to pedagogies of the oppressed that tend to place responsibility for one's plight on social structures or power relations rather than on oneself (Freire 2000), I have called this the 'pedagogy of difference.'

NOTES

1. I am grateful to the Richard and Rhoda Goldman Foundation for funding a visiting professorship at the University of California, Berkeley during the 2008/2009 academic year. Also to Dr. Mitchell Bard of the American Israel Cooperative Enterprise and Dean P. David Pearson of the Graduate School Education (GSE) for exceptional conditions that made writing this chapter possible. I am also indebted to the students in my graduate seminar on citizenship education, participants in the Social and Cultural Studies Speakers Series, and Professor Jabari Mahiri, Chair of the Language, Literacy, Society, and Culture Division of the GSE for helpful comments and suggestions.

2. The very name Palestine for what Jews have historically called Israel was chosen by the Romans after their conquest in the first century ostensibly to indicate that the land belonged not to the Jews but the Philistines, a people who resided in the southwest costal region of that land around eight hundred years earlier. Muslim Arabs arrived in the seventh century and until very recently did not use the designation Palestine for the land. It was reintroduced by the British when they acquired a mandate to rule from the League of Nations in 1917, probably to identify their own empire with that of the Romans. Although people certainly have the right to choose the names by which they prefer to be called, one can only wonder whether the choice of such a name as the national designation for Arab residents of that land after the establishment of the State of Israel in 1948 did not entail an allusion to its anti-Jewish origins. Relations between Jews and Arabs in the region, as I said, are not easily summarized in a single technique of conflict analysis or dialectical reasoning.

BIBLIOGRAPHY

Alexander, H.A. "Moral Education and Liberal Democracy: Spirituality, Community, and Character in an Open Society." *Educational Theory* 53, no. 4 (2004): 367–387.

————. "What is Common About Common Schooling? Rational Autonomy and Moral Agency in Liberal Democratic Education." *Journal of Philosophy of Education* 41, no. 4 (2007): 609–624.

————. "Engaging Tradition. Michael Oakeshott on Liberal Learning." In, *Learning to Live with the Future*, edited by A. Stables and S. Gough, 113–127. New York: Routledge, 2008.

Aristotle. *The Politics*. New York: Penguin Classics, 1981.

Bacon, F. *The New Organon*. Cambridge: Cambridge University Press, 2000.

Ben-Porath, S.R. *Citizenship Under Fire: Democratic Education in Times of Conflict*. Princeton, NJ: Princeton University Press, 2006.

Berlin, I. *The Hedgehog and the Fox: An Essay on Tolstoy's View of History*. New York: Simon and Schuster, 1953.

————. *Four Essays on Liberty*. Oxford: Oxford University Press, 1990.

————. *Against the Current: Essays in the History of Ideas*. Princeton, NJ: Princeton University Press, 1997.

————. *Three Critics of Enlightenment: Vico, Hamann, and Herder*. Princeton, NJ: Princeton University Press, 2001.

Brighouse, H. *On Education*. New York: Routledge, 2005.

Buber, M. *I and Thou*. New York: Scribner, 1970.

Callan, E. "McLaughlin on Parental Rights." *Journal of Philosophy of Education* 19, no. 2 (1985): 111–118.

————. *Autonomy and Schooling*. Kingston and Montreal: McGill-Queen's University Press, 1988.

————. *Creating Citizens: Political Education and Liberal Democracy*. Oxford: Oxford University Press, 2004.

Cicero, M.T. *The Republic and the Laws*. Trans. N. Rudd. Oxford: Oxford University Press, 2009.

Descartes, R. *Discourse on Method and Related Writings*. New York: Penguin, 2000.

Feinberg, W. *Common Schools/Uncommon Identities: National Unity and Cultural Difference*. New Haven, CT: Yale University Press, 2000.

Freire, P. *Pedagogy of the Oppressed*. New York: Continuum, 2000.

Foucault, M. *The Order of Things: An Archeology of the Human Sciences*. New York: Routledge, 2001.

Gramsci, A. *Selections from the Prison Notebooks*. New York: International Publishers, 2008.

Gray, J. *Isaiah Berlin*. Princeton, NJ: Princeton University Press, 1996.

————. *The Two Faces of Liberalism*. London: New Press, 2002.

Gur-Ze'ev, I. *Beyond the Modern-postmodern Struggle in Education*. Rotterdam: Sense Publishers, 2008.

Gutmann, A. *Democratic Education*. Princeton, NJ: Princeton University Press, 1987.

Gutmann, A. and D. Thompson. *Democracy and Disagreement*. Cambridge, MA: Harvard University Press, 1998.

Hegel, G.W.F. *Philosophy of Right*. Oxford: Oxford University Press,1967.

Horkheimer, M. and T. Adorno. *The Dialectic of Enlightenment*. Stanford, CA: Stanford Univ. Press, 2002.

Levinson, M. *The Demands of Liberal Education*. Oxford: Oxford University Press, 1999.

Locke, J. *Two Treaties of Government*. Cambridge: Cambridge University Press, 1988.

Kant, I. *Foundations of the Metaphysics of Morals*. Englewood Cliffs, NJ: Prentice Hall, 1989.

————. *Critique of Practical Reason*. Cambridge: Cambridge University Press, 1997.

Macedo, S. *Liberal Virtues: Citizenship, Virtue, and Community in Liberal Con-stitutionalism.* Oxford: Oxford University Press, 1991.

———. *Diversity and Distrust: Civic Education in a Multicultural Democracy.* Cambridge, MA: Harvard University Press, 2000.

Machiavelli, N. *The Prince.* New York: Bantam, 1984.

MacIntyre, A. *After Virtue: A Study in Moral Theory.* Notre Dame, IN: University of Notre Dame Press, 1981.

MacIntyre, A. *Whose Justice, Which Rationality?* Notre Dame, IN: University of Notre Dame Press, 1989.

Marx, K. *Critique of Hegel's Philosophy of Right.* Cambridge: Cambridge University Press, 1970.

Marx, K. and F. Engels. *Collected Works.* New York: International Publishers, 1998.

McLaren, P. *Life in Schools: An Introduction to Critical Pedagogy in the Foundations of Education.* Boston: Allyn and Bacon, 2006.

McLaughlin, T.H. "Citizenship, Diversity and Education: A Philosophical Perspective." *Journal of Moral Education* 21, no. 3 (1992): 235–250.

———. "Liberalism, Education, and the Common School." *Journal of Philosophy of Education* 29, no. 2 (1995): 239–255.

Mill, J.S. *On Liberty and Other Essays.* Oxford: Oxford University Press, 1998.

Noddings, N. *Caring: A Feminine Approach to Ethics and Moral Education.* Berkeley: University of California Press, 1984.

Nozick, R. *Philosophical Explanations.* Cambridge, MA: Harvard University Press, 1981.

Oakeshott, M. *Rationalism in Politics and Other Essays.* Wichita, KS: Liberty Press, 1991.

Rawls, J. *Justice as Fairness: A Restatement.* Cambridge, MA: Harvard University Press, 2001.

———. *A Theory of Justice.* Cambridge, MA: Harvard University Press, 2005a.

———. *Political Liberalism.* New York: Columbia University Press, 2005b.

Raz, J. *The Morality of Freedom.* Oxford: Oxford University Press, 1988.

———. *Engaging Reason: On the Theory of Value and Action.* Oxford: Oxford University Press, 2002.

Plato. *The Republic.* Trans. R. Waterfield. Oxford: Oxford University Press, 2008.

Sacks, J. *The Dignity of Difference.* London: Continuum, 2003.

Said, E. *Orientalism.* New York: Vintage Books, 1979.

Sandel, M. *Liberalism and the Limits of Justice.* Cambridge: Cambridge University Press, 1998.

Searle, J. *The Construction of Social Reality.* New York: The Free Press, 1997.

Steiner, G. *After Babel: Aspects of Language and Translation.* Oxford: Offord University Press, 1998.

Tamir, Y. *Liberal Nationalism.* Princeton, NJ: Princeton University Press, 1995.

Taylor, C. *The Ethics of Authenticity.* Cambridge, MA: Harvard University Press, 1991.

———. "What is Human Agency?" Chap. 1 in *Human Agency and Language.* Cambridge, UK: Cambridge University Press, 1985.

Tomasi, J. *Liberalism Beyond Justice: Citizens, Society, and the Boundaries of Political Theory.* Princeton, NJ: Princeton University Press, 2001.

Tyack, D. *The One Best System: A History of American Urban Education.* Cambridge, MA: Harvard University Press, 2007.

Walzer, M. *Thick and Thin: Moral Argument at Home and Abroad.* Notre Dame, IN: University of Notre Dame Press, 1994.

Young, I.M. *Inclusion and Democracy.* Oxford: Oxford University Press, 2002.

4 After All, How Small is the World? Global Citizenship as an Educational Ideal

Doret de Ruyter

INTRODUCTION

It is not surprising that the globalization of the market and consumer economy, as well as the globalizing effect of the Internet and other media, have led to a revival of the idea of a certain kind of cosmopolitanism—namely that we are no longer only citizens of a nation state, but that we are citizens of the world. Moreover, this new civic identity is not simply a fact; it is perceived as a desirable state to which persons should aspire. The increased opportunities for First-World citizens to travel the world and interact with people from around the world can be seen as having positive influences on their lives: they are able to explore and learn in unprecedented ways. However, this is not the only side to global citizenship, and it needs to be clearly separated from the moral obligations that follow from such opportunities. The idea that a global citizen is a person who can live everywhere because she is able and willing to understand others is, in my view, but one side of globalization. It is clearly beneficial for the individual, but not necessarily so for others. Under the guise of the moral obligation to be respectful to people in foreign countries, the global citizen may well act primarily in her own interest. She may, for instance, be eager to learn about her new home country in order to become a successful businesswoman. In this case, her respect for others and their cultures is primarily instrumental in character, and 'global citizenship' would merely be a new term for '(capitalist) imperialism.' In order to exclude the possibility of violating the original moral conception of 'cosmopolitanism' as it was found among the Greeks, the moral dimension should be spelled out clearly. Thus, the concept of global citizenship that I offer will be explicitly moral in character. However, this does not mean that being cosmopolitan should not be beneficial to individuals as well, but that the conception of global citizenship will therefore have to balance aspects that are other-regarding as well as self-regarding.

Having to balance moral demands and self-serving qualities is an enormous challenge, particularly at a global scale. Moreover, doing it well is an excellent achievement. These two qualifications seem to indicate that a global citizen is an 'ideal' person. This idea suggests that global citizenship is also an ideal aim of education. In this chapter I will defend the view that cosmopolitanism is indeed an educational ideal aim. I will begin by explaining the concept of 'educational ideals.' Then I will describe what I believe to be the two ideal aims of education, i.e., human flourishing and being morally good. These two aims shape the conception of global citizenship that I will defend as an educational ideal.

IDEALS AND EDUCATION

'Ideals' can be defined as those values a person believes to be excellent or even perfect. To these ideals, she attaches high importance, but they are not realized as of yet. Thus, ideals are a subclass of values and have three characteristics.

Firstly, ideals are values that have a particular quality. Contra Rescher (1987), who claims that ideals refer to perfect values only,[1] I believe that the concept of ideals can also stand for excellent values. This reflects our ordinary language, in which the word 'ideals' is used for excellent values that can be realized as well as perfect values that are unrealizable. For instance, it does not sound awkward to say that one day a Dutch woman may be able to realize her ideal to become the first female prime minister of the Netherlands, but that her ideal of being the perfect ruler of our nation is unachievable because it is impossible for her to be flawless.

Secondly, a person believes her ideals to be of great importance. Ideals therefore have a personal character. An individual may agree with others that a value is excellent or perfect, but it is only an ideal for them if they also believe it is highly important. Of course, the personal character of ideals does not preclude the possibility of a large group of people sharing an ideal. For example, members of a faith community can have similar religious ideals, and professionals pursue ideals characteristic of their profession. Nor does the personal character of ideals imply that a person cannot adopt ideals from others; ideals need to be affirmed by persons, but they do not have to be invented by them. Finally, the personal attachment to ideals does not mean that they are subjective, or that they cannot be evaluated by others through the use of objective standards.

Thirdly, ideals are not yet realized. Their not-as-yet-realized character makes it possible to look at imagined excellent or perfect situations or characteristics of a person from different perspectives and to discover whether or not they would be truly excellent if realized. In reflecting on this, one does not have to take into account whether or not it is actually possible to realize the ideal. On the contrary, not having to do so is precisely what allows people to develop their views on excellent or perfect values. If ideals have to be confined to those values that one can realize, the possibility of developing ideas about perfect values becomes impossible, because perfect values cannot be actualized.

The combination of these three characteristics motivates a person to pursue the realization of the ideal. The fact that ideals refer to perfect or excellent values implies that they are impossible or at least very difficult to achieve. Therefore, it is important that persons be able to combine this implication of ideals with their own wish or drive to realize what they highly value. In other words, their pursuit of the ideal, as well as the expectations of what they can achieve, should be realistic. Without tempering their expectations, persons may either become utterly frustrated and defeated about their own capacities, or they might become fanatical in a relentless mission to accomplish their ideal. These possibilities necessitate that education addresses not only the content of ideals, but also ways in which people pursue them. I will return to this later.

Educational Ideals

'Educational ideals' can be described as the excellent or perfect values that prevail in education, values that are seen as highly important but that are not yet realized. It is possible to differentiate between three clusters of educational ideals: ideal aims, content-ideals, and ideal educational methods or educational approaches.

Firstly, ideals can be aims educators aspire toward or should arguably strive for; for example, that children, once they become adults, will be devout believers, autonomous, happy, successful, or incredibly rich. These examples illustrate two of the characteristics I just described: there are different views about which values are excellent, and secondly, some of these excellences are realizable, albeit with great effort. Ideal aims of education can be diverse, too, in part because children encounter different educators. Therefore, we are faced with the question: Excellent or perfect according to whom? Parents have views on what is excellent for their children, but so do members of society, and the state, as well as those who work as functionaries of the state, such as teachers. Furthermore, not only may the views of these parties clash, it is also possible that they are mistaken or that their intentions lead to undesirable or counterintuitive results.

Here are two examples involving the Dutch government. First, several years ago, the Dutch government warned pregnant women about the consequences of smoking. The reduction in the baby's birth weight was named as one of the negative effects. For some women, however, this information was an incentive to *increase* the number of cigarettes they smoked. By doing so, they aimed at having an easy delivery. Thus, the good intention of the government led to opposite results. Second, The Netherlands Institute for Spatial Research recently accused the government of having obsolete ideals about the Dutch landscape. The institute argued that the government holds on to nostalgic ideals about unspoiled nature and idealistic rural areas. According to the institute, these ideals may have been valid years ago, but that is no longer the case. Therefore, the ideals of the government are mistaken, according to the institute at least.

In order to minimize the possibility of erroneous ideals, we may expect educators to give good reasons for believing that the educational aims they pursue are excellent or perfect, and that they are willing to change their views if they realize that the aims are either not as excellent as they thought or that they conflict with other ideals. In other words, educators need to have a capacity for conception of the good (Rawls 1993). This is important for educators, because what they do affects not only their own lives, but also, or even primarily, affects the lives of others.

Additionally, because ideal educational aims refer to perfections or excellences, they are either impossible or difficult to achieve. That ideals are difficult to achieve is not only related to their excellent character, but also to the potential of children and the circumstances in which educators and children live. Thus, while being able to read, write, and calculate are certainly aims of education, these aims remain ideals for children with dyslexia or dyscalculia, for in their case it would be an excellent achievement if they were able to read or calculate at an adequate level. It may seem that this introduces a new characteristic of ideals, namely that their pursuit and possible realization require a particular level of effort. This is not true. Rather, it illustrates that what we call 'excellence' is also dependent on a person's starting position. However, this does mean that there is a somewhat grey area: educational aims and educational ideal aims cannot always be neatly disentangled.

Second, in addition to ideals as aims, ideals also feature in education as the content of education, i.e., as content-ideals. These are the ideals that educators pursue themselves, as well as those that educators, most likely teachers, believe (or should believe!) an important alternative view on excellent values (see also Brighouse 2005). For instance, while religious parents may foster and pursue the ideal of a theocratic society, teachers will also highlight the excellent qualities of a liberal democracy. Or, while parents may believe that an academic career is the only excellent option for their children if they have the intellectual capacities, teachers may provide excellent examples of other vocations, which for some for children may be more conducive to their flourishing.

The ideals that educators pursue will always play a role in education, even if educators do not intentionally aim for children to adopt these. This is because ideals influence the way in which educators act, and this obviously has an effect on children. For instance, parents or teachers who aspire to be trustworthy or honest will try to act accordingly and will praise children if they do the same, or correct them if they do not.

The distinction between content-ideals and ideal aims might seem a purely analytic one, for we might ask if content-ideals are not simply an aspect of ideal aims. For example, we could interpret the active membership of an organization that challenges unjust situations in the world as a content-ideal, but also as an aspect of the ideal aim that children become good global citizens. However, it is useful to distinguish between these, because while there is a necessary relation between ideal aims and content-ideals, this relation is not sufficient. Parents and teachers with different ideal aims can have the same content-ideals. For instance, both educators who strive for autonomy, as well as parents who hope that their child will become a devout and committed Christian, may wish to instill in their children the ideal of a just world. Likewise, parents and teachers who share the same ideal aim can have different content ideals.

Third, there are ideal ways in which parents and teachers raise and educate children. What is considered an ideal way of educating children needs to cohere with the ideal aims. For instance, if educators pursue the ideal of autonomy, the way they raise and educate children will include the ideals of freedom, critical thinking, open-mindedness, courage, and honesty. However, if they were to use methods of indoctrination to ensure that children will adopt the ideals that they value themselves, they would undermine those ideal aims.

A clear example of the coherence of ideals can be found in William Hare's *What Makes a Good Teacher* (1993). Hare has defended the ideal of open-mindedness in several publications.[2] In his 1993 book, he argues that good teachers should be humble, courageous, impartial, open-minded, empathic, enthusiastic, and able to think critically and use their creative imagination. These qualities of good teachers are characteristic for being open-minded, which means that Hare portrays a good teacher as a person who models this ideal to her pupils and pursues this ideal herself.

Although there are different views about what is excellent and therefore of what diverse educational ideal aims consist, some aims of education can be called ideals for all because they are an excellence for all. This claim, however, is feasible only if the ideals are relatively abstract and open to subjective interpretations. Children need to develop their own interpretation of the excellence because only then will they attach high value to it, and thereby the excellent value can become their ideal too.

In my view there are two ideal educational aims for all: Human flourishing and being a moral person. The ideal of human flourishing I defend is an abstract and formal educational ideal that has objective as well as subjective aspects. Although there are strict or pure objective and subjective well-being theories in both philosophy and psychology, the theories that have most credibility acknowledge the importance of both (see also Griffin 1986).

The following examples illustrate that many theorists who position themselves primarily in one tradition also acknowledge the importance of some aspects of the other.

With regard to the objective theories, Kraut argues that

> They [objectivists] might believe that for each of us there is a large class of ideal lives, and that to be happy we have to come reasonably close to

one of those lives. And an objectivist can also say that different types of individuals have different capacities, so that what is ideal for one person may not be ideal for another. (Kraut 1979, 181).

Meanwhile, the self-determination theory of psychologists Ryan and Deci maintains that there are three innate psychological needs which are functionally required for the flourishing of a person (Ryan and Deci 2000; Reis et al. 2000, 420): the need for autonomy, the need for competency, and the need for being related. However, while these needs are universal, they argue that the way in which they are met is dependent on personal, societal, and cultural circumstances. Thus, a subjective fulfillment of objective and universal goods allows people to flourish.

In subjective theories on well-being or happiness we also recognize ideas of the objective well-being theories. For instance, the subjective well-being theory (SWB) in psychology claims that there are three components to subjective well-being including a cognitive component about satisfaction in life and two affective components, the presence of positive affect and the absence of negative affect (Diener, Suh, and Oishi 1997; Diener, Suh, Lucas, and Smith 1999). Diener, the most important defender of SWB, argues, however, that feelings of happiness or life satisfaction are not sufficient for well-being (Diener and Scollon 2003). He claims research has shown that while happiness is an important value, it is not the most important for all, nor is it the only important value. His studies also demonstrate that persons believe happiness to be of value if they experience positive emotions related to the satisfaction of desires that are important to them. In other words, mere feelings of pleasure are not sufficient.

Based on these two theories, I suggest that persons are able to flourish if they can give their own interpretation to the objective goods and develop as optimally as possible, *and* if the resulting life satisfies them. It is clear that the objective goods of health, having relationships, autonomy, creativity, and intellectual development are general in character. This not only allows but actually *necessitates* that persons give their own interpretation to those goods. Under this conception of flourishing, subjective elements are imported into an objective theory: fulfilling the goods in an optimal way is necessary for the flourishing of people, but they will only do so if this fulfillment is satisfactory to them.

The second educational ideal that is ideal for all is that children develop into moral persons. Similar to the ideal of human flourishing, this ideal needs to be general as well as abstract. It should not be phrased more concretely because there are different views on which excellences are characteristic for a moral person. While some believe that justice is the highest ideal a moral person should pursue, others defend the ideal of care. While some claim that a moral person ideally fulfills all her duties, others perceive a moral person in terms of her virtues. In my ideal conception of human flourishing, being morally good is part of what human flourishing involves.

Although some theories maintain that a person can flourish without being moral or even while being immoral (for instance, see Becker 1992, 26), we would not call this an 'ideal' of human flourishing; we would not say that it is excellent to flourish in a way that does not take into account the flourishing of others too. However, to leave no room for the idea that I would suggest that education should aim for the fulfillment of prudent interests of children only, I present moral goodness as a separate educational ideal aim in addition to human flourishing.

The two ideal aims also lead to a proposal about the content ideals, because educating children to become flourishing adults who are morally good has implications for *what* is being educated. First, objective goods need to be part of the children's upbringing, and of their family life. In other words, parents need to introduce children to objective goods. They also need to have found satisfying interpretations of these goods themselves. These interpretations are the ones they live by and share with their children. Second, ideals need to be part of education. The reason for this claim is based on Joseph Raz's social dependence thesis (2003).

One of the central claims of Raz's thesis is that different practices bring about diverse values. And these values may continue to exist even when the originating practices have changed. The practices, however, are not a uniform whole, but consist of practice 'genres,' which Raz characterizes as follows: "The concept of a genre or a kind of value combines two features: it defines which objects belong to it, and in doing so it determines that the value of the object is to be assessed (*inter alia*) by its relations to the defining standards of the genre" (2003, 39). Thus, while the social dependence thesis leads to value pluralism—i.e., that there are diverse as well as incompatible values—it does not imply relativism. The ground for saying that an action or object is good is relative to a particular genre, but this verdict is absolute within the genre. Thus a piece of art or a social arrangement can be judged by criteria that belong to the respective genre. For instance, Michelangelo's paintings in the Sistine Chapel are exquisite examples of mannerism, while Rothko's work is an excellent illustration of abstract expressionism. Both are good in the absolute sense, yet they are good in different ways. This allows us to say without contradiction that works of art or social arrangements, though completely different, are both good.

Parents and teachers need to teach their children the standards of the particular genres because this enables children to become good judges of values themselves. More importantly, it provides a valuable interpretation of the goods that are conducive to their well-being. Which genre within the objective goods will be good for children is something they have to discover for themselves, but what makes their actions within this genre good is something that educators can teach them. If someone knows what the best within a genre is, that person is able to evaluate current as well as future or alternative practices against these supreme standards. Ideas or images of a trustworthy friend, a reliable colleague, a harmonious family, or a just society can function as regulative ideals.

They can assist people in evaluating what they should do, what they should change or continue doing in order to achieve these ideal standards. These examples illustrate that the interpretation one gives to an objective good is not morally indifferent; on the contrary, they are often moral in character and therefore part of what it means to be a moral person.

Finally, the two ideal aims influence the ideal way of educating children. First, educators need to assist children in developing their ability to reflect on the interpretations of the objective goods, so they may discover which interpretation will be satisfying to them. In other words, the way in which parents and teachers educate children should be characterized by open-mindedness and critical reflection. These qualities are not only of instrumental value to the flourishing of children, they are equally important for the development of children into moral persons. Second, parents have to give their older children the freedom to discover which interpretation of the objective good is right for them, for what parents think is good for their children may not be the right interpretation of the good for them. Alternatively put: children need to have an open future in which they can discover what it is that contributes to their flourishing (Feinberg 1980).

IDEALS AND THEIR PURSUIT

I have already said that the pursuit of ideals can be detrimental both to oneself and to others. While I argued that persons will pursue the realization of their ideals, this does not mean that there is necessarily a causal relationship between the content of ideals and the way in which they are being pursued. Of course, we expect consistency between a person's ideals and her behavior. For instance, if I aspire to be an honest person but regularly tell white lies, then the sincerity of my claims to have this ideal should be questioned. However, as philosophers like Berlin and Emmet (as well as the psychologist Baumeister) have argued, good ideals can lead to evil. Precisely because persons attach such high value to their ideals, there is the possibility that they will strive to achieve their ideals in every possible way. Ideals can then become more valuable than other human beings: a person might not hesitate to sacrifice a few people for the sake of achieving her conception of the Good.

The threat of pursuing ideals in ways that are detrimental to others seems to be particularly prevalent when the two following conditions are combined: when people believe the ideal to be realizable and when the ideal concerns an ideal society. If it is believed that the best society can actually be established because people have a concrete picture—what Dorothy Emmett (1994) calls a 'blueprint' of such a society—they may well aim to create this ideal society at whatever cost. These costs could possibly include the extermination of those who do not believe in the ideal, or the suppression of those with ways of life that do not cohere with the ideal society.

This observation may explain why the most vehement arguments against the pursuit of ideals are about utopias built on a single ideal or a coherent group of ideals. Berlin, for instance, focuses on worldviews that consist of one ideal. This ideal is that "all genuine questions must have one true answer and one only," that "there must be a dependable path toward the discovery of these results," and that "the true answers must necessarily be compatible with one another and form a single whole" (1990 5,6). Even though this ideal is conceptually incoherent, its believers continue pursuing the true answer because they tend to be blinded by their conviction and therefore do not see that they are mistaken, and by doing so, they can create situations with horrific outcomes. In his Agnelli lecture, Berlin proclaims that "the possibility of a final solution turns out to be an illusion; and a very dangerous one. For if one really believes that such a solution is possible, then surely no cost would be too high to obtain it . . ." (ibid., 15).

It would be wrong to deny, therefore, that there are dangers related to pursuing one's ideals. This acknowledgement has implications for a proposal for global citizenship too, because conceptions of the ideal kind of citizen and the ideal kind of society are interrelated. Views on what counts as an ideal society also indicate what is characteristic for an ideal citizen; and conversely, a conception of an ideal citizen also informs how we think of an ideal society. For instance, defining the ideal global citizen as a good Muslim or Christian implies that one believes that a global Muslim or Christian world is ideal and vice versa. The main implication of avoiding the detrimental effects mentioned in this section is to develop a conception of global citizenship that is neither concrete nor precise. The reasons are the same as above: a blueprint of a good global citizen could lead to the conviction that it is possible to actually establish the particular global society of which one is supposed to be a good citizen.

Global Citizenship

Citizenship is regarded as a moral concept; it concerns the way in which citizens are expected to act toward each other and the state. This means that being a global citizen is morally qualified as well—referring here to the way in which inhabitants of the world have to interact or take responsibility for the world in which they live. Thus, global citizenship has to be regarded as an aspect of being a morally good person. This also means that global citizenship qualifies as an educational ideal aim because being morally good, in my view, is one of the two educational ideal aims that should be pursued for all. The educational aim of human flourishing also influences the way in which we have to conceptualize global citizenship, for this is equally an educational ideal aim for all. This leads to the following consequence: The ideal of global citizenship needs to be conceptualized in a way that allows for different subjective interpretations of this ideal. In other words, it has to have a general and abstract character allowing individuals to give their own specific content to the ideal, although this content has to be restricted by the moral imperatives that are equally characteristic for a global citizen.

Following these two ideals, I propose that global citizens should be able to identify with fellow human beings around the world, and that they should be interested in the ways in which others aim to flourish, particularly with regard to what other peoples or individuals perceive to be the ideals of the genres of the objective goods. This leads to a conception of global citizenship that consists of two aspects. First, global citizens have a moral political duty to respect the rights of other people to live their lives as they want to. Second, they ought to have both a moral and self-regarding disposition to be interested in the way other people flourish. The conceptualization of global citizenship that I am outlining here corresponds with two strands that Appiah believes to be characteristic of cosmopolitanism:

> One is the idea that we have obligations to others, obligations that stretch beyond those to whom we are related by the ties of kith and kind, or even the more formal ties of a shared citizenship. The other is that we take seriously the value not just of human life but of particular human lives, which means taking an interest in the *practices and beliefs* (italics DJR) that lend them significance. (Appiah 2006, xv)

The first characteristic of global citizens is that they adhere to public rules in at least a minimally moral and political sense: They have to respect the rights of other people to live according to their own world view or culture, unless their way of life inhibits the rights of others to do the same. Thus, a global citizen should have the moral political capacity to respect the freedom of people around the world to pursue their flourishing in the way that is satisfying to them. This ability is exclusively moral in character and therefore resides completely under the ideal educational aim of becoming a good moral person.

Sypnowich (2005) has developed an interesting conception of global citizenship in relation to human flourishing. In her view, the imperative of global citizenship has to be related to the flourishing of all people on earth, not to the flourishing of the individual (e.g., 2006, 65). In other words, global citizenship is not defended as an aspect of personal flourishing, but as an aspect of the moral responsibility to improve the flourishing of others. Sypnowich acknowledges that grounding it in the flourishing of all people on earth leads to a very demanding conception of global citizenship, most particularly with regard to the redistribution of wealth. Clearly, it would generate the imperative for people in the First World to donate part of their wealth to the Third World. The consequence of a human-flourishing concept of moral worldliness—as she phrases it—requires, in her terms the imperative to provide aid wherever it is needed, regardless of borders or territory. Moreover, insofar as we are concerned that people flourish not just in terms of bodily health, but also in the cosmopolitan's criterion of cultural well being, with scope for human interaction, music, art, and enjoyment of nature, it would seem that the bar for global redistribution is very high indeed. (Sypnowich 2005, 69)

In my own view, this bar is too high if it does not take into account the flourishing of the individuals themselves. Because Sypnowich focuses too much on the moral imperatives of global citizenship, there is a danger that the other ideal educational aim, personal human flourishing, is neglected.

My conception of the duty to respect the rights of others is clearly a more minimal interpretation of the moral obligations that arise out of global citizenship than Sypnowich proposes. Whereas the obligation I propose here is a negative duty, Sypnowich's views entail a positive duty. It could be objected, therefore, that my conception is too minimalist an interpretation of what it means to be a good moral person. This objection would be apposite if this were the only characteristic of a global citizen.

However, being interested in the way other people flourish, which is the second characteristic of global citizens, encompasses obligations that are not minimal in character. The fact that global citizens are obligated to be interested in the lives and the flourishing of other people beyond their own circle—in other words, that they have an expanded circle of sympathy (Rosenblum 1998)—leads to a more than minimal interpretation of their moral capacities: that is, global citizens should have the disposition to contribute to the factors[3] that enable other people to flourish. At this point, one may wonder if Sypnowich's and my proposal are as distinct as I suggested. I think that there are actually two differences.

First, the way in which global citizens encounter other cultures not only requires that they approach them with respect and open-mindedness (in other words, that they are not prejudiced), but also that they evaluate the practices they encounter from an ethical perspective. World citizens should be able to appreciate cultural artifacts for their aesthetic, cultural, or religious value, and rites of passage for their social value. At the same time, however, they should be able to evaluate the accompanying cultural practices and be highly critical of the political and moral circumstances of the countries they visit or live in. For instance, one can be in awe of the beauty and grandeur of Mayan temples but also abhor the practice of offering people to the gods. Likewise, while there may be good reasons for valuing the tribal practice of hunting because those tribes live on the animals they have caught, it is difficult to value the same practice if it is done merely for the sake of pleasure or an archaic tradition, like in Britain.

The second difference is that, in my view, being interested in the ways in which other people flourish has self-regarding characteristics as well. It is not only morally good to want to learn about other ways of life, but becoming culturally knowledgeable is also valuable for the flourishing of the individuals themselves. Cultures generate different forms of artifacts and practices in music, literature, science, and technology. They also generate different kinds of social practices, such as ways in which children are raised, ways in which adults interact, or what they regard as appropriate dress, eating habits, etc. Understanding other ways of life enriches one's knowledge of alternative ideals within different genres. This, in turn, allows one to discover other ways of flourishing than the ways found within one's own culture.

The thesis of Joseph Raz that I introduced previously in this article (the view that social practices can be distinguished into genres) is relevant for the knowledge and understanding of the global citizen, too. In my view, a world citizen is able to recognize a great variety of genres and judge an artifact or practice in relation to the ideals of that genre. As Appiah has it:

> Because you respond, with the instinct of a cosmopolitan, to the value of elegance of verbal expression, you take pleasure in Akan proverbs, Oscar Wilde's plays, Basho's haiku verses, Nietzsche's philosophy. Your respect for wit doesn't just lead you to these works: it shapes how you respond to them. (Appiah 2006, 26)

Thus, being a world citizen may contribute to a person's flourishing because of her increased insights into a variety of cultures and the satisfaction she gets out of these encounters. Her knowledge of a wider range of genres may be beneficial in discovering which genre enables her to flourish, and the ideals that correspond to the genres may assist her to do so in an excellent way.

Now that I have developed a conception of global citizenship that can be defended as an educational ideal, I need to address the question whether or not the pursuit of this ideal could be detrimental to others. Is it possible to realize the global society that mirrors my conception of a global citizen by suppression of alternative views on the ideal society or repression of the defenders of the alternatives?

The ideal society that corresponds to my conception of global citizenship is a liberal democracy. I have already defended the idea that a liberal democracy offers the best possibilities for people to flourish (De Ruyter 2006; 2007). In such a society the state does not impose a particular conception of the good on its citizens; citizens are free to live their private lives as they want to. Precisely because people are able to flourish if they can lead their lives according to an interpretation of the objective goods that is satisfactory to them, it is crucial that they have the freedom to do so[4].

In *Moral Education and the Democratic Ideal* (1989), Israel Scheffler describes the consequences for an education committed to the ideal of democracy. A democratic society requires citizens who are able and willing to make reasoned choices. This means that "[T]o choose the democratic ideal for society is wholly to reject the conception of education as an instrument of rule; it is to surrender the idea of shaping or molding the mind of the pupil" (1989, 139). In requiring that social policy be subject to open and public review, the democratic ideal rejects the rule of dogma and of arbitrary authority as the ultimate arbiter of social conduct. As Scheffler has it, to cultivate the trait of reasonableness is to liberate the mind from dogmatic adherence to ideological fashions, as well as from the dictates of authority. This implies that such an ideal can never be imposed or forced upon societies by an absolute authority or upon children by indoctrination. Moreover, if citizens subscribe to the democratic ideal and contribute to its realization, fanaticism and absolutism become impossible options for them because the ideal excludes these practices by definition.

Furthermore, the actualization of an ideal liberal democracy seems impossible, on a societal as well as a global level. Although societies have developed in the direction of the ideal, the ideal itself will never be achieved. The ideal is too good to be true; it is likely that there will always be aspects of the liberal democracy that can be improved. Moreover, governments and citizens can be mistaken. This requires that citizens be stimulated to use their critical capacity to evaluate the state as well as the world they live in. In other words, the ideal of a liberal democracy functions as a regulative ideal, i.e., an ideal that that sets a direction for a practice and prevents citizens from settling for surrogates (Emmet 1994, 2, 17).

However, even if people were to believe that this ideal could be realized, the ideal would not lead to the detrimental effects for others. As I have claimed, liberal democracies cannot be established by suppression. Moreover, it does not seem feasible to provide a blueprint of an ideal liberal democratic society. Although it is possible to describe its general characteristics and the principles that must prevail in such a society, spelling out what it looks like concretely and saying precisely what the ideal balance would be between the principles of freedom, equality, and fraternity, seems an elusive goal.

Thus, a global citizen defined as a person who respects the rights of others to live their life as they want to[5] and who is interested in the ways other people flourish is, in my view, an ideal aim of education.

IS GLOBAL CITIZENSHIP AN EDUCATIONAL IDEAL FOR ALL?

Global citizenship has universal characteristics because it has to encompass citizens around the entire globe, but is it also a universal ideal? My arguments lead me to the conclusion that it is. Nevertheless, it is not rational for everyone to pursue it. Whether or not it is sensible for individuals to pursue this ideal very much depends on the circumstances they live in.

Inglehart (2000), on the basis of the outcomes of three World Values Surveys (WVS), concludes that there is a positive relation between the economic level of a society and the prevalence of postmaterialist[6] and postmodern values.[7] When a country's wealth increases, its inhabitants no longer have to concentrate on their own survival, but can begin to look at fulfilling other needs. In line with Maslow's hierarchy of needs, the WVS provides evidence that in societies in which people do not have to live in hunger or economic insecurity, there is "a gradual shift in which needs for belonging, self-expression, and a participant role in society became more prominent" (Inglehart 2000, 221). The WVS also show that "postmodern values give priority to environmental and cultural issues, even when these goals conflict with maximizing economic growth" (Inglehart 2000, 223). It is obvious that only the citizens of affluent countries can afford such a stance.

Global citizenship should be interpreted as one of the higher-level postmaterialist values, which means that it is currently untenable that the majority of the world's inhabitants ought to pursue this ideal. It is a vacuous ideal for those who are not able to attend to their basic material needs. This does not mean, however, that we should reject the universal validity of such an ideal. On the contrary, it suggests that there is an additional ideal, namely that everyone should be in the position to become a global citizen. This brings us back to my brief discussion of Sypnowich. I want to reiterate that being a global citizen does not require that one become a moral hero who verges on the brink of denying her own interests. As Wolf has convincingly argued, "moral perfection in the sense of moral saintliness, does not constitute a model of personal well-being toward which it would be particularly rational or good or desirable for a human being to strive" (1982, 419). A global citizen should also take into account her own flourishing. An ideal global citizen is able to find a balance between her moral obligation to look after other citizens in the world as well as her right to look after herself.

NOTES

1. According to Rescher ideals are flawless excellences, i.e., perfect values, which are unrealizable "in this imperfect, sublunary dispensation" (Rescher 1987, 115). He acknowledges that we also have images of something that is "as perfect as we can realistically expect to find" (ibid., 116), but he calls these, slightly disparagingly, mini-ideals.
2. See for instance W. Hare, *Open-mindedness and Education* (Montreal: McGill-Queens University Press, 1979) and W. Hare, *In Defence of Open-mindedness* (Montreal: McGill-Queens University Press, 1985).
3. This would encompass both economic factors (such as sufficient income and appropriate living conditions) as well as moral/political factors (such as freedom).
4. The state is not completely neutral, because it has responsibility to protect the freedom of all citizens. Therefore it needs to place limits on the acceptability of positions and the way in which they are pursued (for instance, see for instance De Jong and Snik, 2002).
5. The respect of the global citizen will, however, be 'limited to' those whose way of life recognizes the rights of others to do the same.

6. 'Postmaterialist values' refer to values that gain importance for a person once her economic situation is relatively secure. If one lives under dire economic circumstances, one is likely to attach importance to materialist values, such as food or shelter.

7. As Inglehart has it, "Postmodern values emphasize self-expression instead of deference to authority and are tolerant of other groups and even regard exotic things and cultural diversity as stimulating and interesting, not threatening" (2000, 223). For example, in a postmodern society sexual norms change from being geared to encouraging reproduction to individual sexual gratification and individual self-expression.

BIBLIOGRAPHY

Appiah, K.A. *Cosmopolitanism: Ethics in a World of Strangers.* London: W.W. Norton, 2006.

Baumeister, R. *Evil: Inside Human Cruelty and Violence.* New York: W.H. Freeman, 1997.

Becker, L.C. "Good Lives: Prolegomena." In *The Good life and the Human Good*, eds. E. Frankel Paul, F.D. Miller, and J. Paul, 15–37. Cambridge: Cambridge University Press, 1992.

Berlin, I. "The Pursuit of the Ideal." In *The Crooked Timber of Humanity: Chapters in the History of Ideas*, ed. H. Hardy, 1–19. London: John Murray, 1990.

Brighouse, H. "Channel One, the Anti-Commercial Principle, and the Discontinuous Ethos." *Educational Policy* 19, no. 3 (2005): 528–550.

De Jong, J. and G. Snik. "Why Should States Fund Denominational Schools?" *Journal of Philosophy of Education* 36, no. 4 (2002): 573–587.

De Ruyter, D.J. "Whose Utopia? Which Ideals? The Importance of Societal and Personal Ideals in Education." In *Edutopias: New Utopian Thinking in Education*, eds. M.A. Peters and J. Freeman-Moir, 163–174. Rotterdam: Sense Publishers, 2006.

———. "Ideals, Education and Happy Flourishing." *Educational Theory*, 57, no. 1 (2007): 23–35.

Diener, E., E.M. Suh, and S. Oishi. "Recent Findings on Subjective Well-being." *Indian Journal of Clinical Psychology*, 1997. http:// www.psych.uiuc. edu/~ediner/hottopic/ paper1.html (accessed 12 December 2006).

Diener, E., E.M. Suh, R.E. Lucas, and H.L. Smith. "Subjective Well-being: Three Decades of Progress." *Psychological Bulletin* 125, no. 22 (1999): 276–302.

Diener, E. and C. Scollon. "Subjective Well-Being is Desirable, But Not the Summum Bonum." Paper delivered at the University of Minnesota "Interdisciplinary Workshop on Well-being," Minneapolis, MN, 23–25 October 2003. http://www. tc.umn.edu/~tiberius/workshop_papers/Diener.pdf (accessed 13 December 2006).

Emmet, D. *The Role of the Unrealisable: A Study in Regulative Ideals.* New York: St. Martin's Press, 1994.

Feinberg, J. "The Child's Right to An Open Future." In *Whose Child? Children's Rights, Parental Authority and State Power*, eds. W. Aiken and H. LaFollette, 124–153. Totowa, NJ: Rowman and Littlefield.

Griffin, J. *Well-being: Its meaning, Measurement and Moral Importance.* Oxford: Clarendon Press, 1986.

Hare, W. *Open-mindedness and Education.* Montreal: McGill-Queens University Press, 1979.

———. *In Defence of Open-mindedness.* Montreal: McGill-Queens University Press, 1985.

————. *What Makes a Good Teacher: Reflections on Some Characteristics Central to the Educational Enterprise.* London, Ontario: Althouse Press, 1993.

Inglehart, R. "Globalization and Postmodern Values." *The Washington Quarterly* 23, no. 1 (2000): 215–228.

Kraut, R. "Two Conceptions of Happiness." *The Philosophical Review* 88, no. 2 (1979): 167–197.

Rawls, J. *Political Liberalism.* New York: Columbia University Press, 1993.

Raz, J. *The Practice of Value.* Oxford: Oxford University Press, 2003.

Reis, H.T., K.M. Sheldon, S.L. Gable, J. Roscoe, and R.M. Ryan. "Daily Well-Being: The Role of Autonomy, Competence and Relatedness." *Personality and Social Psychology Bulletin* 26, no. 4 (2000): 419–435.

Rescher, N. *Ethical Idealism: An Inquiry Into the Nature and Function of Ideals.* Berkeley: University of California Press, 1987.

Rosenblum, N. *Membership & Morals: The Personal Uses of Pluralism in America.* Princeton, NJ: Princeton University Press, 1998.

Ryan, R.M. and E.L. Deci. "Self-determination Theory and the Facilitation Of Intrinsic Motivation, Social Development, and Well-being." *American Psychologist* 55, no. 1 (2000): 68–78.

Scheffler, I. "Moral Education and the Democratic Ideal". in *Reason and Teaching,* I. Scheffler, 136–148. Indianapolis, IN: Hackett Publishing, 1989.

Sypnowich, C. "Cosmpolitans, Cosmopolitanism and Human Flourishing." In *The Political Philosophy of Cosmopolitanism,* eds. G. Brock and H. Brighouse, 55–74. Cambridge: Cambridge University Press, 2005.

Wolf, S. "Moral Saints." *The Journal of Philosophy* 79, no. 8 (1982): 419–439.

5 Education for Global Citizenship and Survival

Randall Curren

The idea of global citizenship suggests a norm of global goodwill or disposition to promote the well-being of others everywhere, present and future, at least to the extent of respecting the requirements of global justice or fair terms of global cooperation. Although the requirements of global justice have not been institutionalized and are still unclear in theory, the global reach and impact of individual actions through economic relations, pollution that damages health and food sources (Connor 2007; Shrader-Frechette 2007, 15ff.; Dodds 2008, 3, 48–62), and climate disruption that already causes an estimated 150,000 deaths each year (WHO 2007), makes the institutionalization of these requirements a moral and practical necessity.[1] Morally, we owe it to each other to discuss the ways our actions impair each other's interests, and to settle what will and will not be recognized as wrongful violations of those interests. Practically, there are no unilateral or regional solutions to global problems of climate disruption and unsustainable aggregate burdens on resources and ecosystems. Globally coordinated action to address these problems is urgently needed, and it is inconceivable that such action will occur except on the basis of global agreements that are mutually advantageous, if not ideally just.

In this context, the contours of global citizenship might be sketched in light of an unrealized ideal of global justice, and education for global justice might be defined parasitically as the education that is most suitable to nurturing citizenship so conceived. An exercise in ideal theory of this sort might have some merit, but the case for instituting such education would be limited by the quality of argument for the ideal. A more serviceable approach would be to conceive of education for global citizenship as educationally preparatory to a just and sustainable world order whose institutional and legal framework is not yet known. It should be predicated on the desirability of universal goodwill and willingness to accept fair terms of cooperation, but it should not attempt to define what those terms of cooperation will be. It should also reflect what is understood of the nature of the hazards to be confronted, and it should aim to enable those being educated to survive and flourish in the face of those hazards, in part by contributing to the transparency of whatever terms of cooperation may be proposed and debated. This is the approach I will adopt. I will focus on the matters of sustainability and survival that provide the most morally and practically compelling case for global cooperation. I will argue that our circumstances require an unprecedented degree of global educational provision, coordination, and reform, and I will outline a 'curriculum of survival' conceived with the US in mind, but adaptable to other settings. To ground this, I will outline the challenges we face and offer a principled defense of a universal education for survival, by which I mean both individual survival and the survival of culturally diverse, intergenerational communities. I will then outline a set of educational proposals. Finally, I will consider the significance of these ideas for the philosophy of education and identify some precedent for them in its history.

HUMANITY *IN EXTREMIS*

Even now, at a time of openly declared 'global food crisis,' tightening oil supplies, and growing public concern about global warming, the most fundamental aspects of the emerging global sustainability crisis are not widely appreciated. This is not surprising because our everyday experience, especially in the prosperous enclaves of the North, provides little insight into the larger patterns and appalling environmental costs of steeply rising global populations and rising intensity of per capita resource use. The human population doubled to two billion between 1800 and 1950, tripled between 1950 and 2000 from two billion to over six billion, and is currently rising by more than 200,000 people per day. On a finite planet this obviously cannot continue indefinitely, and the longer it does continue, the greater the risk will be of a catastrophic population collapse.[2] Yet, with global average fertility rates at 2.8 live births per woman, and not expected to reach replacement fertility (2.06) until 2050, the world's population will continue to grow until 2100 unless pandemics, widespread drought, or something else intervenes (Dodds 2008, 12–16). Average per capita energy use has meanwhile increased more than tenfold since 1800, from less than half a metric ton of oil equivalent per year to about five, and individual water use has nearly quadrupled in that time (ibid., 19–20).

One product of this population growth and rising average material consumption has been a tripling of the human ecological 'footprint' or demand on natural systems between 1961 and 2003. The World Wildlife Fund's *Living Planet Report 2006* estimated human demand on the biosphere at 125 percent of carrying capacity, or 25 percent beyond what is sustainable, having crossed the threshold of unsustainability in the mid-1980s (WWF 2006). Carrying capacity cannot be long exceeded without causing long-term or permanent destruction of that capacity, and the report projects that

> [a] moderate business-as-usual scenario, based on United Nations projections showing slow, steady growth of economies and populations,

suggests that by mid-century, humanity's demand on nature will be twice the biosphere's productive capacity. At this level of ecological deficit, exhaustion of ecological assets and large-scale ecosystem collapse become increasingly likely. (WWF 2006, 2–3)

Another recent analysis projects a 33 percent increase in humanity's footprint in just a decade (Dietz et al. 2007), or a trajectory not unlike the WWF's. In stark numbers, world population, currently 6.7 billion, is projected to reach 9.3 billion by mid-century, at which point human demands on nature might be double what is sustainable. At the higher living standards assumed by the UN, we might be faced with being able to sustain a population of about 4.6 billion or about 2 billion below the current number. At today's standards, 5.2 billion might be feasible. Both numbers assume, of course, that the ecological damage that is occurring does not result in long-term loss of carrying capacity.

The 2005 Millennium Ecosystem Assessment (MA), a comprehensive set of reports sponsored by the UN Foundation, coauthored by 1,350 scientists from ninety-five countries and twenty-two national academies of science, is consistent with this in finding that 60 percent of the world's ecosystems are being "degraded or used unsustainably" (UN Foundation 2005). Walt Reid, the MA's lead author, has noted in interviews that local and regional ecosystem collapses are already occurring, and we are "putting such strain on the natural functions of Earth that the ability of the planet's ecosystems to sustain future generations can no longer be taken for granted."[3] There have been very few mass-extinction events in the past billion years, but human beings are in the process of causing one now. About one-quarter of land mammals, one-third of freshwater fishes, one-third of amphibians, and 70 percent of all plants are at risk of extinction. As many as 300,000 species have become extinct since 1950, and the majority of the ten million or so remaining will probably be destroyed in our lifetimes (Dodds 2008, 42, 70–77). Whether or not one regards this as morally horrific in itself, it is a measure of the hazards to which humanity is subjecting itself.

Many specific aspects of the unsustainability of our collective existence could be mentioned, but energy, water, and climate disruption are pivotal. Global per capita grain yields have been declining steadily since the mid-1980s and are critically dependent upon fertilizer, pesticides, herbicides, and fuel, which are mostly derived from oil and natural gas. World oil reserves will soon peak and begin to decline, if they have not already done so, and we can expect that decline to accelerate, yielding prices high enough to keep demand in equilibrium with declining supplies. There is no ready substitute for the *twenty-five billion* barrels of oil being consumed each year, and the process of shifting from an oil-based economy to one based on other energy sources will be long and energy intensive. Looking a little further down the road, the fossil fuel age will be spent by the end of this century whether or not effective policies to combat global warming are enacted: natural gas supplies are not many years beyond oil in peaking, and coal, though abundant by volume, is a far less concentrated energy source than oil (Goodstein 2004). A focus on the energy yields (energy return on energy invested) of different technologies would counsel the abandonment of biofuels, as well as a preference for wind power over nuclear.[4] The most prudent course will likely involve a rapid conversion to renewable energy sources, but "Surviving [this transition] will of necessity require radical social reorganization" (Tainter, Allen and Hoekstra. 2006, 56). Because modern farming is very energy intensive, it is likely that food prices will rise sharply through the period of transition.

Problems of water availability are already becoming acute in some parts of the world and are getting worse as global warming contributes to drought conditions. The Intergovernmental Panel on Climate Change's (IPCC's) 2007 *Fourth Assessment Report* confirms a global average land temperature increase of nearly 1.8°F (1°C) since 1960, and projects increases of up to 4.5°F (2.5°C) by 2050 and up to 10.4°F (5.8°C) by 2100.[5] This may be enough to cause persistent, severe drought across much of the US and other parts of the world by 2050 (Kolbert 2006, 110–111), and to kill many forms of marine life (Dodds 2008, 45). According to James Hansen, the leading climatologist in the US, the rise in atmospheric carbon dioxide concentrations from the preindustrial level of 275 ppm to today's 385 ppm is already enough to raise ocean levels by several meters (Hansen, 2008). Writing in *The New York Review of Books* in the fall of 2006, Bill McKibben observed that "Very few understand with any real depth that a wave large enough to break civilization is forming, and that the only real question is whether we can do anything at all to weaken its force" (McKibben 2006, 24).

How much higher atmospheric carbon dioxide levels could rise without eventuating in utter catastrophe is a matter of debate, but recent findings suggest Earth's climate system is more sensitive to rising levels of greenhouse gasses than previously estimated. "Compared with the original [climate] models of a few years ago," writes McKibben, "ice is melting faster; forest soils are giving up more carbon as they warm; storms are increasing much more quickly in number and size. . . . methane [is] leaking from Siberian permafrost at five times the predicted rate" (McKibben 2006, 23). The IPCC's current estimate of climate sensitivity suggests a stabilization target of 425 ppm is safe, though figures as low as 350 ppm are now defended (Hansen 2008). Staying within the politically canonical target of 450 ppm would require that emissions begin to decline now, fall by 65 percent globally by 2050, and be more or less eliminated by 2100 (Athanasiou and Baer 2002, 50–62; Eilperin 2008). Lower stabilization targets would require even bolder steps to prevent much of the planet from becoming uninhabitable.

All told, it is becoming clear that in one way or another and before long there will be major adjustments in the ways we live, though most people remain even with respect to energy problems, "aware neither that there is a problem, nor how short is the time (viewed historically), nor how large are the stakes, nor how great are the uncertainties" (Tainter, Allen and Hoekstra 2006, 57). Geopolitically, events seem to be moving towards intensifying competition for shrinking basic resources, through means that include wars over land, water, oil, timber, and minerals.[6]

WHY SUSTAINABILITY PROBLEMS CALL FOR AN EDUCATIONAL REPONSE

I will now offer some reasons why the global circumstances I have outlined require a vigorous and global educational response. Specifically, I will argue that all children are entitled to learn about these things and be prepared to deal with them constructively, and that public institutions should be designed to provide such education as well as continuing education of this kind for all ages. The obstacles to universally providing this education give some indication of the urgent need for globally coordinated action. Most notably, there are cultural barriers to educating girls in many parts of the world, and there are half a million people per week being added to the roughly 1 billion inhabitants of urban slums, which lack not only schools but every other basic service and prerequisite of human dignity (Davis 2006, 22, 126, 155).

The simplest and most compelling reason I will describe for providing education for global citizenship and survival is that everyone is entitled to it. I will offer four supporting arguments for the existence of such an entitlement. The second reason is that there are moral and prudential grounds for cooperating to solve the problems of sustainability and survival, and the desirability of cooperation makes desirable the education I am calling for. The third reason I will identify is that in our present circumstances, the education I am calling for is a prerequisite for sustaining any other reasonable educational goals we may have.

A first argument for thinking everyone is entitled to an education for global citizenship and survival is that human beings, being born helpless and needy, are entitled to have their needs met and to be prepared so as to be able to meet their needs themselves as they mature. The opportunity to acquire the understanding and ability to survive and meet one's needs in the world one will inhabit would seem to be a basic entitlement, to the extent one can be provided with that opportunity. Because we are social beings who must often act collectively to protect and advance our well-being, there is a civic aspect to this entitlement. Civic education that enables one to be an informed and capable participant in democratic processes is one aspect of a well-rounded preparation to responsibly secure the satisfaction of one's needs. In the circumstances I have described, this civic education must have a global dimension, since the well-being of individuals everywhere will depend upon the quality of global cooperation. As it pertains to both the conduct of one's private affairs and one's participation in public affairs, the education called for should promote 'effective agency,' or the development of not only one's knowledge, abilities, and value orientation, but also the development of capacities to critically examine and improve the state of all three related aspects of one's agency (Curren 2006, 465–68).

A second argument I will describe for thinking everyone is entitled to the education for global citizenship and survival is that it is arguably a condition of a just society that individuals not be denied substantial opportunities to live well "as an avoidable result of the design of social institutions" (Brighouse 2006, 18). This is a quite minimal requirement of justice, and certainly less demanding than a principle of fair equality of opportunity. It should thus be widely acceptable in societies, such as the US and UK, that acknowledge the importance of fair equality of opportunity. It follows from this principle that justice requires schools and other institutions be designed to enable children to meet the challenges they will face and live well, to the extent this is possible. This a requirement of justice that creates a fundamental social entitlement.

Third, one could appeal to a notion of universal human rights linked to a conception of the capabilities people must be able to exercise in order to live a life of human dignity. This version of the 'capability approach' provides a direct foundation for regarding the universal, global provision of education as a basic human right, since education is "the key to all the human capabilities" (Nussbaum 2006, 322). Because capabilities are understood as abilities to function in various ways within an institutional, economic, social, and physical context, the education required as a basic human right must be suitable to the world as it is and will be.

A fourth perspective on educational entitlements may be found in Allen Buchanan's appeals to our inevitable and significant epistemic reliance on others in defending liberal institutions, characterized as institutions that reduce *prudential and moral risk* by sorting truth from error and disseminating truth (Buchanan 2004). We all have fundamental interests, both prudential and moral, which are served by truth, he argues: we have an interest in truth, both to advance our own well-being and to avoid doing harm to others. From this perspective, we all have a prudential and moral interest in the existence of educational institutions, including but not limited to schools, and an interest in their thoroughness in disseminating the truths we most need to know in order to live well and without fault. Given the state of the world as I have described it, those truths would surely include the ones I have mentioned and a great deal more. This is a useful perspective, in noting the significance of education beyond schools and emphasizing that we all have a common interest in knowing the truth—even those among us who perceive public education as a burden whose benefits flow exclusively to other people's children.

I will now argue that the moral and prudential grounds for cooperating to solve the problems of sustainability and survival give us reasons to implement the education I am calling for.

At the beginning of this paper, I noted the global reach and impact of our actions, and I said that morally we owe it to each other to acknowledge the ways our actions impair each other's interests, and to settle what will and will not be recognized as wrongful violations of those interests. From a Kantian moral perspective, there is indeterminacy in the content of our concrete rights and duties—e.g., who owns what, and how much risk it is morally acceptable to impose on others (Kant 1991, § 6). Because this is so, and because this indeterminacy can only be remedied by establishing a body of common law, we have in Kantian terms a moral duty to settle the details of our moral relations with each other—with *all those with whom we cannot help associating or interacting*—by binding ourselves by mutual consent under a body of common law and legislative and judicial capacity. In an age of global interaction involving incremental impacts on resources, health, and climate, this implies a moral duty to enter into a system of global governance with enough power to create and enforce fair terms of cooperation. If a world state is too fraught with tyrannical prospects, we can nevertheless imagine a "thin, decentralized, and yet forceful global public sphere," an array of enforceable environmental, trade, and labor regulations, and various other accords and treaties that can be incorporated into the domestic laws of the world's still independent countries (Nussbaum 2006, 319–320). This would make concrete and specific the general moral duties we already owe each other, and it would almost certainly extend the forms of self-restraint entailed by duties not to injure others' property and health, for instance by establishing equitable limits on greenhouse gas emissions and compensation mechanisms to alleviate some of the harms that are no longer preventable (Adger, Paavola, Huq and Mace 2006).

If global cooperation is thus morally compulsory, then education for global citizenship is required on two grounds. It is required first of all because the facilitation of cooperation requires understanding of the value of cooperating; a well-informed critical capacity to guard against the strategies used by corporate front groups and others to misinform, discourage, and subvert cooperation; understanding of the possible institutional bases of cooperation, such as the United Nations; and the understanding, skills, abilities, and knowledge that may be needed to participate in cooperative arrangements. Little of the learning that could facilitate global cooperation is widely available to students in the US, and few have any comprehension of the extent to which their impressions of environmental matters are shaped by an array of well-financed corporate strategies.[7]

A second related consideration is that education for global citizenship is required to secure the *legitimacy* of whatever terms of cooperation might be negotiated. Legitimacy rests on transparency, which requires understanding of what is at stake, hence a wealth of relevant education for all who may be directly or indirectly parties to the negotiation or subject to the terms of cooperation it yields—in short, everyone in the world. Legitimacy also requires that the terms of cooperation be imposed—that compliance be obtained—as much as possible through voluntary cooperation based on a sound understanding of what is at stake and how the cooperative arrangements have been arrived at. Creating a semblance of a global rule of law is, like instituting any rule of law, an essentially educative enterprise (Curren 2000; 2002). However far we may be from settling on fair terms of global cooperation, it is not too early to lay the groundwork for this to occur in a legitimate way.

As I have said, global cooperation to address problems of sustainability and survival is not only morally required, but prudent. Faced with the declining resilience and capacity of global commons—the atmospheric and oceanic systems—on which human life fundamentally depends, the longer the nations of the world approach these matters competitively and without self-imposed collective limits, the more difficult life will become. This makes it prudent, in addition to morally compulsory, to favor the cooperation whose educational requirements I have just outlined.

To the extent that this concerns climate disruption, a contrary view, expressed frequently and with some truth, is that there will be 'winners' and 'losers.' What is true is that *below some threshold* of warming, some are more vulnerable than others (Adger et al. 2006). It doesn't follow from this that it would be prudent of those who currently may be less vulnerable to withhold the cooperation necessary to stay within that threshold. In the absence of effective coordinated action, there is little assurance there will be any 'winners' much longer, and even less reason to think the interests of the 'winners' of today wouldn't be harmed enough to make cooperation worthwhile. A planet altered to the profound detriment of all life on it for hundreds of years, if not far longer, is not in the interest of anyone who feels any personal stake in a civilized future for humanity.

There are, to be sure, countless unresolved questions about the terms of the cooperation needed. Most vexing may be the tradeoffs between population size and quality of life. Faced with a status quo that allocates substantial reproductive rights through markets that will increasingly deny those who are poor the means to sustain the lives of any children they bear, one can speculate that before long it may seem fair and most humane to conceive of reproductive rights not as unlimited liberty rights, but as limited welfare rights.[8] What can be said within the parameters of the present inquiry is that the various reasons adduced in support of the education I am defending are all reasons to believe that everyone in the world should be enabled to make reproductive decisions informed by knowledge of the momentum and impact of unsustainable human demands. A step toward this, which would go a long way toward reducing fertility by promoting a greater capacity to exert reproductive choice, is simply universal basic education for girls.

To the foregoing arguments may be added the consideration that the curriculum called for by the circumstances of unsustainability is arguably a prerequisite for the prudent advancement of any other educational ends we might reasonably impute to schools. Whether our aim as educators is to enable children to lead flourishing lives, to facilitate the conscious reproduction of democratic communities, to preserve and transmit the best of what human beings have achieved, or to secure any other good whose fulfillment requires an indefinite civilized future, our educational mission requires the survival of a civilized world order and must take some responsibility to incorporate a curriculum of survival.

I suggested at the outset that global citizenship requires a willingness to act for the well-being of others everywhere by respecting the requirements of global justice or fair terms of global cooperation. I have argued that as a matter of individual right and institutional legitimacy, such willingness must rest on a rational, free, and informed understanding and acceptance of those terms. The prospects of reaching agreement on any such terms, and of securing cooperation with them, rest similarly on understanding and acceptance of this kind. Beyond this, cooperation and individual well-being will require understanding, resourcefulness, adaptability, and sacrifice.

A Curriculum of Survival

The curriculum that seems to be called for may be outlined as a set of nine recommendations.

Teach Environmental Studies More Systematically

The environmental studies curriculum should include the relevant science, the problems, the regional and global distribution of impacts, and the state of cooperation or noncooperation in solving the problems. It is important that students not just learn science, but be able to understand what is happening in the world around them through the methods and explanatory resources of science. This is a tall order, yet without such understanding and openness to scientific inquiry, science learning will be inert and offer little foundation for conviction about what must be done to solve our problems. To say that adequate education in environmental science should be supplemented with other forms of environmental education—concerning the problems, distributions of impacts, and state of cooperation or noncooperation—implies an extension of student learning and inquiry into matters that are vitally important, but also controversial. Students in wealthy countries will need to understand far more than most now do about poverty and the distribution of environmental benefits and burdens both globally and within their own countries. To understand these things, they will need to learn some very distressing truths about the vast resources devoted to suppressing the truth about pollution, environmental damage, and their enormous and inequitably distributed burdens on human health (Shrader-Frechette 2002; 2007).

Integrate This with Honest History and Prehistory

This should begin with what we know of the patterns and dynamic of societal collapse and survival (see Tainter 1988; Redman 1999; Wright 2004; Diamond 2005). Every child should know the story of deforestation fueled by status competition on Easter Island, of irrigation and ecological catastrophe in the Fertile Crescent, and the population overshoot and collapse of the Maya. They should understand the analytical models through which anthropologists, geographers, and others understand societal complexity and collapse, and they should understand how those models apply to their own world and lives.

In the spirit of UNESCO's wide conception of 'environmental literacy,' history and social studies curricula should also address the role of competition for scarce resources in the genesis of war and genocide.[9] This is best accomplished through detailed case studies, including some that provide background for ongoing conflict, most obviously in the Middle East. In the United States, textbook adoption practices in the largest states, Texas and California, yield school books that are notoriously devoid of 'controversial' content, no matter how well-established on the evidence that content may be.[10] We are thus not likely to see many legislatively adopted texts in the near future that deal honestly with the role of water rights in the Israeli–Palestinian conflict, or US and British oil interests in the political history of the Middle East. It is nevertheless very much within the rights and in the interest of children in the US, as well as children in the Middle East, to know the specific truths and general lessons of such history. It is surely in their interest to understand the extent to which the case for war is often built on obfuscation, disguising unacknowledged private interest as a common national or international interest. Indeed, there can be little doubt that, in the age of scarcity looming before us, global citizenship and security of every kind will require far more vigilant resistance to the seductions of war than most of us are accustomed to.[11]

Integrate Economics with These Environmental Studies

Students can benefit from honest instruction in production methods, both agricultural and industrial, and the environmental controversies surrounding them. They should come away knowing how much energy and water resources are consumed in the production of common products (800 gallons of water for a hamburger, for instance, and 1,700 for a gallon of corn ethanol), and how atmospheric carbon and other wastes are released. Here, and throughout the curriculum, the focus on critical and inventive thinking should be as effective as possible and engaged with vital questions: How can production, marketing, and distribution systems be redesigned to be more environmentally friendly? How can we best live without economic growth, if growth is precluded? To what extent would more egalitarian distributive policies help? Who, if anyone, gains from growing populations and growing demand for property, goods, and services, and who doesn't?

Encourage Resourcefulness, Inventiveness, and Adaptability

Schools can promote a readiness to examine, rethink, and redesign every aspect of how we live, in order to promote the most rapid adjustment to a sustainable human ecological footprint. In connection with this, they can nurture skills in diverse practical arts, with an emphasis on design, economy, and adaptability. This may be considered not only collectively beneficial as a basis for adapting how we live, but also a form of individual insurance against the risk inherent in being prepared only for white-collar occupations that may become less lucrative or cease to exist. The collapse or simplification of social hierarchies has been associated historically with the depletion of usable energy reserves, and it requires little imagination to grasp that this could easily happen within the lifetimes of today's school children.[12]

With regard to adaptability and the potentially calamitous price of cultural intransigence, public schools should at the very least provide lessons in the hardship that societies have brought upon themselves by failing to adapt. The failure of the Greenland Norse to abandon maladaptive aspects of their European heritage provides one vivid illustration of this (Diamond 2005, 211–276). Another telling case study could be constructed around the culture and economics of gold. Many people continue to regard the exchange of gold (e.g., in weddings) as a cultural necessity, even as the environmental toll of producing gold far eclipses any substantial good achieved by it. The decision to buy gold should at least be informed by a vivid understanding of the fact that the world's remaining gold ore is of such poor quality that the extraction of a single ounce—the gold in one ring—requires *thirty tons* of ore and commonly involves the use of a cyanide leaching process that contaminates the thirty tons (minus one ounce) of debris that remains, as well as everything downstream and downwind (Perlez and Johnson 2005; Perlez and Bergman 2005). In the interest of dietary adaptability, which could reduce the American carbon footprint by 20 percent (Singer 2007), schools could provide students with experiences calculated to broaden their culinary horizons.

Encourage the Enjoyment of Environmentally Friendly Activities as a Basis for Flourishing Lives

Such activities would include intellectual, musical, athletic, and social pastimes, with modifications from their present forms as needed, such as to reduce demands on transportation and energy resources. The growing body of research on what actually makes people happy, why they buy things, and the surprising extent to which shopping and buying things makes them *less* happy, can be taught as one component of this (Kasser 2002).

De-Commercialize Schools

Commercial messages to consume, to define one's identity through consumption, and to address one's problems though material consumption should be banned from schools, except as objects of critical-thinking exercises. This would be one modest step toward making it easier for children to distinguish between what they need and what they want, and to resist inducements to excessive and imprudent consumption. As modest as this step would be, however, it requires that we muster renewed belief in the importance of preserving public spaces, including schools, in which we can conduct the public's work, in the public interest, through public reason, free of the dominating influence of commercial interests.[13]

Teach Children to Distinguish the Truth from Propaganda

Most or all of the foregoing will be denied and subverted by many whose short-term commercial and political interests and positional advantages are at stake. In light of this, it bears repeating that throughout the curriculum, the focus on critical and inventive thinking should be as effective as possible and engaged with vital questions. This requires sustained, direct instruction in methods of critical thinking, practice in thinking critically and creatively about the vital questions at issue, and a critical study of the media and propaganda. Surely we owe children the wherewithal to protect themselves against campaigns of misinformation and misleading argument.

Prepare Children for Global Cooperation

There is much that could contribute to an openness and ability to participate in global cooperation, beginning with serious instruction in geography, languages, world affairs, the history of the United Nations, and an understanding of poverty and the faltering capacity of existing governments to secure a livable future for their citizens. If it is ever appropriate to inculcate patriotism at all, which is doubtful, it should be counterbalanced by the cultivation of sympathetic attachment to a global community and institutional basis of international cooperation.[14] Writing in 1916 during the First World War, John Dewey suggested that schools treat national sovereignty as "provisional" (Dewey 1916, 98). I would second this, at least to the extent of urging openness to accepting limitations on national sovereignty as the price of escaping the hazards of a global state of nature.

Prepare Everyone for a World with Lower Fertility Rates and the Prospect of Fewer Human Beings

The human population of Earth will almost certainly be lower at the end of this century than it is today. What is uncertain is how humane or inhumane the path of descent will be, and how and to what extent decisions will reflect the trade-offs between population size and quality of life. It is not clear how best to prepare children for this, but any approach taken must seek to equip them with the imagination, understanding, and critical capacity to make rewarding lives for themselves in ways we may not now envision. Literature and the arts will surely play a role.

THE PRESENT, PAST AND FUTURE OF PHILOSOPHY OF EDUCATION

The idea of education for survival may seem outlandish and marginal to the traditional and contemporary concerns of philosophy of education. I'll suggest in this concluding section that apart from it being necessary, it is a natural extension of other recent developments in philosophy of education, and not completely without precedent in the history of the field. A focus on the limits to growth and associated need for equity would return the field to an important aspect of its roots.

The language of survival does appear in one major strand of contemporary philosophy of education, but invariably with a narrow focus on cultural survival and the limits of a cultural group's right to impose the education of its choice (see e.g., Appiah 1994 and Reich 2003). Many of the world's language and ethnic groups are indeed threatened with extinction through assimilation and genocide and through cultural, economic, and geographic encroachment; national minorities often "demand various forms of autonomy or self-government to ensure their survival as distinct societies" (Kymlicka 1995, 10).[15] They are "concerned with ensuring that the larger society does not deprive them of the conditions necessary for their survival," where that "survival . . . is heavily dependent on protection of their land base . . . [which] is vulnerable to the greater economic and political power of the larger society" (Kymlicka 1995, 38, 43). Political philosophers and others have argued that all of these groups should have the wherewithal to survive as distinct groups, if that is their wish, and some have advanced qualified defenses of minority rights (to certain forms of representation, self-governance, and cultural protection) as a counterweight to the political advantages that accrue to national majorities. The educational debates associated with these matters have focused on language rights and tensions between the cultural autonomy of adults, the future autonomy and well-being of children whose parents and communities may use their educational discretion to discourage deviations from cultural norms, and the claims of liberal-democratic societies to establish educational standards consistent with a liberal-democratic political culture.[16]

At the heart of these debates is a conception of autonomy focused on the 'conceptions of the good' available within a culture. Largely overlooked is the culture or society's capacity to provide the *means* to live well or secure those goods, the global context of that capacity, and the contributions of education to preserving or destroying that capacity. This is not a trivial oversight, and it's what I've addressed here: the material basis of the survival of diverse cultural groups and their members, and the moral basis and shape of a curriculum of global citizenship and survival adequate to the challenges of global interdependence and emerging sustainability crises. Survival has thus been on the agenda of contemporary philosophy of education, but we are in need of a wider discussion of the educational dimensions of survival than what has been transacted in the conceptual space of cultural identity, autonomy, and citizenship. The focus on domestic, cultural politics must be absorbed into a larger focus on global, intergenerational, and environmental justice and a curriculum of survival that is in part a curriculum of global citizenship.

Will Kymlicka, a prominent liberal theorist of minority rights, notes repeatedly that cultural survival depends in part on a culture's material basis and ability to control and ensure the adequacy of that material basis. He notes the fundamental importance to some cultures of fishing and hunting rights, and that "indigenous struggles over land are the single largest cause of ethnic conflict in the world" (Kymlicka 1995, 43). "Fishing is an important aspect of some Aboriginal cultures, and guaranteed fishing rights ensure that they are not outbid or outvoted by the larger society on decisions regarding access to fishing," he writes (Kymlicka 1995, 44). It would be easy to concede this point and consider it beyond the concern of *educational* philosophy, were it not becoming clear that it is beyond the power of individual countries to provide meaningful long-term guarantees of fishing rights, or water rights, or rights to land that can sustain life. The collapse of fisheries; the disappearance of mountain ice packs and other transnational water sources; the impact of human-induced drought, soil loss, and salinization; and the global population pressures that outstrip any foreseeable growth in basic commodities or public services are conspiring with other aspects of globalization to transfer the focus of political philosophy to a world stage on which the fate of individual countries, let alone national minorities, is not in their own hands—a global stage on which a commitment to establishing fair terms of cooperation in the survival of diverse ethnic groups may matter to the survival of a civilized way of life in general. Educational philosophy must follow suit, and adopt a perspective that is both global and comprehensive in its understanding of the prospects for human well-being.

Looking back across the history of the field, there are reasons why one would scarcely expect in the modern period to find any concern with such matters as limits to the growth of population or aggregate consumption. Among noted educational thinkers, the most direct concern with survival we find is in the work of Jean-Jacques Rousseau. In Book III of *Emile*, he invokes the specter of revolutions that upset the social ranks assumed by conventional education:

You trust in the present order of society without thinking that this order is subject to inevitable revolutions, and it is impossible for you to foresee or prevent the one which may affect your children. The noble become commoners, the rich become poor, the monarch becomes subject. Are the blows of fate so rare that you can count on being exempted from them? (Rousseau 1979, 194).

The lesson Rousseau draws is that education should be predicated on equality, the value of work that provides the necessities of life, and the premise that no one is too good or too secure to master a trade and prepare to secure the necessities of life with his own hands. Education should prepare one to survive without the conveniences of rank in a system bound to collapse (Rousseau 1979, 195–96).

Rousseau could see that only so much destitution and opulence could coexist side-by-side in one society, but he was a philosopher of his time and place in focusing on the proportionality of individual production and consumption, and not on the inevitable limits to aggregate production and consumption. Why would Rousseau, or John Locke, or any other European philosopher of the seventeenth or eighteenth century concern himself with such limits when vast continents lay at hand, when nature's 'harmony' seemed sufficient proof of a divine plan in which a human future was assured?

Post-Enlightenment Greek antiquity offers a contrasting view still shaped by cultural memory of civilizations *in extremis*. Philosophically, Plato's *Republic* is most of all about the nature of justice or goodness, and the relationship between goodness and happiness. If we inquire about the nature of the background concerns that animate the dialogue, however, the answer in a word is 'overconsumption.' The theme of excessive and ruinous consumption is invoked through the language of greed and injustice, and more specifically of "unnecessary" and "lawless" desires.[17] The "true" and "healthy" city of Book II (Cooper 1997, 369–372) is contrasted with the luxurious "city with a fever" (ibid., 372e, 373).[18] People in the former live simply, and everyone's needs are met even in old age (ibid., 372d); the city is sustainable across generations (ibid., 372d); it is a classless, unregulated partnership, with free and mutually advantageous exchange of goods (ibid., 369dff., 372c); people enjoy sex but limit children to "no more than their resources allow" (ibid., 372b–c); they thereby avoid both poverty and war (ibid., 372c). This 'healthy' city might be Plato's image of Eden.

The unhealthy city is, expressly or by implication, none of these things. Its first unhealthy choice is to eat meat, which requires hunters, herds, more land, and doctors (ibid., 372b–d). The addition of further luxuries requires more resources, even more land, and hence an army and a policy of military expansionism. This is a portrait of Athens itself, which mitigated class conflict by exporting a large proportion of its poor over time to colonies established in conquered territories, until the Peloponnesian War brought an end to that. The story of the ensuing books of the *Republic* is one of restoring the luxurious city of Athens to a healthy state of equilibrium, a state of social harmony achieved through equity in the distribution of limited resources. The justice and education that establish this equilibrium are deeply equalizing in the sense that they steer those who hold political and military power away from material indulgence, and toward the enjoyment of the 'highest' goods—those of the mind—which are goods that can be enjoyed simultaneously and equally by an unlimited number of people (provided their basic material needs are met).

We know from other texts that Plato's concerns about sustainability and excessive consumption were not limited to the relationship between war-making and limited resources. By the time Plato was born, the landscape of Greece had already suffered from overgrazing by sheep and hillside deforestation, which had given rise to a number of legislative acts to replant hillsides and limit erosion (Ponting 1991, 76–77; Williams 2006, 62ff.). Writing with a sound understanding of floods, erosion, and water scarcity caused by deforestation, Plato observes in the *Critias* that "Attica of today is like the skeleton revealed by a wasting disease, once all the rich topsoil has been eroded and only the thin body of the land remains" (Cooper 1997, 111b). He goes on to describe a mythical city of Atlantis as densely populated, incessantly occupied with commerce, and ultimately ruined by intoxication with luxury and wealth (ibid., 117–121). The lesson, as in the *Republic*, is that when "possessions become pursued and honored" (ibid., 121a), human beings exceed the limits of prudence and justice and come to a bad end. The antidote he prescribes is an education that combats materialism and injustice.

There are some echoes of these Platonic themes in Aristotle's *Politics*, especially in his remarks about misguided accumulation of wealth (1256b27–1258b8), the importance of limiting population (1265a38–b16, 1326a5–b25, 1327a15, 1335b21–27), and his insistence that injustice is the most important general cause of the collapse of regimes (1301a36–b4). It is instructive to note his observation that education that gives unfettered expression to a culture is not the same thing as education that is most conducive to a culture's survival. He notes in Book V of his *Politics* that the education that enables a regime to survive is not what members of the ruling class typically prefer. "Democratic education," or education that preserves a democracy, is not as singularly favorable to the poor, nor is "oligarchic education" as singularly favorable to the rich, as the friends of unfettered democracy (defined as lawless rule by the poor) or oligarchy (lawless rule by the rich) imagine (1310a20–26). What preserves a regime is education that is constitutionally moderating, or conducive to an equitable distribution of political power among constituent groups and conducive to cooperation in the direction of that power toward an equitable distribution of the means to living well.[19]

In our world, a world in which much of the material basis of a sustainable human existence is imperiled by overreaching, the education that will enable individual governments and societies to survive is not likely to be the education of our partisan dreams and patriotic pride. An example from close to home is the culture of the American suburbs, which is unsustainable and already staggering under the weight of rising costs and debt.[20] In the meantime, the schools in these suburbs are for the most part blindly replicating a culture of consumption that is not only doomed, but also hard to reconcile with any conceivable terms of global cooperation compatible with the survival of many other linguistic and ethnic groups.[21]

NOTES

1. For a vivid account of the global reach of economic relations, see Davis 2006.
2. For accounts and explanatory analyses of such collapses in the past, see Tainter 1988, Redman 1999, Wright 2004, and Diamond 2005.
3. Quoted in "The State of the World? It is on the Brink of Disaster," *The Independent,* 30 March, 2005, online edition. http://news.independent.co.uk/world/science_technology/article8480.ece.
4. The net energy loss on corn ethanol, when all energy inputs are accounted for, has been calculated at 43 percent, and the loss on switch grass ethanol, if that became feasible, would be about 70 percent, since it would require the processing of two to five times more biomass. Even if there were a net energy gain, the vision of large-scale use of biofuels is fundamentally misguided. Photosynthesis is such an inefficient way of capturing the energy of sunlight (0.01 percent versus 2 percent for photovoltaic cells) that it would require 80 percent of all vegetation in the US to replace 15 percent of US gasoline consumption by 2017 (Pimentel 2008). The energy yields on nuclear fission reactors are also quite inferior to those of wind generation (Tainter 2008), and the limited reserves of fissile material make it at best a short-term solution requiring exceedingly long-term investments in securing radioactive waste against leakage (Goodstein 2004, 106–07; Shrader-Frechette 2002, 95–116).
5. The IPCC is a scientific and member government body established by the World Meteorological Organization and the United Nations Environmental Programme, charged with providing periodic assessments of the state of climate science and knowledge of climate change. Its comprehensive report, the *Third Assessment Report* (IPCC 2001), was attacked by skeptics but strongly endorsed in a report by the US National Academy of Sciences requested by the Bush administration (US National Academy of Sciences, 2001). The IPCC's *Fourth Assessment Report* was released in 2007 and strengthened the basic conclusions of earlier assessments. See IPCC 2007 for the summary of findings addressed to policymakers. Although the assessments represent the work of thousands of scientists, the role of member governments in approving assessment reports typically injects some politically motivated dilution of the strongest conclusions reached on the basis of the science.
6. On genocide in Rwanda and the critical role of land hunger, see Diamond 2005, 311ff. and related references. On the role of climate change and displacement from land in the Darfur conflict, see Borger 2007. On conflict over water and other resources, see Ward 2002 and Klare 2002.

7. On the role and extent of misinformation campaigns in suppressing public awareness of environmental risks, see Shrader-Frechette 2007. The book's specific focus is public awareness of the public health risks of pollution, but its detailed exposé of corporate-funded regulatory capture, private interest science, legal settlement nondisclosure provisions, public relations strategies, lobbying, and industry front groups reveals much about the uphill battle any environmental or sustainability public education campaign would face.

8. One could find philosophical support for this in David Archard's account of children's rights and limitations on the right to bear children (Archard 2004, 141), and in the implications of Martha Nussbaum's conception of human rights for reproductive rights. On her view, the securing of a right is an "affirmative task" to put people "in a position of capability to function" in a specified way (Nussbaum 2006, 287). In circumstances of declining resources, the substantial and affirmative character of the right would demand that it be limited.

9. See UNESCO 2005a and 2005b. UNESCO has announced a UN Decade of Education for Sustainable Development (UNDESD) with the intention of promoting environmental integrity, economic viability, and justice. Its environmental component is focused on the natural resources and ecosystem goods and services "essential for human development and indeed survival." Environmental "literacy" is understood broadly to include "the capacity to identify root causes of threats to sustainable development and the values, motivations and skills to address them" (UNESCO 2005a, Quality Education). This would surely include a capacity to recognize when wars are being contemplated and fought out of unwillingness to accept just and peaceful distributions of scarce resources.

10. On the role of major 'adoption' states and the extent to which US school books are censored, see Delfattore 1992.

11. For related analysis of the proper stance of school curricula toward US foreign policy, see Miller 2007. On the relationships between justice, security, and war, see Curren 2005.

12. On the "massive transformation in employment patterns" and "reduced economic circumstances" entailed by a transition to renewable energy sources (in effect, from energy mining to energy farming), see Tainter, Allen, and Hoekstra 2006. The paper identifies general patterns in energy resource transitions on the basis of both historical and biological case studies.

13. For background, see Manning 1999; Schor 2004; Brighouse 2005; Raley 2006.

14. Much has been written about the forms and presumed benefits and costs of patriotism. See Fullinwider 1996, Nussbaum 2002, Brighouse 2007, and Blum 2007. I agree with Brighouse that the inculcation of patriotism by a government or its schools undermines the legitimacy of that government.

15. By 'national minority' Kymlicka means a nation, or "historical community, more or less institutionally complete, occupying a given territory or homeland, sharing a distinct language and culture," which is embedded within a country dominated by a different national culture (Kymlicka 1995, 11).

16. See Callan 1997, Dwyer 1998, Levinson 1999, Curren 2000, Galston 2003, McDonough and Feinberg 2003.

17. Balot 2001 documents the widespread attention to these themes in Athens and their importance for understanding Plato's work.

18. All the translations from Plato's works relied on here are from Cooper 1997.

19. See Curren 2000, 100–109. References to Aristotle's *Politics* are to the book, chapter, page, column, and line numbers of Immanuel Bekker's 1831 edition of the Greek text. These appear in the margins of most modern editions and translations.

20. I use the word 'culture' here in the sense of the customs of a group or 'lifestyle enclave' (Kymlicka 1995, 18).
21. For helpful discussion of earlier drafts of this paper, I owe thanks to Jason Blokhuis, Yvonne Raley, Chris Schlottman, Barb Stengel, Kenneth Strike, Elaine Unterhalter, and my audiences at the annual meetings of the Philosophy of Education Society, the Philosophy of Education Society of Great Britain, and the Human Development and Capability Association, in March, April, and September of 2007. I also owe a debt to my sustainability interns, Gena Aktas, Daniel Muller, and Rayna Oliker, who researched and talked me through a wealth of sources and themes pertaining to the theory and practice of education for sustainable development in the summer of 2008. The first three sections of this paper incorporate material from chapters one, four and five of my book, *Education for Sustainable Development: A Philosophical Assessment*. London: PESGB, 2009.

BIBLIOGRAPHY

Adger, W. N., J. Paavola, S. Huq and M. J. Mace, eds. *Fairness in Adaptation to Climate Change*. Cambridge, MA: MIT Press, 2006.

Appiah, A. "Identity, Authenticity, Survival: Multicultural Societies and Social Reproduction." In *Multiculturalism: Examining the Politics of Recognition*, ed. Amy Gutmann, 149–163. Princeton, NJ: Princeton University Press, 1994.

Archard, D. *Children: Rights and Childhood*. 2nd ed. New York: Routledge, 2004.

Athanasiou, T., and P. Baer. *Dead Heat: Global Justice and Global Warming*. New York: Seven Stories Press, 2002.

Balot, R. *Greed and Injustice in Classical Athens*. Princeton, NJ: Princeton University Press, 2001.

Blum, L. "Best Traditions Patriotism." *Theory and Research in Education* 5, no.1 (2007): 61–68.

Borger, J. "Darfur Conflict Heralds Era of Wars Triggered by Climate Change, UN Report Warns." *The Guardian*, 23 June 2007. http://www.guardian.uk/environment/2007/jun/23/sudan.climatechange

Brighouse, Harry. "Channel One, the Anti-Commercial Principle, and the Discontinuous Ethos." *Educational Policy* 19, no. 3 (2005): 528–49.

———. *On Education*. London: Routledge, 2006.

———. "Should We Teach Patriotic History?" In *Philosophy of Education: An Anthology*, ed. R. Curren, 528–38. Oxford: Blackwell Publishing, 2007.

Buchanan, A. "Political Liberalism and Social Epistemology." *Philosophy and Public Affairs* 32, no. 2 (2004): 95–131.

Callan, E. *Creating Citizens*. Oxford: Clarendon Press, 1997.

Connor, S. "World's Most Important Crops Hit by Global Warming Effects." *The Independent*, 19 March 2007. Archived at http://news.independent.co.uk/environment/climate_change/article2371569.ece.

Cooper, J. *Plato: Complete Works*. Indianapolis, IN: Hackett, 1997.

Curren, R. *Aristotle on the Necessity of Public Education*. Lanham, MD: Rowman and Littlefield, 2000.

———. "Public Education and the Demands of Fidelity to Reason: A Response to Dwyer, Feinberg, Hourdakis, Pendlebury, Robertson, Strike, and White." *The School Field* 13, no.1 (2002): 79–105.

———. "Public Reason and the Foundations of Security." Chap. 13 in *Homeland Security: Controversies, Strategies, and Impact*, ed. Nawal Ammar. Kent,

OH: Kent State University Press, 2005. Available at http://upress.kent.edu/ Ammar/13%20Curren.htm.

———. "Developmental Liberalism." *Educational Theory* 56, no. 4 (2006): 451–468.

Davis, M. *Planet of Slums*. London: Verso, 2006.

Delfattore, J. *What Johnny Shouldn't Read: Textbook Censorship in America*. New Haven, CT: Yale University Press, 1992.

Dewey, J. *Democracy and Education*. New York: Macmillan, 1916.

Diamond, J. *Collapse: How Societies Choose to Fail or Succeed*. New York: Viking, 2005.

Dietz, T., E. A. Rosa, and R. York. "Driving the Human Ecological Footprint." *Frontiers in Ecology and the Environment* 5 (2007): 13–18.

Dodds, Walter. *Humanity's Footprint: Momentum, Impact, and Our Global Environment*. New York: Columbia University Press, 2008.

Dwyer, James. *Religious Schools v. Children's Rights*. Ithaca, NY: Cornell University Press, 1998.

Eilperin, Juliet. "Carbon Output Must Near Zero to Avert Danger, New Studies Say." *Washington Post,* 10 March 2008.

Fullinwider, R. "Patriotic History." In *Public Education in a Multicultural Society*, ed. R. Fullinwider, 203–227. Cambridge: Cambridge University Press, 1996.

Galston, W. "Church, State, and Education." In *A Companion to the Philosophy of Education*, ed. Randall Curren, 412–429. Oxford: Blackwell Publishing, 2003.

Goodstein, D. *Out of Gas: The End of the Age of Oil*. New York: W. W. Norton, 2004.

Hansen, James. Interview on *The Diane Rhem Show*, 23 June 2008. Archived at http://www.wamu.org/programs/dr/08/06/23.php#20635.

Intergovernmental Panel on Climate Change (IPCC). *Third Assessment Report: Climate Change 2001*. http://www.ipcc.ch/ipccreports/assessments-reports .htm

———. *Climate Change 2007: Synthesis Report*. http://www.ipcc.ch/ipccreports/ ar4-syr.htm

Kant, I. *The Metaphysics of Morals*. Trans. Mary Gregor. Cambridge: Cambridge University Press, 1991.

Kasser, T. *The High Price of Materialism*. Cambridge, MA: MIT Press, 2002.

Klare, M. T. *Resource Wars*. New York: Henry Holt, 2002.

Kolbert, E. *Field Notes from a Catastrophe: Man, Nature, and Climate Change*. New York: Bloomsbury USA, 2006.

Kymlicka, W. *Multicultural Citizenship*. Oxford: Clarendon Press,1995.

Levinson, M. *The Demands of Liberal Education*. Oxford: Oxford University Press,1999.

Manning, S. "Students for Sale: How Corporations are Buying Their Way into America's Classrooms." *The Nation,* 27 September 1999.

McDonough, K., and W. Feinberg. *Education and Citizenship in Liberal-Democratic Societies*. Oxford: Oxford University Press, 2003.

McKibben, B. "How Close to Catastrophe?" *The New York Review of Books* 53, no. 18 (2006): 23–25.

Miller, R. "Unlearning American Patriotism." *Theory and Research in Education* 5, no. 1 (2007): 7–21.

Nussbaum, M. *For Love of Country*. Boston: Beacon Press, 2002.

———. *Frontiers of Justice*. Cambridge, MA: Harvard University Press, 2006.

Perlez, J., and K. Johnson. "Behind Gold's Glitter: Torn Lands and Pointed Questions." *The New York Times,* 24 October 2005. http://www.nytimes. com/2005/10/24/international/24GOLD.html?th+&emc+th&pagewa.

Perlez, J., and L. Bergman. "Tangled Strands in Fight over Peru Gold Mines." *The New York Times* 25 October 2005. http://www.nytimes.com/2005/10/25/international/americas/25GOLD.html?th+&emc=th.

Pimentel, D. "Global Energy Challenges and Solutions." Paper presented at the Sustainable Energy Symposium, University of Rochester, Rochester, NY, 5 April 2008.

Ponting, C. A. *Green History of the World*. London: Penguin, 1991.

Raley, Y. "Food Advertising, Education, and the Erosion of Autonomy." *International Journal of Applied Philosophy* 20, no 1 (2006): 67–79.

Redman, C. *Human Impact on Ancient Environments*. Tucson, AZ: University of Arizona Press, 1999.

Reich, R. "Multicultural Accommodations in Education." In *Education and Citizenship in Liberal-Democratic Societies* by K. McDonough and W. Feinberg, 299–324. Oxford: Oxford University Press, 2003.

Rousseau, J.-J. *Emile*. Trans. A. Bloom. New York: Basic Books, 1979.

Schor, J. *Born to Buy*. New York: Scribner, 2004.

Shrader-Frechette, K. *Environmental Justice*. New York: Oxford University Press, 2002.

———. *Taking Action, Saving Lives*. New York: Oxford University Press, 2007.

Singer, P. "Richard J. Franke Lecture." Chicago Humanities Festival, Chicago, IL, 1 November 2007.

Tainter, J. *The Collapse of Complex Societies*. Cambridge: Cambridge University Press, 1988.

———. "Energy Gain, Organization, and Sustainability." Keynote address, Sustainable Energy Symposium, University of Rochester, Rochester, NY, April 5, 2008.

Tainter, J., T. Allen, and T. Hoekstra. "Energy Transformations and Post-normal Science." *Energy* 31(2006): 44–58.

United Nations Foundation (UNF). *The Millennium Ecosystem Assessment*. Washington, DC: UNF, 2005. Summary with links available at http://www.unfoundation.org/features/millenium_ecosystem_assessment.asp

United Nations Educational, Scientific, and Cultural Organization (UNESCO). Education for Sustainable Development: United Nations Decade (2005–2014). Paris: UNESCO, 2005a. Available at http://portal.unesco.org/education/en/ev.php-URL_ID=23279&URL_DO=DO_TOPIC&URL_SECTION=201.html

———. Guidelines and Recommendations for Reorienting Teacher Education to Address Sustainability. Paris: UNESCO, 2005b. Available at http://unesdoc.unesco.org/images/0014/001433/143370E.pdf

United States National Academy of Sciences. *Climate Change Science: An Analysis of Some Key Questions*. Washington, DC: National Academies Press, 2001.

Ward, D. R. *Water Wars*. New York: Riverhead Books, 2002.

Williams, M. *Deforesting the Earth: From Prehistory to Global Crisis (An Abridgment)*. Chicago: University of Chicago Press, 2006.

World Health Organization (WHO). *Climate and Health*. Geneva: WHO Media Centre, 2007. Available at http://www.who.int/mediacentre/factsheets/fs266/en/.

World Wildlife Fund (WWF). *Living Planet Report 2006*. Available at http://www.panda.org/about_our_earth/all_publications/living_planet_report/living_planet_report_timeline/lp_2006

Wright, R. *A Short History of Progress*. Toronto, Canada: House of Anansi Press, 2004.

Part II

New Pedagogical Approaches

6 Why They Hate Us
A Pedagogical Proposal

Irfan Khawaja

INTRODUCTION

The explanation of human action is both an everyday task and an occasion for the most perplexing of methodological dilemmas. On the one hand, we unreflectively ask for, offer up, and receive action explanations as a matter of daily routine: we need to know *why* someone acts as he does in order to deal with him at all, and do so in everyday contexts without necessarily being stymied into paralysis. On the other hand, when we pause to reflect on the philosophical presuppositions of action explanations, we're quickly led to questions of sufficient complexity to keep philosophers occupied for generations.

Issues in action theory acquire a yet greater degree of complexity when we focus on the explanation of a morally and politically charged category of actions, like 'terrorism' or 'Islamic terrorism' or 'Islamic terrorism in the late twentieth and early twenty-first centuries.'[1] The intensification of complexity arises in part from the specifically political and historical dimensions of the topic: what was previously a difficult exercise in action theory becomes, in this context, a yet more difficult interdisciplinary exercise in action theory, legal theory, religious studies, history, and international relations. To explain the actions of an Osama bin Laden or Muhammad Atta, we need the apparatus of action theory, *plus* a conceptual framework for talking about terrorism, *plus* a working knowledge of Islamic theology, *plus* a working knowledge of the history of the modern Near East. And even the metaphor of addition is insufficient to capture what we need; we need to sum what we know and put the results into an integrated and coherent whole.

This topic might at first seem wildly inappropriate as the basis of a pedagogical proposal, as opposed to a professional research program: too complex, too emotionally fraught, and too political. Perhaps counterintuitively—drawing on themes in the work of Gerald Graff[2]—I argue in what follows that teaching it *is* appropriate, and in fact urgently necessary in American higher education. In my experience, American undergraduates want to understand Islamic terrorism, but lack a context in which to study it. The result is that such students are uniquely vulnerable to the pseudoex-planations of terrorism offered up by ideologues and conspiracy theorists. To preempt that possibility, and simply to educate students to understand the world around them, I argue in what follows that the explanation of ter-rorism ought explicitly to be thematized and taught. Though challenging and not without risk, I argue that the venture can, under the right circum-stances, be successful.

PEDAGOGY AND THE STUDY OF ACTION

Philosophers since Aristotle have typically made a distinction between actions on the one hand and events on the other, and have marked out the former as the subject of a special and systematic topic of study. An action is something *done*; an event is something that merely *happens*. In this sense, though both human and animal action are voluntary and goal-directed, human action is uniquely subject to specifically moral appraisal: not just voluntary but free, and not just goal-directed but intentional. So understood, action is a ubiquitous phenomenon that demands constant and assiduous attention. We can scarcely go a day without in some sense having to deal with, think about, engage in, and/or appraise actions, whether our own or those of others.

In a wide variety of contexts, action confronts us as an interpretive puz-zle mediated by 'why' questions. In the simplest case, someone acts a cer-tain way, and we wonder why she's done as she has. Or else we ourselves act without conscious deliberation, and then wonder why we did. These simple cases vary greatly, but variation aside, what we seek in asking such 'why' questions is *intelligibility*. We want to make sense of the action, and the answer to the 'why' question does that by identifying its cause and putting the action in a broader context. Such demands for intelligibility are made in two very different contexts which, risking oversimplification, I'll call the 'everyday' and the 'academic.'

The everyday approach to action involves four interlocking (but typi-cally unarticulated) assumptions that seem, at least prima facie, to cohere in a seamless way. The first concerns the nature of the explanandum; call it 'methodological individualism.' The actions we seek to explain in everyday life are the actions of identifiable individuals; hence 'why' questions are of the form 'Why did S do x?' where 'S' denotes such an individual and 'x' denotes an action.

The second assumption is a presupposition of explanation; call it the 'causal assumption.' Every action is produced by some cause or network of causes, and every 'why' question seeks to identify the causes that produced the action requiring explanation. So the answer to 'Why did S do x?' is a claim of the form 'Because . . .' where the causal force of that word is to be taken literally.

A third assumption concerns the relevant causes themselves; call it the 'character assumption.' The thought here is that the causes that best explain an action lie in the interaction between S's character and S's circumstances. We identify the deepest and most fundamental causes when we identify the relevant connections between S's traits of character and the circumstances of her action that, in conjunction with those traits, 'triggered' the action.

A final assumption involves the normative status of the causes; call it the 'agency assumption.' While character functions as a cause, its formation is still in some sense up to us, and thereby a candidate for ascriptions of moral responsibility and moral appraisal. It's worth noting that the agency assumption need not involve any commitment, implicit or explicit, to 'compatibilism' as that term is understood in analytic philosophy. Where 'compatibilism' denotes the compatibility of *determinism* and responsibility, the agency assumption merely entails the compatibility of *causation* and responsibility, a commitment compatible with compatibilism (so to speak), but not equivalent to it.

Put in a nutshell, then, the everyday explanatory framework consists in the following ostensible truisms: actions are produced by individuals who freely do what they do in virtue of the interaction between their character and their circumstances; the explanation of an act and the moral evaluation of the causes that produced it are inextricable parts of the same inquiry. An action is produced by the agent's virtues or vices. In the first case, the agent is to be praised and/or rewarded for the action, in the latter, to be blamed and/or punished. But the same cause explains the action as supplies the basis for judging it.

Now consider academic approaches to the study of action. In this case we can, broadly speaking, distinguish two distinct approaches to the subject. On the one hand, we have what might be called the 'first-order disciplines,' i.e., the social sciences, along with those of the natural sciences that focus on the explanation of human action. Here the task is to explain action in particular contexts without worrying too much about second-order issues about the nature of action as such. If we want to explain, say, an action or a trend, we take a certain explanatory framework for granted, and apply it to the relevant data. The basic challenge is to find the best explanatory fit between data and hypothesis, not to raise questions about action as such.

On the other hand, we have what might be called the 'second-order disciplines,' most prominently philosophical action theory. Here the task is to tackle second-order conceptual issues about the nature of action without bothering too much with the job of explaining concrete cases of it. In this case, for instance, we want to know what counts as an action, whether actions can in principle be free, and if so, how freedom relates to determinism, responsibility, and moral judgment. The challenge here is to generate a coherent and plausible conceptual scheme, not to apply it.

Despite the differences between them, both of the preceding academic approaches to explanation exist in tension with what I called the everyday approach to action—a fact with a series of pedagogically relevant consequences.

Imagine that a student comes to university adhering unreflectively to the everyday explanatory framework I described above, and encounters or majors in one of the first-order disciplines. She soon discovers at least two problematic things.

She discovers, first, that the everyday approach is flatly incompatible with the academic. For one thing, the academic approach flatly denies methodological individualism. It assumes the existence of irreducible social facts and of structural types of causation not reducible to individual action. So individuals no longer take center stage.

Further, the academic approach delegitimizes the importance of character traits in explanation. Reference to such traits is essentially incompatible with the decision-theoretic or evolutionary frameworks now prevalent, and is likewise incompatible with the insistence that genuinely scientific explanations of action involve measurable variables that 'maximize concreteness' and eliminate reference to moral or evaluative predicates.[3]

Finally, the academic approach delegitimizes ascriptions of moral responsibility, at least as a feature of the explanatory enterprise. The agency assumption as I described it above is essentially at odds with the causal models that are taken for granted in the first-order disciplines, where explanations are deterministic, probabilistic, or stochastic but typically ignore the question of how action can, consistent with its etiology, be *up* to the agent (especially in a strong libertarian sense).[4] Thus the single assumption held in common both by the everyday and the academic approach is the causal assumption, but this nominal agreement evaporates in the context of the other, more substantive disagreements. Both approaches agree that explanation is causal but disagree about what that amounts to.

Having made this first discovery, our student quickly makes a second: that her everyday explanatory framework is *irrelevant* to academic study. The governing assumption of a great deal of first-order teaching and inquiry is that the student of a first-order discipline is, qua student, being inculcated into the explanatory framework of the discipline to which she is apprenticed: she is being invited to 'think like' an economist, a political scientist, or a historian. To fail to think in this way, according to standard textbook presentations, is not necessarily to think falsely but to fail to live up to an academically defined role. The choice is either to accept the role and its assumptions, or forswear the respectability that the role confers. The assumptions of the everyday framework are not therefore to be refuted or rejected; they're to be set aside in deference to the imperatives of professionalism.

Suppose now that the student comes to university with the same everyday explanatory framework but goes into philosophical action theory, a second-order discipline. In this case, the student will very likely have to grapple with explicit challenges to every element of her everyday framework. She may well come to vindicate elements of that framework. She could, for instance, become an agent-causal libertarian about free will and/or a nonreductionist virtue ethicist about character. But whether she vindicates or undermines the everyday framework, she will typically study the subject in abstraction from the everyday task of explanation. She might, for instance, come to vindicate metaphysical libertarianism by reflecting on 'Frankfurt counterexamples' or Van Inwagen's 'consequence argument' but have no idea how this bears on the explanation of a single everyday action, much less anything more complicated than that.[5] She might likewise become an enthusiast of virtue ethics by reading Foot or Hursthouse, but as this material is usually taught, it is irrelevant either to second-order questions about the explanation of action or to first-order explanations.[6] And a survey of about twenty logic/critical thinking text-books convinces me that explanation is one of the least discussed topics in courses on logic and critical thinking. When it *is* discussed (e.g., in the context of inductive logic), textbook examples and exercises on the topic are usually drawn from the natural, not the social sciences, wherein the explananda are events, not actions.

These tensions between the everyday and academic approaches to explanation are exacerbated by tensions within the academic approach. I noted above that the academic study of action divides along first- and second-order lines—and obviously, along lines of division within each of these categories. These various divisions in the academic approach to the subject tend to produce a certain compartmentalization. Each discipline has its own distinctive approach, occasionally overlapping with, but occasionally subversive of, the claims of others. Meanwhile, philosophy tends to pursue its own autonomous lines of inquiry, mostly without reference to the claims of any of the first-order disciplines.

Predictably, this compartmentalization of inquiries gives rise to a dizzying variety of perspectives on the subject of action within the academy, with each perspective saying wildly different things about action and embodying incompatible methodological or substantive approaches to it, but no single discipline devoted to the comparative study or integration of the different claims. Thus a student can learn about free will versus determinism in introductory philosophy, but have no sense of the connection of that topic to her study of 'the causes of World War I' in international relations. She can study 'thick description' in a class on area studies or anthropology,[7] but have no sense of the relation between thick description there and an economist's explanations of the behavior of 'the sovereign consumer' in the local supermarket. Our student can study intention and foresight in the sociology of law without being aware that the very same subjects are discussed in a very different way in moral philosophy. And she can, in criminology, take for granted that crime is produced by 'negative reinforcement,' but never encounter explanations of crime from evolutionary psychology, much less explanations via the id, the ego, or moral agency.[8] As a result of this compartmentalization, 'action' disappears as an object of study, to be replaced by 'action as seen through the lens of discipline X.'

My point here is not to lament the delegitimization of the everyday approach by the academic, but to suggest that the failure to confront their incompatibility in an explicit way leads students to a sort of epistemic schizophrenia.[9] Given the incompatibilities between the everyday and academic approaches (as well as within the academic), a student has two basic options: either adopt one consistent approach to the explanation of action, or acquiesce in incoherence. The student who opts for acquiescence ends up committed to a sort of methodological relativism, according to which one's choice of an approach to the explanation of action is unregulated by principle; we can adopt any approach to action without worrying about its incompatibilities with other approaches.[10] The student who opts for consistency faces two further options: either consistently affirm the everyday approach to action, or consistently affirm (some brand of) the academic. In the first of these cases, the student is obliged to regard academic inquiry as a relatively pointless exercise unrelated to everyday life. In the second case, bracketing the (unguided) choice of which academic perspective to adopt, she is obliged to apply a radically revisionary explanatory perspective to everyday life without ever explicitly addressing whether the revision might entail a serious loss of intelligibility—or indeed, whether the revisionary perspective is true.

Epistemologists tell us that coherence is (at least) a necessary condition of epistemic justification and so, of knowledge. If so, there is a sense in which academic life, ironically enough, unfits students for knowledge about the explanation of action. What it produces, to paraphrase Bernard Williams, is a situation in which *education destroys knowledge*: the more students believe what they study, the more they undermine the coherence of their beliefs.[11] The easiest strategy for achieving coherence would appear to be to believe as little as possible, but that, unfortunately, is also the quickest recipe for apathy and cynicism.

If this is right, there is an epistemic case to be made for making the study of action a topic (an interdisciplinary course or even a program) designed for advanced undergraduates and graduate students in the humanities and social sciences. If coherence is a necessary condition of knowledge, it requires both the removal of obvious inconsistencies in our belief-sets, as well as the concerted attempt to bring coherence to apparently divergent approaches to a common subject matter. In the present case, it requires students to bring coherence to their beliefs about the explanation of action at multiple levels: between everyday and academic approaches, within different aspects of the everyday approach, and within different aspects of various academic approaches.

Though certainly ambitious, such a project would reap important pedagogical dividends. For one thing, it would ensure that students left the university with the resources to leverage what they had learned about action in the classroom and apply it to 'real life.' It would, in addition, give them a certain capacity for knowledge in their personal lives, while affording them a more critical and intellectually resourceful outlook in law school (or legal practice), graduate school, or work pertaining to business and/or government.

What goes for action generally goes for the study of particular types of it. 'Terrorism' and 'Islamic terrorism' are action-types of particular significance in contemporary life. Could the preceding approach to action improve understanding of those topics?

PEDAGOGY AND THE EXPLANATION OF TERRORISM

Most of us, I suppose, remember where we were on September 11, 2001. I certainly do. I left my apartment that morning around 8:30 and ambled into Princeton University's Firestone Library one minute before American Airlines Flight 11 struck One World Trade Center. Lacking the slightest sense that anything was wrong, I went into the basement of the library so that I could work undisturbed and remained there, undisturbed, until about 1:00 p.m. Around that time, I walked home, intending to eat lunch and drive out to my own institution, The College of New Jersey, to teach my 2:00 p.m. introductory philosophy class. The subject that day was (ironically enough) supposed to have been Ruth Benedict's defense of cultural relativism. I walked in the front door of my apartment and to my bewilderment found my partner home from work hours earlier than usual, watching what I took to be an action film. Except that it wasn't an action film. "You haven't heard," she said, grimly, turning off the television. "Heard what?" I asked.

It took a full five minutes to comprehend what sounded to me to be her bizarre and implausible answer to that question, which I flatly disbelieved at first, and came to believe only after insisting on independent verification of the morning's events on CNN. Unable to think very clearly at that point, and unable to get through to anyone at the college, I robotically insisted on driving there to teach. Having gotten there, I found a memo on the bulletin board from the provost, asking that faculty hold classes rather than cancel them, in order to "facilitate" students' need to "process" the day's events. That, I confess, was the precise moment at which I decided to cancel class: I myself hadn't processed the day's events, and was in no position to facilitate anyone else's attempt to do so.

We all, eventually, did come to process that day's events, and on my campus at least, as well as campuses nearby, many of us made attempts to facilitate our students' attempts to do so. Some of this did real good and some of it didn't, but in one clear respect, I thought then and continue to think that a 'teachable moment' was squandered and eventually lost. The teachable moment concerned the then-ubiquitous, and very urgent, 'why' question about the original event, which was no sooner posed than forgotten about. The point was put with perfect sensitivity to the zeitgeist by the journalist Christopher Hitchens in a piece in the London *Guardian* called "The Morning After." "One day into the post-World Trade Center era," Hitchens wrote, "and the question 'how' is still taking precedence over the question 'why.'"

> With cellphones still bleeping piteously from under the rubble, it probably seems indecent to most people to ask if the United States has ever done anything to attract such awful hatred. Indeed, the very thought, for the present is taboo. . . .
>
> In general, the motive and character of the perpetrators is shrouded by rhetoric about their "cowardice" and "shadowy" character, almost as if they had not volunteered to immolate themselves in the broadest of broad blue daylight. On the campus where I am writing this, there are a few students and professors willing to venture points about United States foreign policy. But they do so very guardedly, and it would sound like profane apologetics if transmitted live. So the analytical moment, if there is to be one, has been indefinitely postponed.

Noting that "fighter planes are the only craft in the sky over New York and Washington," and that the "National Guard is on the streets," Hitchens ended the piece with the following mordant and prescient observation:

> Yes, it does give the impression that we are "at war," all right. But being on manoeuvres is not the same as warfare, and "preparedness" and "vigilance" are of little value if they contribute to the erection of a Maginot Line in the mind.[12]

We've been at war in the full-blooded sense for nearly eight years now, and though I can inevitably speak only of my own experiences and students (several hundred, at six institutions) I'm inclined to say that the 'analytic moment' remains postponed, and the mental Maginot Lines remain formidably present. For many students (not all, obviously, but a sizable number), the events of 9/11 are now old hat—'history' in the weirdly pejorative sense of that term—and have come to blur into the background of historical events, belonging to the distant and hence irrelevant past. Descriptions of the event itself abet this interpretation. '9/11' is typically seen as a single, one-time, *sui generis* event without context or precedent, unrelated to anything before it, and likewise disconnected from the present and the future. On this conception, it neither bears an intelligible relation to anything we might have done to provoke it, nor for that matter to an entirely self-generated campaign by the terrorists themselves. It was simply a singular bolt from the blue, on par with any natural disaster, appearing as causelessly and inexplicably as its failure to happen again—an event, not an action.

Though it sounds uncharitable to put the point this way, I've also found from hard experience that when asked to discuss 9/11 or terrorism generally, students are capable at best of remembering the events of the day and emoting about them, but can do little of an analytical or cognitive nature with what they remember. Eight years after the fact, they evince a flabbergasting ignorance of key names, places, dates, and chronologies, and a predictable incapacity to make sense even of ordinary newspaper or magazine stories on the subject. One Middle Eastern country is to them the same as every other, as is one Middle Eastern face, leader, grievance, or atrocity. So it is with Islam. Multiculturalism tells them to respect it, folk wisdom tells them to fear it, but few have any idea of what it is, what it says, or what relevance it has to any real-world event.

"And yet," as Hitchens puts the point in a different essay, "there is still an unmet need, an unanswered yearning, for an intelligible past," which "finds its expression in surrogate forms, like the 'referred pain' of a complex ailment. . . ."[13] Unfortunately, one of these "surrogate forms" consists in evading the issues altogether, and then festering in a sort of muted rage or anxiety about the unintelligible evil of 'Muslims' or 'the Bush Administration.' Another closely related form is dogmatic allegiance to propaganda and conspiracy theorizing. I've met as many students who believe that Saddam Hussein was behind 9/11 as believe that the Israelis were. Students in this predicament face two choices: either a wholesale acquiescence in the unintelligibility of the social world they confront, or intelligibility purchased at the price of epistemic virtue.[14]

Some of this, to be sure, arises from perfectly straightforward causes and has relatively straightforward remedies. Obviously, to the extent that students are ignorant of history, politics, or Islam, they need courses in history, politics, and religious studies. To the extent that they're apathetic about the world around them, they need to be motivated to take it seriously. To the extent that they're in the grips of a facile multiculturalism or of bigotry or conspiracy theories, these need to be explicitly challenged and debunked. But while important, these features of the problem tend to conceal deeper problems, problems that persist even after the narrowly informational deficiencies are remedied.

To begin to explain an event like 9/11, at a bare minimum we need an adequate characterization of the explanandum—literally, an account of *what* we're talking about. As many commentators have noted, the very designation '9/11' evades this task: '9/11' is a conveniently neutral set of numbers that presupposes, in Americocentric terms, that the most important phenomenon taking place on the planet that day involved four hijacked jetliners in the airspace of New York, Pennsylvania, and Washington. But even if we make this assumption, we are left with the far-from-trivial question of how to characterize the phenomenon itself.

I take for granted here (contrary to many conspiracy theories) that an attack did take place, and that the conventional account of it is essentially

accurate.[15] If the question, then, is why this attack took place, our focus is ipso facto a moral or political one, involving the motivations and actions of those who launched the attacks, and not a technical or scientific one about the strictly mechanical events of the day—e.g., the physics and chemistry of fuel-laden projectiles, falling towers, melting steel, and crumbling walls, or even how it is that the attackers succeeded in subverting the defense apparatus of the targeted country. Our starting point, then, has to be the attackers themselves.

It is tempting to think that if this is our starting point, the character-ization of the relevant actions is entirely obvious: 'nineteen Arab-Muslim hijackers hijacked four American commercial jetliners, ramming two of them into the World Trade Center, one into the Pentagon, and (having been overcome by the passengers) crashing one in a field in southwestern Pennsylvania.' But though every fact in the preceding sentence is true, its truth doesn't by itself entail that the sentence itself is the one incontestably correct description of the event, or of the explanandum. For one thing, it immediately becomes clear that given almost any plausible criterion of rel-evance, the actions relevant to characterizing 9/11 didn't all take place on September 11, 2001. Many of the relevant actions long preceded that. But how far back should we go? Which actions are relevant?

A bit of reflection on these questions makes clear that even if we insist that the explanandum specifically put al-Qaeda at the center of the action—a highly contestable assumption[16]—we see that 9/11 was not an isolated or random act, but part of a long-standing conflict that began (depend-ing on one's interpretation) in 1917, 1923, 1947, 1967, 1989, 1993, 1996, 1998, or if one really wants to stretch things, 610 A.D.[17] Regardless of one's appraisal of the act, then, 9/11 was part of a broader historical context. We thus face another series of questions preliminary to the task of generating an explanation (or explanatory hypotheses): should we try to explain 9/11 as a single event, or the campaign that gave rise to it? In the first case, why dissociate the one event from its broader context? In the second case, how should we conceptualize the relevant context?

Suppose we decide that our explanandum is not '9/11' as such, but the campaign of which it was (and is) a part. In that case, we soon come to see that the campaign was itself the product of a huge number of individuals, extended in space and time, making choices and forming beliefs, desires, and intentions in response to events around them. Clearly, the choices, beliefs, desires, and intentions are relevant to characterizing the event, but if the mental states make reference to further events, how relevant are these further events? And which events are relevant? This may seem an overly abstract question, but the answer to it makes the difference between describ-ing 9/11 as an 'unprovoked act of mass murder' and describing it as 'propor-tional retaliation for grievances suffered over the course of a century.'

Suppose we decide, on some principled basis, to identify the relevant actors and delimit the relevant mental states and events. In that case, we face yet another crucial choice. We have, let's say, an account of what al-Qaeda takes itself to be accomplishing in its campaign against its enemies, and thus understand 9/11 in the context of this account. We can at that point either take that account at face value or appraise and judge it from a perspective alien to it, say, our own. In either case, the standards of rationality and morality that we apply (or don't apply) and our manner of applying them will have momentous consequences for the very description of what happened.[18] Again, are we explaining an episode in a nihilistic campaign of terrorist violence, a battle in a holy war, or the expression of nationalist grievances against foreign occupation?

The preceding questions merely scratch the surface of the complexity involved in the task of explanation. What becomes apparent on engaging with them is that there is no obvious way to characterize what happened on 9/11, and so no trivial or self-evident way of specifying the explanandum of any proposed explanation of 'the event.' Virtually every assumption here is contested territory, regardless of the apparent 'obviousness' of any given claim by any given party. The very characterization of the event is a controversial matter and is the product of a complex inquiry, not its self-evident starting point.

Suppose, however, that we get the characterization of the explanandum under control. '9/11,' let us say, is best conceived not as a single event, but as one component in an interconnected series of terrorist attacks by al-Qaeda, its allies, and fellow travelers, each attack being part of a single relatively concerted quasi-military campaign inaugurated by Osama bin Laden's August 1996 "declaration of *jihad*" against the United States.[19] Let's stipulate (ex hypothesi) that we regard this campaign as irrational and evil, thereby rejecting the attackers' claims to be engaged in a (genuinely, as opposed to perceivedly) just war against the United States and its allies. At this point, we run into questions of equal if not greater difficulty and complexity, questions that attend any attempt to explain evil and make it intelligible to those who adamantly reject its claims.

One problem is metaphysical and epistemological. We want to know why the attackers did as they did. In other words, why did they choose evil as against good? On the one hand, the search for answers to these questions entails that we ought to seek causal explanations of the relevant actions. On the other hand, the very nature of the questions suggests that the answers ought to facilitate ascriptions of moral responsibility and predications of moral judgment. But the search for causal explanation presupposes that the relevant acts are part of a network of causes, so that our explanation succeeds only if it picks out the relevant causes. Meanwhile, the tasks of ascribing responsibility and making moral judgment presuppose that the relevant acts are free, and on a common view of things, are *not* produced by any network of causes. The question we face, then, is how to construct a causal explanation while preserving the freedom required to make moral appraisals of the very same actions.[20]

The preceding metaphysical–epistemic problem is complicated by a closely related psychological one.[21] We can in principle take two very different perspectives on an action, which I'll call 'agential' and 'observational.' The agential perspective is the first-personal perspective of the agent performing the act, a perspective we can take up when explaining the acts of others by engaging in a sort of vicarious introspection on their acts.[22] When I introspect vicariously on another's act, I put myself in the position of that agent, to see the world (as much as possible) from within his consciousness, experiencing what it's like to exercise his agency. By contrast, the observational perspective is the second- or third-personal perspective of a spectator on someone else's act. From this perspective, I view the agent as yet another object in the world, subject to causal influence by the world (including factors internal to the agent himself). Both perspectives seem necessary for full understanding of an act, but each perspective stands in psychological tension with the other.

On the one hand, to understand the act, and construct an explanation of it, I have to take the agential perspective on it. But the judgment that an act is evil typically produces revulsion at the act in proportion to its evil, and if the act is sufficiently evil, my revulsion can be so extreme as to vitiate my capacity to take the agential perspective on it in any genuine way. Indeed, it can seem immoral to try, for the more motivationally real I make another's evil, the narrower the gap between thinking about the act and doing it; the narrower that gap, the more it seems that I have to alter my character in the direction of evil to make it motivationally attractive.[23] Unchecked revulsion will incline one to demonize or bestialize those we regard as evil: given our incapacity to take up their perspective, we will tend to assume that their perspective is itself inhuman and, in a fundamental sense, inexplicable.

On the other hand, to explain the act, I also have to take an observational perspective on it. I have to bracket how the agent saw his environment, and focus on the environment itself—those aspects of it that, when cognized, have a propensity to motivate action. In other words, I have to identify the forces acting on the agent, whether internal or external, whether acknowledged by the agent or not. Notice, however, that if I take the observational perspective on the act but refuse the agential, I omit something essential to the act: the agency by which it was produced. I treat the agent as an object acted on by forces beyond his control. This perspective will (despite the protestations of its practitioners) tend to evoke a certain *sympathy* or *pity* (however grudging) for the agent, for from this perspective, the agent is merely pushed or pulled into the action by what is not-him.[24] But if I succumb to this temptation, I subvert my understanding of the very phenomenon I set out to explain—namely, evil.

I list these puzzles not because I regard them as irresolvable paradoxes,[25] but because one cannot begin to explain terrorism, or evil generally, without confronting and resolving them. And though terrorism is of course studied in universities, often with great seriousness and sophistication, I think it is safe to say that one cannot even begin to address the puzzles I've raised by the sources or methods of area studies, postcolonial studies, conventional historiography, social science, or journalism. Students who come to the study of terrorism with nothing but these tools at their disposal are (unless they are miraculously lucky) foredoomed to getting the fundamentals of explanation wrong.[26] One sees the result of this failure in otherwise well-informed students whose attempted explanations of Islamist terrorism oscillate between the claim that terrorists engage in terrorism because the victims deserve it, and the claim that they engage in terrorism from some inexplicable demonic-bestial propensity that inheres in them.

As may be apparent, the conundrums I've discussed here are just special cases of the issues I discussed in the preceding section. They are, in effect, the unresolved tensions between the everyday and academic perspectives, coming home to roost.

THE PROPOSAL AND SOME OBJECTIONS ANSWERED

I lack the space here to describe the specifics of my pedagogical proposal in any detail, so for present purposes, a broad overview of the proposal will have to suffice, followed by a brief discussion of some objections.

What I envision is a course, sequence of courses, or program involving an action-theoretic approach to the study of terrorism, intended for advanced undergraduates in majors pertaining to the study of terrorism. The overall aim of the course would be to integrate what the rest of the curriculum leaves unintegrated about explanation, and to bring an integrated understanding of explanation to bear on the facts. In effect, its subject matter would be the very topics I've been discussing in the preceding sections of this chapter, made intelligible to an undergraduate audience.

For ease of exposition, imagine a single course. The first third of the course would focus on philosophical action theory. Here the governing concern would be to induce the student explicitly to address the conflict between the everyday and academic approaches to action. For example, how (if at all) do we reconcile the social scientist's conception of causal explanation with our everyday approach? Is such a reconciliation possible? If not, which approach is true? A second third of the course would involve the presentation of essential factual content relevant to terrorism: history, politics, and religion. Here, the essential point would be to master the essential factual background concerning (say) Near East history, politics, and fundamentalism required to follow debates about (say) Islamist terrorism. The last third of the course would be devoted to students' appraising existing explanations of terrorism in the literature, and having them produce explanations of their own—applying the lessons learned in the first two parts of the course to the literature, and to the world.

It might be wondered whether the proposal I have in mind is pedagogically feasible. Could students actually study a topic framed in such an abstract, theoretical way?

I think so. I should stress that, as an upper-division course, the proposal I have in mind is intended for a specific subset of students, not the student population as a whole. The material is admittedly demanding and presupposes a background in a relevant area of study as well as an aptitude for interdisciplinary study. But I don't see that the material of the course is any more difficult than, say, calculus, biochemistry, organic chemistry, fluid dynamics, electrical engineering, or philosophy of language, all of which are taught at the undergraduate level. Indeed, for advanced students in philosophy, Near East Studies, or forensic psychology/criminology, some parts of the course may well seem too easy, compensated for by the difficulty of less-familiar parts.

Unlike calculus, biochemistry, and the rest, however, we might think that the study of terrorism involves emotional demands that make it inappropriate as an academic subject at the undergraduate level. Is the proposal, then, too emotionally fraught?

Certainly, the course involves material that would likely produce intense emotional reactions in students, and an instructor would have to know how to deal with the expression of conflict and emotion in the classroom. But the expression of intense emotion is a sign that students have a strong stake in the issues. As long as the expression of emotion doesn't lapse into dogmatism or abuse, I would say that the expression of emotion is a potential ally of inquiry and ought to be capitalized on. A pedagogical skill worth cultivating is the ability to tease out the evaluative judgments expressed through emotion, to lay them out, and to make them amenable to rational analysis. That skill is as necessary in any class on contemporary moral issues, bioethics, or Near East Studies as it would be in the course I'm proposing.[27]

Finally, is there not a danger that a course of the proposed sort lends itself too easily to politicization? Isn't the underlying motivation here the same as that of the "know the enemy" pedagogies we've seen in the past? If so, doesn't the proposal in some sense subordinate the classroom to the national security imperatives of the state?

In one sense, I would admit right from the start that the analysis and proposal I've offered are explicitly and unapologetically political. I assume throughout that Islamist terrorism (and terrorism generally) is something that will occupy center stage in world affairs for the foreseeable future, that it is desirable to have a citizenry capable of dealing with this phenomenon, and that given the pedagogical status quo, we are not apt to get such a citizenry. This is controversial, and in some sense political, but it's neither indoctrinative nor propagandistic.

Having said that, I am emphatically not proposing a "know the enemy" course in the conventional sense of that term, where X is presupposed as "the enemy," and the student's task is to inculcate dogmas about this enemy.[28] Given all that I've said here, a student enrolled in the course I propose could, compatibly with the aims of the course, come to think of terrorism as a justified form of holy war or liberation struggle, sympathize entirely with al-Qaeda, explain 9/11 as an act of condign justice, and reach the conclusion that four million Americans really do deserve to die in retaliation for the malfeasances of American foreign policy.[29] But a student could, compatibly with the aims of the course, come to exactly the reverse views.

The point of the course, as I see it, is not to inculcate any particular view of terrorism, but to get students to come to grips with the relevant challenges of describing, evaluating, and explaining it for themselves. So understood, the purpose of the course rules out indoctrination of any kind—the use of the classroom to impose a specific ideology on students, to penalize them for dissenting from the instructor's views, or to deceive them into regarding the range of permissible debate as narrower than it in fact is.

I make no pretense, however, that the proposal is somehow 'neutral' in the sense that instructors must entirely abstain from the expression of their own considered philosophical or political views in the classroom. Discussion about terrorism is inherently contentious: after all, terrorism itself arises from political strife. Once students are brought up to speed in understanding the foundational issues, they have to learn to deal with the fact that the topic at hand is almost entirely contested territory. The best way of dealing with this fact is to habituate them to dealing in a productive way with conflict itself. To that end, what students need is an instructor who can exemplify the process of constructive disagreement in a way that helps them reliably distinguish that from dogmatism, indoctrination, and evasion.[30] A conflict-laden syllabus, then, is not enough. What is needed is an instructor at home with the conflicts in it.

CONCLUSION

"I have carefully labored," writes Spinoza in the Introduction of his *Political Treatise*, "not to mock, lament or execrate, but to *understand* human actions. . . ."[31] At first glance, this aspiration may seem ill-suited to the study of terrorism. For one thing, it seems to imply that understanding should somehow preclude the execration of evil, and trump the lamentation of its consequences. Worse yet, in common English usage, 'understanding' seems either to imply sympathy for the object of understanding, or to connote the clinical orientation of someone detached or alienated from human action as such. At first glance, then, Spinoza's aspiration seems the very opposite of a desirable pedagogical ideal.

But I think it *is* the ideal. For Spinoza's claim does not imply (as might first appear) that there are no actions worth lamenting or execrating; it demands instead that understanding precede and regulate our emotional reactions. And though understanding has (for reasons worth investigating) come over time to connote sympathy, detachment, or alienation, what it denotes, in the context of action, is the fullest grasp of the significance of the action—the capacity to identify its causes, to ascribe responsibility for it, to hold it up for moral judgment, to integrate one's account of the act with the rest of one's knowledge, and to put it into the widest and most informative context. Terrorism is perhaps the most-discussed phenomenon of our age. Spinoza's maxim makes the demand that we know *what* we're talking about.

In my view, current pedagogical practices do little to promote that aspiration. My hope is that the proposal I offer here holds out the possibility of the sort of understanding that does promote it, and in doing so, promotes attitudes toward terrorism worth having, and policies worth enacting.[32]

NOTES

1. I focus throughout on Islamic terrorism, but this focus is not necessarily inherent to the proposal as such. Obviously, not all terrorism is Islamic, and the proposal might with appropriate changes be made to apply to the study of other forms of terrorism. Thanks to Magi Ibrahim for pressing this point.

2. See G. Graff, *Beyond the Culture Wars: How Teaching the Conflicts Can Revitalize American Higher Education* (New York and London: Norton, 1992), hereafter *BCW*.

3. G. King, R. O. Keohane, and S. Verba, *Designing Social Inquiry: Scientific Inference in Qualitative Research* (Princeton, NJ: Princeton University Press, 1994), 6, 109–112.

4. King, Keohane, and Verba, *Designing Social Inquiry*, chap. 3.

5. For a typical textbook presentation of both issues, see R. Kane, ed., *Free Will* (Malden, MA: Blackwell Publishers, 2002). For an explicit attempt to decouple the topic of free will from that of explanation, see R. Clarke, "Toward a Credible Agent-Causal Account of Free Will," in *Agents, Causes, and Events: Essays on Indeterminism and Free Will*, ed. T. O'Connor (New York and Oxford: Oxford University Press, 1995), 210–11.

   On Frankfurt counterexamples, see H. G. Frankfurt, "Alternate Possibilities and Moral Responsibility," *Journal of Philosophy* LXVI, no. 23 (1969), reprinted in *The Importance of What We Care About: Philosophical Essays* (Cambridge: Cambridge University Press, 1988), chap. 1. On the consequence argument, see P. Van Inwagen, *An Essay on Free Will* (Oxford: Clarendon, 1983).

6. See P. Foot, *Natural Goodness* (Oxford: Clarendon, 2001); R. Hursthouse, *On Virtue Ethics* (Oxford: Oxford University Press, 2001). One notable exception to this rule is the work of Alasdair MacIntyre. See chaps. 7 and 8 of his *After Virtue: A Study in Moral Theory*, 2nd ed. (Notre Dame: University of Notre Dame Press, 1984). In my experience, however, instructors usually omit MacIntyre's views on explanation from courses on virtue ethics. The professor in my Twentieth Century Ethics seminar in graduate school assigned us almost all of *After Virtue* to read, but told us to "skip the chapters on social science," since "they've got nothing to do with ethics." My

undergraduate professors in political philosophy (at a different institution) said and did about the same thing.

7. C. Geertz, "Thick Description: Toward an Interpretive Theory of Culture," *The Interpretation of Culture* (New York: Basic Books, 1973), 3–30.

8. Cf. Graff, *BCW*, chaps. 6–7.

9. Cf. Graff, *BCW*, chap. 6.

10. I don't think that the problem can be circumvented by differentiating contexts of explanation and employing some methods in some contexts, and others in others. For one thing, we would need a principled account of how to individuate and differentiate contexts, and need an account of why each context required methods that were (not just different but) *incompatible* with those in other contexts. It's not clear that that's possible. Second, notice that the everyday question asks 'Why did S do x?' In this form, the question makes no reference to context; it simply demands the explanation of an action as such. Thus if the presuppositions of the question are correct, the question cannot affirmatively be answered by an explanation relativized to a context: to give such an answer is to fail to answer the question as asked. But if the only possible explanations are relativized to contexts, the presuppositions of the question as asked must simply be illegitimate, since the question asks for the impossible. I think the alternatives are exhaustive, and their exhaustiveness sharpens the dilemma described in the text. Thanks to Yvonne Raley for pressing this issue.

11. B. Williams, *Ethics and the Limits of Philosophy* (Cambridge: Harvard University Press, 1985), 147, 168–70. We could, in principle, ignore the tensions I've described in the text, proceeding as though they weren't there or weren't important, but this gambit would necessarily have to come at the expense of coherence, and if coherence is necessary for knowledge, at the expense of knowledge. Thanks to Yvonne Raley for pressing this point.

12. C. Hitchens, "The Morning After," reprinted in *Love, Poverty, and War: Journeys and Essays* (New York: Nation Books, 2004), 407, 408, 409.

13. C. Hitchens, "Why Americans Are Not Taught History," in *Love, Poverty, and War*, 265.

14. For an illuminating discussion of 9/11 conspiracy theorizing, see S. J. Al Azm, "Islam, Terrorism, and the West," *Comparative Studies of South Asia, Africa and the Middle East* 25, no. 1 (2005): 6–15.

15. In what follows, I accept the essential veracity of *The 9/11 Commission Report*, authorized ed. (New York: W. W. Norton, 2004).

16. Contestable because Khalid Shaikh Muhammad, "the principal architect of the 9/11 attacks," was not a member of al-Qaeda but "enjoyed considerable autonomy" in planning his own independent terrorist campaigns. See *9/11 Commission Report*, p. 145, and generally, pp. 145–50. The word *qaeda* in Arabic means 'base' or 'foundation' and therefore implies the existence of a superstructure supported by the base but not identical with it.

17. An explanation for the significance of the dates in the text: 1917 represents the date of the Balfour Declaration; 1923, the end of the Ottoman Caliphate; 1947, the proposed partition of Palestine; 1967, the (to Arabs) most traumatic of the Arab–Israeli wars; 1989, the Soviet retreat from Afghanistan; 1993, the first attack on the World Trade Center; 1996 and 1998, the dates of Osama bin Laden's first and second *fatwas* against the US, respectively; and 610 A.D., the Prophet Muhammad's assumption of the prophecy.

18. Cf. A. MacIntyre, "Rationality and the Explanation of Action," in *Against the Self-Images of the Age: Essays on Ideology and Philosophy* (Notre Dame: University of Notre Dame Press, 1978), chap. 21.

19. Reprinted as chapter 3 of *Messages to the World: The Statements of Osama bin Laden*, ed. B. Lawrence, tr. J. Howarth (London and New York: Verso, 2005).

20. For two contrasting accounts of this issue, see T. Nagel, *The View from Nowhere* (Oxford: Oxford University Press, 1986), chap. 7 (hereafter *VFN*), and T. O'Connor, "Agent Causation," in *Agents, Causes, and Events*, 173–200.

21. My account here, though highly influenced by Nagel's philosophy of mind, departs radically from it in ways that I cannot discuss here. See Nagel *VFN*, 120–24; "What Is It Like to Be a Bat?" *Philosophical Review* 33, October 1974, reprinted in T. Nagel, *Mortal Questions* (Cambridge: Cambridge University Press, 1979), 165–80.

22. I get the phrase "vicarious introspection" from J. Stern, *Terror in the Name of God: Why Religious Militants Kill* (New York: Harper Collins, 2003), xvii. Cf. Nagel: when we hold someone responsible for an action, "the result is not merely a description of his character, but a vicarious occupation of his point of view and evaluation of his actions from within it" (*VFN*, 121).

23. For a brilliant fictional depiction of this problem, see I. Murdoch, *The Nice and the Good* (New York: Penguin, 1968). Cf. E. H. Carr's discussion of a similar point in *What Is History?* (New York: Vintage, 1961), 26–29.

24. Stern offers a sensitive account of this problem; see the Introduction of *Terror in the Name of God*.

25. *Pace* Nagel, *VFN*, 113, 117, 123, 124, 137.

26. I include in this assessment social scientists who adopt the explanatory framework of R. A. Pape's *Dying to Win: The Strategic Logic of Suicide Terrorism* (New York: Random House, 2005), widely regarded as a model of explanatory success in the social sciences. Yet Pape deals with none of the topics I discuss in this paper, and offers an explanation of suicide terrorism that equivocally ascribes it to "foreign occupation" and to *perceptions of* foreign occupation (e.g., 20–24). Thus his account treats veridical cognition of real occupations and delusions about nonexistent ones as a single unitary causal factor in the production of suicide terrorism. But it is hardly clear that incompatible phenomena can, by mere conjunction, be regarded as unitary causal factors. It is also highly disputable that explanations of action that abstain from judgments of rationality about the explananda, as Pape's does, are genuinely explanatory of those actions. An action is arguably not intelligible until we can judge its rationality, but we cannot judge this from a perspective that is professedly neutral as between veridical cognition and self-delusion. (On this latter point, see MacIntyre, "Rationality and the Explanation of Action," cited note 18 above.) If either of these points can be vindicated, Pape's explanation becomes a paradigm of explanatory failure, not success.

    For a critique of the methodological assumptions of postcolonial theory, see my "Essentialism, Consistency, and Islam: A Critique of Edward Said's *Orientalism*," *Israel Affairs* 13, no. 4 (2007): 689–713.

27. Cf. Graff, *BCW*, 148.

28. Cf. Graff's discussion of this issue in *BCW*, 153–155. See also my review of William Bennett's *Why We Fight: Moral Clarity and the War on Terrorism* in *Teaching Philosophy* 27, no. 1 (2004): 61–65.

29. Bin Laden's spokesman, Suleman Abu Gheith, has argued that four million Americans deserve to die in retaliation for what he takes to be indiscriminate killing of Muslims by the United States. See "Why We Fight America," Middle East Research Institute, Special Dispatch Series No. 388 (12 June 2002), http://www.memri.org/bin/articles.cgi?ID=SP38802.

It's worth remembering that if a course of this sort were taught in a Muslim-majority country, most students would have as much sympathy for al-Qaeda as American students have for the American military. As I say in what follows in the text and imply in the discussion of "narrowly informational deficiencies," I do not mean to imply that an instructor should remain neutral about a student's sympathy for al-Qaeda. The view needs to be challenged. But it is not the *purpose* of the class to ensure that students have or lack such sympathy. Thanks to Yvonne Raley for pressing this issue.

30. For an excellent discussion of philosophy instructor as discursive model for students, see C.-A. Biondi, "Socratic Teaching: Beyond *The Paper Chase*," *Teaching Philosophy* 31, no. 2 (2008): 119–140.

31. B. de Spinoza, *A Political Treatise*, tr. R. H. M Elwes (New York: Dover, 1951), I.4, 288 (my emphasis).

32. Thanks to George Abaunza, Fahmi Abboushi, Sadik al Azm, Carrie-Ann Biondi, Richard Burnor, Hilary Persky, and Yvonne Raley for helpful conversations on the subject of this essay, and to Carrie-Ann Biondi and Yvonne Raley for comments on the essay itself. Thanks also to audiences at The College of New Jersey and Felician College for the opportunity to present related material.

7 Global Aspirations for Gender Equality in Education
What Kind of Pedagogy?[1]

Elaine Unterhalter and Amy North

Since the late 1990s there has been widespread acceptance of a shift in economic power from the nation-state to the global market. While analysts disagree on the extent of economic control that remains with governments and on the nature of the political and social realignments that have accompanied this change, virtually no one disputes that a significant alteration in relationships has taken place (Lauder et al. 2006). Thus, for example, the global market price for oil, securities, or the skills of highly trained mobile teachers have marked effects on economies and education systems around the world, which governments have only a limited range of strategies to mitigate. These changes have profound implications for how we think about schooling and pedagogies. Drawing on some discussions of the nature of globalization and its implications for education (Baylis and Smith 2001; Green 1997; Rizvi 2003) this chapter develops a taxonomy that distinguishes three different ways to understand how these processes frame ideas about pedagogy associated with the global aspirations for gender equality in education.

Gender equality in education holds a special place in contemporary global social justice policies and practices. Two-thirds of the one billion people in the world with little or no schooling are women and girls (Unterhalter 2007, xii). Aspirations for gender equality are central to two Millennium Development Goals (MDGs), initially agreed by virtually all the governments of the world in 2000. These remain a touchstone for UN organizations, many national government departments, and a large number of civil society organizations. MDG 2 aims at universal primary education, and its target entails that by 2007, all girls and boys of primary-school age should have entered school to enable them to complete eight years' study by 2015. MDG 3 aims to achieve gender equality and the empowerment of women. Its first target was for gender parity (that is, equal numbers of girls and boys) in primary school by 2005. The dates for the gender and education targets were set earlier than those associated with the other MDGs (all of which are to be accomplished by 2015) because education generally, and gender equality in education more specifically, is seen to underpin the achievement of all the MDGs (Vandemoortele, 2003). The MDGs have been scrutinized both by those who are close to the implementation effort (Birdsall and Vaishnav 2005; Sachs 2005), and by those who are critical of the attempt (Antrobus 2005; Black and White, 2003). We do not intend to take on the debate regarding the efficacy of the MDGs, although we have written elsewhere regarding some of the assumptions they make and the problems associated with failures to meet targets (North 2006; Unterhalter 2005, 2007). Instead, in this chapter we attempt to explore some of the pedagogic approaches associated with different engagements with the question of gender equality in education as a global aspiration as expressed in, but not only confined to, the MDGs.

One view of globalization links it with the struggle between global market relations and nation-states. Global space, in this view, is understood as constituted by the interaction between global market forces and nation-states, which sometimes advance economic globalization and sometimes oppose or seek to regulate it. The space of the global and the national are distinct with the global set 'above' the national. It is argued that global market forces, accelerated by information communication technologies, enthusiasm for trade liberalisation, privatisation, and the growth of finance capital, weaken the power of nation-states. Although some moves have been made to regulate global markets, these are generally inadequate in addressing the speed, rapacity, and greed associated with hyperglobalization (Held et al. 1999; Elliott and Atkinson 2008). This view is associated with the idea that economic growth has been primarily linked with the development of knowledge economies, and that education systems and investments in skills will be key vehicles for leaping from the level of the national 'up' to the more intoxicating air of global market action (Powell and Snellman 2004). A form of what we term 'inter/national contestation' between countries and corporations is generated by economic globalization with competition between nation-states to 'upskill' and 'tune up' education systems. The assumption is that states offer fertile conditions for economic growth through enhanced education provision and skills development. We identify below a pedagogic approach associated with this agenda based on skills and competition. While economic competitiveness is a major driver, the international approach is also associated with limited programs for social inclusion, partly so that the disadvantaged do not threaten national and global stability. The form of gender equality associated with this entails the expansion of education for girls and boys to enhance skill formation and social cohesion.

A second view of globalization and pedagogy we have named 'in/ternational,' because contestations are not framed by national political economics, but by the intermingling and flow between global and local cultural processes, each of which is inside the other. This view, sometimes identified by the term 'glocalisation,' is strongly associated with the work of Arun Appadurai (1996). He argues that the new global cultural economy cannot be understood in terms of older center–periphery models, but requires an appreciation of the disjuncture between culture, economy, and politics. He links these disjunctures with aspects of global cultural flows, in which imagined landscapes of sameness and difference shape the ways in which we understand ethnicity, media, technology, finance, and ideas about consumption. This view is associated with discussions of pedagogy that highlight its potential as a form of critique of the discourse of skills and marketization. In this work there is an appreciation of the critical potential of pedagogies to disrupt the notion of education as a tool for economic growth or 'simple' social inclusion. The stress is on pedagogic practices that are deconstructive, generating questions regarding the authority of science, the official curriculum, and the worldview shaped by the minority world (Hooks 1994; Lather 1991a, 1991b; Luke and Gore 1992; Ntuli 1999; Spivak 1993). Forms of pedagogic practice concern the ways in which languages and cultures are negotiated and their meanings expanded or diminished in relation to global processes. The discourses that frame knowledge production and circulation have been an important area of discussion (Bhabha 1994; Hickling-Hudson and Ahlquist 2003; Said 1978). A key pedagogical activity entails the revelation of formations of in/ternational understanding, where the intermixture of global and local practices and identities are evident (Carrim, forthcoming; Rampal, forthcoming). Pedagogy is thus not a simple matter of instruction in particular forms of knowledge or understanding, but a deconstructive process, constantly examining its own discursive formation.

A third view of globalization is associated with attempts to build global regulatory institutional machinery across nation-states to tame global market forces, effect redistribution, enhance participation, and assert some equality of status between people. This position, generally associated with the writings of David Held (2004) on a global covenant, is also evident in a range of positions on cosmopolitanism (Appiah 2006; Brock and Brighouse 2005; Rapport and Stade 2007) and assessments of attempts by global social movements to deepen practices of participation and discussion and hold states and markets accountable for promises made on advancing equalities (Cohen and Rai 2000; Edwards and Gaventa 2001; Mundy and Murphy 2001; Okin 2003). This position is associated with a range of writings on pedagogies that take seriously some of the normative questions entailed by thinking about global justice (Boni 2008; Nussbaum 1997; Walker 2006). Some writers advocate teaching global dispositions, not just deconstructing the discourses that frame globalization (Bourn 2008; Davies et al. 2005). A number of accounts document teacher and learner views in classrooms where human rights, global citizenship, and inequalities are explicitly discussed (Marshall and Arnot 2007; McCowan 2008). Nira Yuval-Davis (1997; Stoetzler and Yuval-Davis, 2002) has elaborated the notion of transversal dialogue. This offers rich resources for formulating pedagogies that take seriously participatory processes to foster critical understanding of the historical location of the self as learner and teacher, and engagement with discussion across difference with others. This dialogic process of transversalism appears a key component of actions for reconstructing global justice, not simply deconstructing or evading it (Unterhalter 2007, 32). We have termed the pedagogic approaches associated with an attempt to change existing global social and pedagogic relations 'international' in that they do not refuse some of the frameworks provided by nation-states, as is typical of writers in the second group, but stand very far from the uncritical endorsement of competition around skills and alignments of national assessment or quality assurance regimes associated with the first group of writers. In this pedagogic approach there is a critique of nation-states for being insufficiently attentive to participatory processes, global inequalities, forms of the global market, and the exclusions associated with current forms of decision making. Nancy Fraser's (2005) concern to bring together a politics of redistribution, recognition, and participation provides a useful framing for some of these international pedagogies. Jennifer Chan illuminates both the ontological and epistemological dimensions of an emancipatory pedagogy that draws on some notion of reconstructed global relations when she writes:

> A dialogical model of recognition to global justice sees education beyond merely a good investment or basic freedom; it is a core component of an emancipatory project for recognizing and positively valorizing cultural diversity, and transforming the institutionalized patterns of cultural value in our collective pursuit of global democracy. (Chan 2007, 373)

Her vision entails both a form of reconstructed international relations where participation and debate form part of some of the processes of regulation, and also a set of relationships where gender equality is linked with a larger emancipatory project concerned with global justice.

This taxonomy of different approaches to pedagogy associated with different understandings of globalization allows us to distinguish some different emphases in the ways in which gender equality in education as a global aspiration is put into practice.

CONTRASTING APPROACHES TO GENDER EQUALITY IN EDUCATION AS A GLOBAL ASPIRATION

Each view of globalization and the associated pedagogies is linked with a different orientation to the issue of gender equality in education as a global aspiration. Thus for the hyperglobalists, there is concern to get girls and boys into school, partly to enhance social stability and partly to develop skills. Sufficient education for girls and boys to ensure 'no child left behind' or 'meeting basic learning needs' is the major policy goal. Inequalities in education, in earnings, or in national power may remain, but the remit of global policy is only to intervene to bring every child up to the minimum level of schooling or income. As we discuss below, this (inter/national) policy is associated with a minimalist reading of gender equality in the MDGs. It is linked with an approach to global education policy where there is a strong conviction that global organizations and nation-states can get equal numbers of girls and boys into school to advance the development of the global market.

The second position on globalization, associated with the formation of in/ternational pedagogies, tends to problematize the construction of gender, race, ethnic, or national identities within and through schools. These are seen as relational, culturally located, and intersecting dimensions of social division. For writers associated with this position, the MDG project is highly problematic regarding gender parity in schooling. It fails to understand or take seriously the complexity of local histories and cultures. It does not give attention to reversing social and cultural languages of exclusion and oppression, and it refuses the participatory and deconstructive politics so central to in/ternational pedagogies.

The third position (the international) entails some form of global social compact on gender equality and education. This is associated with the formulation of pedagogies concerned with building global networks and institutions, developing processes of participation, and revising current forms of understanding so that we can advance and evaluate intersecting demands for gender equality, women's rights, human rights, and global social justice.

Inter/National Pedagogies as Interventions for Gender Equality

For supporters of globalization, education—and in particular, girls' education—is seen as a catalyst for the development of dispositions for the global knowledge economy. The argument, based on a cost–benefit analysis of education, is that educated girls and women make better mothers with fewer, healthier, and better-educated children and are more productive workers, thereby contributing to faster economic growth (Herz and Sperling 2004). Links are also sometimes made between education and women's empowerment, although what is actually meant by 'empowerment' is not always clear. There is an emphasis on technical rather than political interpretations of empowerment, and empowerment is often not conceived multidimensionally, as characterizes the work of a number of feminist and critical commentators (Gaventa 2003; Kabeer 1999), but as a set of technical attributes such as voting or participating in the formal economy (World Bank 2001). Women's empowerment and gender equality are themselves often linked instrumentally to economic development: the World Bank's 2007 Global Monitoring Report's "Key message" number two is that "investing in gender equality and empowerment of women is *smart economics*" (our emphasis) because "greater gender equality helps to create a fair society, raises economic productivity, and helps advance other development goals" (World Bank 2007, 3).

This position is associated with seeing learning as primarily a matter concerning the economic outcomes of gender-equitable education. Learning is thus not linked with processes that develop understanding of the gendered power relations within which schooling and pedagogies are embedded. Indeed, in much of the literature that advocates expanding girls' enrollments or supporting progression, there is little or no discussion of what goes on within schools, how gendered hierarchies and inequalities play out within them, or the way in which these are affected by the broader social context within which they are situated. The assumption is that schools are bounded neutral spaces in which the transfer of skills from teacher to student occurs. As long as girls are in school and have teachers, textbooks, and adequate management, appropriate skills will be learned (Hill and King 1995; Schultz 2002).

Gender is thus understood as a noun. It simply refers to the numbers of girls (and boys) in school. The principal strategy for ensuring access to and progression through school is intervention—for example the abolition of school fees, stipend programs for girls, or food for school (Unterhalter 2007). There is some concern with building supportive institutions for girls' schooling (Unterhalter 2007), but little attention is given to critically examining conditions within schools, developing participatory processes for gender equality, or exploring pedagogies that make connections outside the formal school space.

The narrow focus in MDG 2 on gender parity suggests an understanding of gender equality restricted to gender as a noun. The setting of the first MDG target—gender parity in primary and secondary school by 2005, ten years before the rest of the MDGs—is indicative of the view that gender equality in education is instrumental for the achievement of the broader MDG agenda. This invites an orientation to pedagogy that stresses the ways in which it is primarily a form of intervention to develop particular skills.

This approach is dominant within many of the global institutions that work without an explicit critique of inter/national relations and seek to implement frameworks such as the MDGs. For example, the World Bank provides direct support to national education systems though credits and loans, participates in global education policy formulation as a member of the High-Level Advisory Group, and hosts the Education For All–Fast Track Initiative (FTI), a compact between donor agencies and developing countries that seeks to mobilize and coordinate funding to accelerate progress towards the Millennium Development Goal of universal primary education by 2015. An approach to gender equality and education that focuses on interventions to get girls and boys into and through school is central throughout this work. It is reflected, for example, in the 2005 Education

Sector Strategy Update, which emphasized education strategies that "maximize the impact of education on economic growth," and outlined the Bank's intention to work toward strengthening "education as a basis for a knowledge economy" (World Bank 2005, 3). Gender equality is given little attention beyond the recognition of a need to accelerate "the rate at which the gender gap is closing" through interventions such as stipend programs or tutoring programs for girls (World Bank 2005, 101).

The work of the FTI exemplifies the lack of engagement with gender equality beyond the consideration of gender as a noun. The FTI made a commitment in 2005 to pay greater attention to gender in its processes. This had been prompted by recommendations in a report commissioned by the United Nations Girls' Education Initiative (UNGEI) (Seel and Clarke 2005). However, since 2005 there has been little action to give the commitment effect. In the FTI's most recent progress report (FTI 2007) there is a focus on the progress made to get children into school and on the resources needed for this to continue. There is barely any mention of gender beyond the identification of girls in "hard to reach" groups and an analysis of progress made toward gender parity in FTI countries. Any wider concerns with equality are off the page.

The United Nations Girls' Education Initiative, which was established in 2000, coordinated by UNICEF as a partnership including the UN agencies, governments, donors, and civil society, seeks to narrow the gender gap in primary and secondary education (UNGEI 2006). While some global social movements initially saw UNGEI as a vehicle to advance wider concerns with gender and participation, its focus has largely been limited to interventions for getting girls into school, rather than a broader vision of gender equality within and beyond school and some of the pedagogic resources required for this. This narrow remit is reflected in UNGEI promotional literature (see for example UNGEI 2006) and in a recent report documenting UNGEI's experiences (Chung 2007). However, interviews conducted in 2008 with senior figures in UNGEI indicate efforts within the organization to engage with gender equality more holistically and build the organization at country level, although the effects of this are still to be assessed (North 2008).

The approach to learning associated with inter/national pedagogies is predicated on a particular understanding of the relationship between the global and the local—the North and the South. Learning in a school is understood primarily as a top-down process involving the transfer of knowledge and skills from an expert/teacher to the learner. At the global level this translates into a top-down transfer of funds, technical skills, and knowledge from 'global experts' who advise nation-states and local organizations on 'what works' (Herz and Sperling 2004) for girls' education. International policy documents and frameworks are produced and agreed by experts working at the global level. There is an expectation that funding for national and local governments or local NGOs will be tied—explicitly

or implicitly—to adherence to globally established priorities. This sometimes sits uncomfortably alongside affirmations on support to nationally
owned, autonomous education plans, a tension that is clearly illustrated by
the stated aims of the FTI:

> [the FTI aims] to provide the incentives and resources to empower poor
> nations to build and implement sound education plans. Developing na-
> tions are responsible for taking ownership of crafting national educa-
> tion plans, with budget accountability and a greater commitment of
> political and financial resources, while donor nations commit to pro-
> viding the additional technical know-how to ensure that no country
> that met its obligations would fail for a lack of resources or technical
> capacity. (FTI 2002)

But in the work of the FTI there is little concern with the context in which
governments make plans or fashion accountability (Rose 2005).

The approach is not attentive to power relations in schools and, in a
similar vein, tends to ignore the power relations that shape the relationship between the global and the local—the North and the South. The
inter/national assumptions suggest these are all players in a global marketplace, and that the historical and contemporary forms of inequality are
not salient. In this view, globalization is seen as a set of useful technical
processes based on competition and skills development that speed up and
facilitate the transfer of information and delivery of plans between nation-
states, or from the global to the local. This means that there is little scope
for questioning the relations of inequality associated with global capitalism
or considering the impact these have on global learning. In inter/national
pedagogies, the local is expected to listen to and learn from the global,
while those who work at the global level have little obligation to learn
from or with the local. Those who drive policy are concerned to teach, but
not to learn. They stress instruction and forms of intervention to get girls
into school, for example, but do not see dialogue or attention to the conditions within which dialogue can occur as particularly pressing. The understanding of gender equality emphasizes technical processes, which focus on
transferring skills and knowledge. There is no obligation for global institutions to engage in discussions regarding gender either within their own
organizations or in wider global social relations.

International Pedagogies and Critiques of Global Initiatives

The limited interpretation of pedagogies associated with the international
version of gender equality in education draws a wide array of criticism.
One group of writers who cluster around an in/ternational understanding
of globalization highlight the complexity of the contexts for implement-
ing policy, and they question the sharp binaries between global and local,

school and non-school knowledge, and gender identities (Bronfen and Kavka 2001; Cornwall et al. 2007). These critics stress the way in which gender and poverty are enacted in multiple sites of education, linked with multifaceted and relational dimensions of difference, diversity and negotiations over resources, meanings or outcomes (Mohanty 2003; Vavrus 2005). They tend to highlight gendered power relations and their intersection with race, class, and postcolonial processes. Often their work, informed by poststructuralism and postcolonialism, deploys theories of discourse and identity to explain the complex pedagogic processes associated with an in/ternational understanding of globalization. The relational gender dynamic associated with people moving across spaces and shifting identifications is a major concern. In this work there is a clear realization that gender equality in education can never be a simple matter of policy roll-out because of local conditions marked by gender inequalities, struggles over power, the complexities of historical context, and the ravages of global capitalism. A number of critical studies are based on practical experiences of working in particular local settings and experiencing inter/national flows as disjunctures and discontinuities (Chapman and Miske 2007; Vavrus 2003).

The problems of conservative backlash and multiple forms of negotiation are just one of a number of reasons these writers are highly critical of the confident assertions associated with the framing of inter/national pedagogies. Some draw powerfully on the work of grassroots organizations or social/indigenous movements, or on ethnographic studies (Aikman 1999; Vavrus 2003). For many writers in this group, the relationship between culture and gender is a complex one. Some point to the need to recognize and consider the way in which gender may be constructed in different contexts. They argue that it is not possible to consider a universal definition of equality, and that gender identities are embedded in local identities and hierarchies linked to ethnicity and caste (Robinson-Pant, 2004). There is often a tension between gender and culture, with culture—as a collective identity—sometimes being privileged over concerns with gender inequality (N. Rao and Robinson-Pant 2006; S. Rao, 1999; Robinson-Pant 2004). This is sometimes evident when global economic or security forces place particular cultures under threat, forcing cultural solidarities across gender divisions. In the process, educational and other social achievements for gender equality are undermined (Yuval-Davis 1997).

Rather than stressing the economic and socially integrating outcomes of education, these critics tends to be more concerned with the processes of learning and the ways in which diverse activities are embedded within locally situated contexts of power and exclusion. There is a stress on learning as a social practice through which identities are constructed, bounded by the power dynamics of languages, cultures, national curricula, or gendered conditions of knowledge production (Braidotti 1994; Mohanty 2003). They tend to celebrate pedagogies that construct—rather than deny—difference. They are concerned with processes that take place beyond the confines of the school—within the community, in adult education classes, or in local political and activist spaces (Higgins and Rwanyange 2005).

Many in this group are critical of actions for gender and education based on interventions and the establishment of institutions, which are seen to be imposed by northern donors or trading partners who link cultural assimilation to the views of dominant elites (Rampal, forthcoming). They advocate approaches based on participation as equals in decision making, critique, dialogue, and revisioning the rules of the game, rejecting the 'top-down' forms of relationship that characterize some of the inter/national writing. For example, writing about education policy in Uganda, Higgins and Rwanyange point to the need to look critically at discourse around partnership and ownership, and the way in which "the realization of nationally (and globally) set goals and targets is complicated by the dynamics of the complex interplay of cultural and social forces at local level" (2005, 8).

These critics reject the privileged position given to global actors associated with the first position we mapped. They question the validity of 'global experts' and assert the value of local expertise and locals as experts (Longwe 1998). They challenge the global—or those in global positions of power—to learn from and listen to the local, to respect and value diversity, and to recognize the unequal global power dynamics within which exchanges occur. Pedagogy for this group is therefore a bottom-up process that starts with/ from the local and contextually specific. Their localist vision makes thinking about global action or a global project for gender equality and education challenging. For this group, political action, forms of analysis, and pedagogic practice all must of necessity become diverse, relational, and contextually specific. Global obligations are to recognize and respect difference, but formulating a pedagogy that goes beyond the fragments is very difficult.

International Pedagogies for Gender Equality in Education

A second group of critics are not inherently opposed to the idea of global aspiration or the notion of a pedagogy that develops larger horizons than those suggested by local relationships. For this group, overarching values such as human rights, cosmopolitanism, and global social justice offer opportunities to refashion the MDGs, make connections with global social movements, and develop pedagogies that take seriously new forms of global interconnection (Kabeer 2005; Molyneux 2007; Unterhalter 2008).

This group has no single view of gender or education. Sometimes writers associated with it delineate gendered sites of power and intersecting relational identities and discourses, but sometimes they stress women's rights, gender and capabilities, and shifting sites of empowerment. They often draw more on political economy analyses than those linked to cultural studies, but critiques of gendered exclusions, hybrid identities, and forms of gendered becoming distinguish their work from writers associated with the first position who simply note the presence or absence of girls or boys. However, while there are some similarities between this group of writers and those advocating in/ternational pedagogies in their definitions of gender, there are differences in relation to how they view global markets and poverty. Proponents of in/ternational pedagogies generally view the growth of global markets as wholly destructive, inevitably associated with exploitation, exclusion, and the establishment of a reserve army of labour. However, many writers contributing to developing analysis of international pedagogies look to forms of the development state, redistributive policies, and forms of global regulation to direct and regulate economic growth toward gender equality. They are more optimistic that there may be forms of economic growth and development that make it possible to overcome gender and other inequalities, and thus form fairer societies expressing strong notions of national and global obligations for social justice and equality. It is to this work that pedagogies to develop forms of global understanding and connection are directed.

Pedagogies that work with notions of empowerment (Gaventa 2003; Kabeer 1999) have considerable potential to underpin the international approach. Discussions of empowerment suggest the importance of bringing together and evaluating resources (such as trained teachers, curricula, and learning materials), the development of a critical form of agency in learners and teachers, and attention to overcoming global and local inequality in the outcomes of education. Gaventa's 'power cube' (2007) provides an important method for approaching pedagogy, suggesting the process assists learners and teachers to understand the nature of closed, invited, and created spaces for participation in global governance, and the visible, hidden, and invisible forms in which power is exercised. The struggle to articulate forms of empowerment in relation to practice is evident in some UNICEF documents. Thus, for example, a joint publication in 2007 from UNICEF and UNESCO (UNICEF/UNESCO 2007) outlined a vision of a rights-based approach to education. Rather than being instrumentally linked to economic returns, education is seen as necessary for the realization of other rights; and there is concern with not only access to school, but also conditions within school, including those that affect gender equality such as freedom from violence and teaching and learning materials free from gender stereotypes. While the pedagogic detail is not elaborated, the potential for thinking beyond the top-down frame is evident. While these pedagogies of rights and empowerment await further work to make them concrete in curriculum design and classroom practice, they suggest an approach that accepts global interconnections, yet points to different values—not those simply given by the unregulated market.

INTERSECTING PEDAGOGIES: THE GLOBAL CAMPAIGN FOR EDUCATION

In practice, the distinctions between the three positions outlined above are not always clear-cut. Despite inherent tensions between the three approaches, many organizations display elements of each in different aspects of their work, and organizations may oscillate between one approach and another as they adapt their work and communications to particular contexts, moments, and audiences. Many global civil-society organizations working on education appear to move uneasily between the three positions. Some have explicit commitments to women's and girls' rights in and beyond school, a focus on gender not limited to counting numbers of girls in schools, and a critical perspective on globalization and the role of global institutions. However, in their policy documents a concern with 'what works' to get girls in school often dominates as they seek to influence or appeal to policy makers—donors, governments, or multilateral organizations. Meanwhile, they may engage with local partners who have critical perspectives on gender, education, and issues relating to cultural identity and diversity.

The Global Campaign for Education (GCE) provides an interesting example of how these three pedagogical approaches intertwine. The international alliance was founded in 1999 to ensure that the World Education Forum held in Dakar in 2000 resulted in "concrete commitments and viable policies to implement the Education For All goals" (GCE 1999). GCE brings together civil-society organizations, including nongovernmental organizations (NGOs), community based organisations (CBOs), and teacher unions campaigning on Education For All around the world. Building links globally through democratic structures that connect member organizations working on education in the North and South has been key to GCE's practice and identity (Mundy 2007; Mundy and Murphy 2001). The notion of education as a right and a concern with the most deprived sections of society, including women, is central to the GCE's aims. According to their mission statement,[2]

> The Global Campaign for Education promotes education as a basic human right [and] mobilizes public pressure on governments and the international community to fulfil their promises to provide free, compulsory public basic education for all people, in particular for children, women and all disadvantaged, deprived sections of society.

The campaign itself is thus explicitly framed within a rights-based approach as well as around the broader Education For All agenda, which expresses concerns with gender equality in education (Aikman and Unterhalter 2005).[3] Therefore, although gender equality in education and pedagogies to advance this is not the main or central focus of the GCE's work, the campaign does have an interest in rights, participatory processes, and strategies which wish to advance the MDGs beyond the narrowest reading.

Some GCE activities and policy reports have focused specifically on gender equality in education, and align their work with the international stream. In 2005, the year in which the first MDG target to get as many girls as boys into primary and secondary school was missed, the GCE released Girls Can't Wait (GCE 2005a). This report, like a similar one published in 2003 (GCE 2003), went beyond a simple consideration of gender parity, taking a more nuanced approach to gender equality in education that included attention to wider equality issues. Instrumental understandings of gender were combined with language around rights and emphasis on the intrinsic importance of gender equality. Alongside a focus on the need for interventions such as abolishing schools' fees to get girls into school, suggestions were also put forward for addressing issues of gender equality within schools that go beyond issues of access.

However, despite these efforts, the space given to concerns with gender equality in GCE's main work and higher profile campaigns and policy materials is limited. The arguments presented for investment in gender equality and education often reflect an unproblematized approach to policy roll-out. The School Report, produced yearly by the GCE, ranks governments on their commitments to Education For All (GCE 2005b, 2006, 2007, 2008). It makes explicit use of 'what works' language in its efforts to mobilize resources to get children—girls and boys—into school. The emphasis is on what can be achieved and the wider economic and social benefits that greater numbers of children—including girls—in education will bring about. As with the literature associated with inter/national pedagogies discussed above, gender is given little emphasis beyond a concern with increasing parity.

The pedagogical eclecticism associated with the mixed alignments of GCE is evident in the teaching it supports in schools. In April of every year, Global Action Week is a focal moment in the GCE's campaigning when members coordinate campaigning efforts around a particular theme. In 2008, the focus was on breaking the record for the world's biggest lesson. More than 7.5 million people took part in the planned lesson, which focused on Quality Education to End Exclusion[4]. The global lesson utilized the GCE's networks in the North and the South to bring together education organizations, campaigners, school children, politicians, and celebrities from around the world and build and strengthen connections between different groups. Thus—in contrast to the inter/national top-down notion of learning and its formulation of sharp distinctions between global and local—the global lesson was concerned with building a sense of a shared international global vision. In this, while stressing the importance of local affiliations, there was also an acknowledgement of the strategic gains from global connection.

The lesson plan focused on what constitutes a quality education and the groups currently excluded from receiving this. There was scope for learner participation as students were invited to suggest their definitions of 'quality education.' A number of national coalitions adapted the plan to fit with their national curricula and incorporated issues relevant to their national context. For example, in Kenya the lesson included a focus on the education needs for children and young people who had experienced violence and exclusion in the postelection crisis. Thus, the lesson did not suggest context was irrelevant, but the particularities of context came to be connected with a wider discussion of quality and exclusion. All of these were elements of a pedagogy associated with reconstructed international relations and pedagogies with the potential to express transversal dialogue. However, in order to be recognised as an official world-record attempt, which was important for GCE publicity, and in order to facilitate a sense of connection between participants in different places, the lesson followed a similar format in every country. This included a 'test' at the end in which participants were tested on what they had learned. This prescribed formula meant that space was limited for the expression of diverse local forms of learning and experimentation with pedagogical practice. Despite the focus on quality and exclusion, within the lesson plan itself there was little attention to the way in which processes of exclusion take place both outside and within school, and the ways they are affected by power inequalities at global, national, and local levels. Gender issues were barely mentioned beyond giving girls as an example of an excluded group.

The aim of the Global Lesson was to raise awareness of the numbers of children still excluded from school and to put pressure on governments and global leaders to invest more in education. As such it probably achieved these limited inter/national objectives. However, wider pedagogic concerns to collectively engage in a critical examination of global processes concerning justice or inequality were addressed only as a side issue.

The Global Lesson in many ways illustrates both the strengths of the GCE and the challenges that come with building a global movement around gender equality and education. Much of the GCE's success so far has been in their ability to mobilize very large numbers of people across borders and bring different constituencies together through the Global Action Week, building up very real pressure for change. Yet this very process involves negotiating between the competing priorities and perspectives of different groups. To some extent simple 'top line' campaign messages do not encourage the exploration of more complex, nuanced and controversial issues such as gender equality or ideas around identity, difference, local complexity and global inequality. The high profile of these messages reflects strategic decisions to prioritise influencing key global players, and a missed opportunity to consolidate meaningful outward links to the global women's movement or other civil society networks working on social justice, or participatory and critical pedagogies.

CONCLUSION

This chapter has counterposed three different ways of understanding globalization and drawn out the implication for thinking about pedagogies associated with gender equality in education. The most limited, but also the most widely circulating meaning of gender equality, is that which aspires only to have parity in the numbers of girls and boys in school. This view is associated with pedagogies concerned with transmitting skills and fostering inter/national participation in a global marketplace. Critical views of pedagogy that develop a sense of the complexity of gender and different forms of globalization struggle for articulation. Even when the UN or large civil-society organizations have policy supporting these, they are difficult to put into practice. The strategic challenge for advocates of gender equality in education as a global aspiration is to assess how much useful collaboration is possible with the agenda of skills and free markets, and where and how to stage the important contestations regarding expanded notions or equality, empowerment, and critical pedagogies.

NOTES

1. This chapter expands ideas initially discussed in working papers developed as part of the ESRC funded research project Gender, Education, and Global Poverty Reduction Initiatives (Award number RES 167–25–0260). We are grateful to fellow members of that research team (Jenni Karlsson, Herbert Makinda, Jane Onsongo, Veerle Dieltiens, and Chris Yates) and advisory committees in Kenya and South Africa for comments on earlier drafts. Special thanks to Yvonne Raley for very helpful advice on the development of the initial paper for this volume.
2. See GCE's constitution at http://www.campaignforeducation.org/about/about_constitution_en.html
3. http://www.unesco.org/education/efa/ed_for_all/dakfram_eng.shtml.
4. http://www.campaignforeducation.org

BIBLIOGRAPHY

Aikman, S. *Intercultural Education and Literacy: An Ethnographic Study of Indigenous Knowledge and Learning in the Peruvian Amazon.* Amsterdam: Benjamins, 1999.
Aikman, S. and E. Unterhalter. *Beyond access: transforming policy and practice for gender equality in education.* Oxford: Oxfam GB, 2005.
Antrobus, P. "Critiquing the MDGs from a Caribbean Perspective 1." *Gender and Development* 13, no. 1 (2005): 94–104.
Appadurai, A. *Modernity at Large: Cultural Dimensions of Globalization.* Minneapolis and London: University of Minnesota Press, 1996.
Appiah, K. *Cosmopolitanism: Ethics in a World of Strangers (Issues of Our Time).* New York: W. W. Norton, 2006.
Baylis, J., and S. Smith, eds. *The Globalization of World Politics: An Introduction to International Relations.* 2nd ed. Oxford and New York: Oxford University Press, 2001.
Bhabha, H. K. *The Location of Culture.* London: Routledge, 1994.
Birdsall, N., and M. Vaishnav. "Education and the MDGs: Realizing the Millennium Compact." *Journal of International Affairs* 58, no. 2 (2005): 257–264.

Black, R., and H. White, eds. *Targeting Development: Critical Perspectives on the Millennium Development Goals*. London and New York: Routledge, 2003.

Braidotti, R. *Nomadic Subjects*. New York: Columbia University Press, 1994.

Boni, A. "Using the Capability Approach and Power Theories to Analyse Competency Discourses in Higher Education." Paper presented at the seminar organized by the education thematic group of the HDCA (Human Development and Capability Association), Nottingham, England, March 2008.

Bourn, D. "Education for Sustainable Development in The UK: Making the Connections Between the Environment and Development Agendas." *Theory and Research in Education* 6, no. 2 (2008): 193–206.

Brock, G., and H. Brighouse. *The Political Philosophy of Cosmopolitanism*. Cambridge: Cambridge University Press, 2005.

Bronfen, E., and M. Kavka, eds. *Feminist Consequences: Theory for the New Century*. New York: Columbia University Press, 2001.

Carrim, N. "Human Rights and the Limitations of Releasing Subaltern Voices in a Post-apartheid South Africa." In *International Handbook of Comparative Education*, eds. R. Cowen and A. Kazamias. Berlin: Springer, forthcoming.

Chan, J. "Between Efficiency, Capability and Recognition: Competing Epistemes in Global Governance Reforms." *Comparative Education* 43, no. 3 (2007): 359–376.

Chapman, S., and S. Miske. "Promoting Girls' Education In Africa: Evidence from the Field Between 1996 and 2003." In *The Structure and Agency of Women's Education*, ed. M. Maslak, 87–106. Albany: State University of New York Press, 2007.

Chung, F. *Making UNGEI Work: Lessons From Four African Countries*. Nairobi: UNICEF Eastern and Southern Africa Regional Office, 2007.

Cohen, R., and S. Rai, eds. *Global Social Movements: Towards a Cosmopolitan Politics*. London: Athlone Press, 2000.

Cornwall, A., E. Harrison, and A. Whitehead, eds. *Feminisms in Development: Contradictions, Contestations and Challenges*. London: Zed Books, 2007.

Davies, I., M. Evans, and A. Reid. "Globalising Citizenship Education? A Critique of 'Global Education' and 'Citizenship Education.'" *British Journal of Educational Studies* 53, no.1 (2005): 66–89.

Edwards, M., and J. Gaventa. *Global Citizen Action*. Boulder, CO: Lynne Rienner Publishers, 2001.

Fast Track Initiative (FTI). Education For All–Fast Track Initiative. 2002. Available at http://www.worldbank.org/education/efafti/overview.asp (accessed 19 May 2008).

Fraser, N. "Mapping the Feminist Imagination: From Redistribution to Recognition to Representation." *Constellations* 12, no.3 (2005): 295–307.

Elliott, L., and D. Atkinson. *The Gods That Failed*. London: Bodley Head, 2008.

Gaventa, J. *Power After Lukes: An Overview of Theories Of Power Since Lukes and Their Application To Development*. Brighton: Participation Group, Institute of Development Studies, 2003.

———. "Participation and Citizenship: Exploring Power for Change." Paper presented at the ODI/IDS Development Horizons Seminar, 2007. Available at http://www.odi.org.uk/events/horizons_nov06/22Jan/John%20Gaventa.pdf

Global Campaign for Education (GCE). *A Fair Chance: Attaining Gender Equity in Basic Education by 2005*. Johannesburg: Global Campaign for Education, 2003.

———. *Girls Can't Wait: Why Girls' Education Matters, and How To Make It Happen Now*. Johannesburg: Global Campaign for Education, 2005a.

———. *Missing the Mark: A 'School Report' on Rich Countries' Contribution to Universal Primary Education by 2015*. Johannesburg: Global Campaign for Education, 2005b.

————. 'Underachievers': A 'School Report' on Rich Countries' Contribution to Universal Primary Education by 2015. Johannesburg: Global Campaign for Education, 2006.

————. 'Not Up To Scratch': A 'School Report' on Rich Countries' Contribution to Universal Primary Education by 2015. Johannesburg: Global Campaign for Education, 2007.

————. Global School Report 2008: No Excuses! A Global Report Card Ranking Governments Efforts To Achieve Education for All. Johannesburg: Global Campaign for Education, 2008.

Green, A. Education, Globalization and the Nation State. New York: St. Martin's Press, 1997.

Held, D. Global Covenant: The Social Democratic Alternative to the Washington Consensus. Cambridge: Polity, 2004.

Held, D., A. McGrew, D. Goldblatt, and J. Parraton. Globalization. Global Governance 5 (1999): 483–496.

Herz, B., and G. Sperling. What Works In Girls' Education: Evidence and Policies From The Developing World. New York: Council on Foreign Relations, 2004.

Hickling-Hudson, A., and R. Ahlquist. "Contesting the Curriculum in the Schooling of Indigenous Children in Australia and the United States: From Eurocentrism to Culturally Powerful Pedagogies." Comparative Education Review 47, no. 1 (2003): 64–89.

Higgins, L., and R. Rwanyange. "Ownership in the Education Reform Process in Uganda." Compare 35, no. 1 (2005): 7–26.

Hill, M., and E. King. "Women's Education and Well-Being." Feminist Economics 1, no. 2 (1995): 21–46.

Hooks, B. Teaching To Transgress: Education As the Practice Of Freedom. London: Routledge, 1994.

Kabeer, N. "Resources, Agency, Achievements: Reflections on the Measurement of Women's Empowerment." Development and Change 30, no. 3 (1999): 435–464.

————. "Gender Equality and Women's Empowerment: A Critical Analysis of the Third Millennium Development Goal." In Gender and the Millennium Development Goals, ed. C. Sweetman. Oxford: Oxfam GB, 2005.

Lather, P. Feminist Research In Education: Within/Against. Geelong, Vic.: Deakin University Press, 1991a.

————. Getting Smart: Feminist Research and Pedagogy With/in the Postmodern. New York: Routledge, 1991b.

Lauder, H., P. Brown, J.-A.Dillabough, and A. H. Halsey, eds. Education, Globalization and Social Change. Oxford: Oxford University Press, 2006.

Longwe, S. H. "Education for Women's Empowerment or Schooling for Women's Subordination?" Gender and Development 6, no. 2 (1998): 19–26.

Luke, C., and J. Gore. Feminisms and Critical Pedagogy. New York: Routledge, 1992.

Marshall, H. and M. Arnot. "Competing curriculum agendas for gender justice: The implications of EFA and global citizenship education." In Girls' Schooling at a Critical Juncture: conceptual frameworks and global engagements, eds. S. Fennell and M. Arnot. London: Routledge, 2007.

McCowan, T. Enacting Citizenship: A Study of Three Educational Initiatives. PhD thesis, Institute of Education, University of London, 2008.

Mohanty, C. T. Feminism Without Borders: Decolonizing Theory, Practicing Solidarity. Durham, NC: Duke University Press, 2003.

Molyneux, M. "The Chimera Of Success: Gender Ennui and the Changed International Policy Environment." In Feminisms In Development: Contradictions, Contestations and Challenge, eds. A. Cornwall, E. Harrison, and A. Whitehead, 227–240. London: Zed Books, 2007.

Mundy, K. "Global Governance, Educational Change." *Comparative Education* 43, no. 3 (2007): 339–357.

Mundy, K., and L. Murphy. "Transnational Advocacy, Global Civil Society? Emerging Evidence from the Field of Education." *Comparative Education Review* 45, no. 1 (2001): 85–126.

North, A. "Missed Target Triggers Call For Bold Steps—Will They Be Enough?" *Equals* 16, (2006): 1–3.

———. Notes from interviews conducted with senior figures within UNGEI/UNICEF, London/New York, July 2008.

Ntuli, P. P. "The Missing Link Between Culture and Education: Are We Still Chasing Gods That Are Not Our Own?" In *African Renaissance: The New Struggle*, ed. M. W. Makgoba. Sandton/Cape Town: Mafube/Tafelberg, 1999.

Nussbaum, M. C. *Cultivating Humanity*. Cambridge, MA: Harvard University Press, 1997.

Okin, S. M. (). "Poverty, Well-Being, and Gender: What Counts, Who's Heard?" *Philosophy & Public Affairs* 31, no. 3 (2003): 280–316.

Powell, W. W., and K. Snellman. "The Knowledge Economy." *Annual Review of Sociology* 30, no. 1 (2004): 199–220.

Rampal, A. "An Indigenous Discourse to Cradle Our Cognitive Discourse and Script Our Aspirations." In *International Handbook of Comparative Education*, eds. R. Cowen and A. Kazamias. Berlin: Springer, forthcoming.

Rao, N., and A. Robinson-Pant. Adult Education and Indigenous People: Addressing Gender In Policy and Practice. *International Journal of Educational Development* 26, no. 2 (2006): 209–223.

Rao, S. "Woman-As-Symbol: The Intersections of Identity Politics, Gender, and Indian Nationalism." *Women's Studies International Forum* 22, no. 3 (1999): 317–328.

Rapport, N., and R. Stade. "A Cosmopolitan Turn—Or Return?" *Social Anthropology* 15, no. 2 (2007): 223–235.

Rizvi, F. "Democracy and Education after September 11." *Globalisation, Societies and Education* 1 (2003): 25–40.

Robinson-Pant, A. "Education For Women: Whose Values Count?" *Gender and Education* 16, no. 4 (2004): 473–489.

Rose, P. "Is There A 'Fast-Track' to Achieving Education For All?" *International Journal of Educational Development* 25, no. 4 (2005): 381–394.

Sachs, J. *The End Of Poverty : How We Can Make It Happen in Our Lifetime*. London: Penguin Books, 2005.

Said, E. *Orientalism*. London: Penguin Books, 1978.

Schultz, T.P. "Why Governments Should Invest More To Educate Girls." *World Development* 30, no. 2 (2002): 207–22.

Seel, A., and D. Clarke. *Integrating Gender into Education For All–Fast Track Initiative Processes and National Education Plans*. Washington: UNGEI, 2005.

Spivak, G. C. *Outside in the Teaching Machine*. New York: Routledge, 1993.

Stoetzler, M., and N. Yuval-Davis. "Standpoint Theory, Situated Knowledge and the Situated Imagination." *Feminist Theory* 3, no. 3 (2002): 315–333.

Education for All–Fast Track Initiative (FTI). *Quality Education For All Children: Meeting The Challenge* (Annual Report, 2007). Washington, DC: World Bank, 2007.

United Nations Girls' Education Initiative (UNGEI). Factsheet. New York: UNGEI, 2006. http://www.ungei.org/resources/files/Ungeifactsheet_Nov06.pdf (accessed 13 May 2008).

UNICEF/UNESCO. *A Human Rights-Based Approach to Education For All: A Framework for the Realization Of Children's Right To Education and Rights Within Education*. New York/Paris: UNICEF/UNESCO, 2007.

Unterhalter, E. "Mobilization, Meanings and Measures: Reflections on Girls' Education." *Development* 48, no. 1 (2005): 110–114.

———. *Gender, Schooling and Global Social Justice.* London: Routledge, 2007.

———. "Cosmopolitanism, Global Social Justice and Gender Equality In Education." *Compare* 29, no. 3 (2008): 539–553.

Vandemoortele, J. *The MDGs and Pro-poor Policies: Can External Partners Make a Difference?* Policy paper, United Nations Development Programme. New York: UNDP, 2003.

Vavrus, F. *Desire and Decline.* New York: Peter Lang, 2003.

———. "Adjusting Inequality: Education and Structural Adjustment Policies in Tanzania." *Harvard Educational Review* 75, no. 2 (2005): 174–201.

Walker, M. *Higher Education Pedagogies: A Capabilities Approach.* Maidenhead, UK: Society for Research into Higher Education/Open UP, 2006.

World Bank. *Engendering Development.* New York: Oxford University Press, 2001.

———. *Education Sector Strategy Update: Achieving Education For All, Broadening our Perspective, Maximizing our Effectiveness.* Washington, DC: The World Bank, 2005. http://siteresources.worldbank.org/EDUCATION/Resources/ESSU/Education_Sector_Strategy_Update.pdf (accessed 12 May 2008).

———. *Millennium Development Goals: Confronting the challenges of gender equality and fragile states.* Global Monitoring Report 2007. Washington, DC: The World Bank, 2007.

Yuval-Davis, N. *Gender and Nation.* London: Sage, 1997.

Yuval-Davis, N., and M. Stoetzler. "Imagined Boundaries and Borders: A Gendered Gaze." *European Journal of Women's Studies* 9, no. 3 (2002): 329–344.

8 'Let Us Now Praise...'
Rethinking Role Models and Heroes in an Egalitarian Age

Moira Lavinson[1]

INTRODUCTION

Martin Luther King Jr. is indisputably an American hero. In a recent Gallup poll, he came in second only to Mother Teresa as the most admired person from the twentieth century (Newport 2006). He and Christopher Columbus are the only two non-presidents to have national holidays designated in their honor. Last year, a full two-thirds of high school students surveyed in a nationally representative sample named Martin Luther King Jr. as one of the five "most famous Americans," easily vaulting him into first place on the list. A parallel survey of adults similarly earned King one-third of the vote, putting him second only to Benjamin Franklin (Wineburg and Monte-Sano 2008; although it is important to note that respondents were explicitly told to exclude presidents and their wives from the possible list of "most famous"). King's popularity presumably reflects, at least in part, his ubiquity in American history textbooks that cover the period, every US civics book, literally thousands of trade books for children and adults, and almost every classroom and media outlet across the country during Black History Month. There is little doubt that Martin Luther King is widely taught and recognized as an "American hero" (Bond 1993).

What are the civic implications of Americans' recognition and elevation of King as a heroic figure? These are much harder to discern. The techniques used by King and his colleagues in the civil rights movement are arguably moribund, despite the fact that our country faces a multitude of ills (and commits a multitude of sins) that threaten justice, equality, and liberty as much now as fifty years ago. Civil disobedience, collective action among thousands of citizens for a sustained period of time, nonviolent protest—these are evident neither in school curricula, which tend to treat King as a towering figure who single-handedly led Americans into 'the promised land,' nor in American civic or political practice in the early twenty-first century.[2] Young people (and probably adults, too) fail to recognize even that they could carry forward King's work in any but the most anodyne ways. Among the thousand or so middle school students that I taught over the course of about a decade, for example, almost all expressed fervent admiration for Martin Luther King while never thinking to try to put his techniques into action. They would speak generally of King's perseverance, his standing up for what he believed in, his willingness to sacrifice himself to the cause, and other such platitudes. But they rarely if ever referenced his broader civic leadership or his empowerment of others to advance the causes for which he and they stood. Furthermore, even the sanitized and "antiseptic" (Bond 1993) personal characteristics they did identify did not motivate them to act in a different way on a day-to-day basis. This is admiration devoid of emulation.

Why does this matter? Why should it matter that at least one—and I would actually argue many more—of America's 'most famous' heroes lives on in words but not in deeds? In part, I think it matters because our democracy would be stronger, and we as citizens would be better, if we were to emulate King in addition to venerating him. I think that young people as developing citizens *should* learn about the power of collective action, such as by learning and practicing the techniques for identifying and working with allies on behalf of a common cause. I also think that we would do well to recognize that the goals that King fought so tirelessly to achieve are not yet fully realized, and to feel an obligation to promote those goals ourselves. It is no diminution of his heroic stature to admit that the struggle needs to continue if his and others' hard-fought gains are to be sustained. In this respect too, it is disturbing and even a bit bizarre that so many Americans profess deep admiration for King while failing to actually work to advance the causes for which he fought.

On the other hand, there are some ways in which our worship of King in words but not in deeds are perfectly acceptable. Heroes are frequently referred to as symbols of what people or a nation identify with, care about, or see themselves as standing for. Rev. Peter Gomes remarks, for example, that "a discussion about heroes and heroines is essentially an exercise in self-discovery and cultural introspection; and in choosing to honor certain persons as heroes and certain actions as heroic, we invest those persons and actions with ideals that we ourselves value and admire" (Gomes 2002, xi). In this respect, the fact that we hold up Martin Luther King—a liberal African American who crusaded for social and economic justice, civil rights, and racial equality, among other goals—as an American hero is itself worth celebrating.[3] Whether or not we actually emulate him, the fact that we hold him up as a symbol of what's good about our country is itself a valuable good.

The purpose of this essay is to delve more deeply into the complicated network of relationships among heroes, role models, and democratic civic education in the US in the early twenty-first century. In this essay, I argue that while heroes have historically served many purposes in educating young citizens and shaping and sustaining the *civitas*, these purposes are frequently being lost or even undermined because of heroes' diminishing stature and changing roles in the United States today. Much ink has been spilled bemoaning the loss of heroes in the modern American imagination. Arthur Schlesinger complains, for example, that "Ours is an age without heroes. . . . Today no one bestrides our narrow world like a colossus; we have no giants" (Schlesinger 1968, 341). Charles I. Glicksberg concurs, "What is wrong with their age is that it has lost its faith in the greatness or the capacity for greatness of man" (Glicksberg 1968, 357; see also Boorstin 1968; Porpora 1996; Gibbon 2002). Unlike these authors, I do not bemoan this state of affairs, in part because it's not entirely true, as the example of Martin Luther King shows;[4] in part because I think our country is stronger, and certainly our understanding of history is more accurate, when we recognize and discuss individuals' complexities, nuances, and even failings; and in part because we can achieve the same civic goals for which we used to use heroes in other ways. But to do so, we need to be thoughtful and intentional, and I would argue that these characteristics have been missing in much democratic civic education both taught in schools and promoted through the media.

The rest of the essay is structured as follows: first, I examine the various reasons that people have given for needing heroes, creating heroes, and/or teaching about heroes. I focus in particular on the civic uses of heroes, and give examples of how civic educators in the past used heroes to advance these purposes. In the second section, I consider whether these uses of heroes are appropriate for democratic civic education in the United States in the early twenty-first century. This question has two components: (1) Are the goals themselves that heroes were used to promote actually worthy of democratic civic education? And (2) to the extent that they are, is it possible in this day and age to use heroes to achieve such goals? Question (1) is essentially a normative and political question, while (2) is essentially a sociological, psychological, and pedagogical question. In the third section, finally, I consider how we might achieve worthwhile goals of democratic civic education in twenty-first-century America without the widespread use of civic heroes, as well as highlighting where and how heroes can still play an effective role in democratic civic education. With respect to the latter, I suggest that in order truly to learn from heroes, students need to learn more about their techniques—their step-by-step mechanisms for achievement. As we teach this, we and our students will discover that many heroes are public symbols for the important work and efforts of many 'behind the scenes' individuals. In this vein, I will also argue that we should spend at least as much time in school helping students learn about these 'behind the scenes' participants and activists, particularly in students' own communities, as we spend studying the 'heroes' in the front. Sustained study of and interaction with these 'ordinary role models,' I suggest, can take us a long way toward motivating simultaneous admiration and emulation—and thus overcome the paradox with which I opened this essay. I conclude with some brief reflections on the potential implications of Barack Obama's presidency with regard to these issues.

TEN CIVIC FUNCTIONS OF HEROES

Society's elevation and recognition of heroes may serve many civic functions—at least ten, by my count. In particular, social and civic recognition and elevation of heroes may:

A. model expectations by
   (1) providing models for emulation by citizens;
   (2) imparting and reinforcing common civic values and norms;
   (3) establishing touchstones for the qualities citizens should expect of elected officials and other civic leaders;
   (4) teaching citizens their place by contrasting their own ordinariness with heroes' extraordinariness;
B. promote civic unity and identification by
   (5) inspiring patriotism;
   (6) unifying the country via establishment of a civil religion;
   (7) unifying the country via establishment and reinforcement of symbolic, inclusive membership;
C. inspire greatness of character and action by
   (8) combating historical fatalism and thus inspiring potential leaders to grasp the reins of power and citizens in general to become civically engaged;
   (9) motivating citizens to look for and realize greatness within themselves;
   (10) symbolizing human possibility.

Although these functions are often conflated in theory and overlapping in practice, it is important to tease out their conceptual and empirical distinctions in order to understand what we have potentially lost in losing common civic heroes, and hence also in order to reflect sensibly on how we can overcome or at least minimize those aspects of this loss that are troubling. In the rest of this section, therefore, I explain each of these civic functions of heroes and provide evidence of their historic use in civic education inside and outside schools.

Provide Models for Emulation by Citizens

One of the most basic functions that the public elevation of heroes has served in the past—and I will argue in Part II below that 'role models' have taken over today—is that of providing models for emulation. We valorize and teach our children about heroes in order to inspire ourselves and our children to behave like them and thus be better people in general—and from a civic perspective, better citizens in particular. Thus, "[t]extbook writers typically used statesmen like George Washington as exemplars of republican character" (Tyack 2001, 337). A typical nineteenth-century school recitation taught, for example:

> Perhaps the reason little folks
> Are sometimes great when they grow taller,
> Is just because, like Washington,
> They do their best when they are smaller. (Wecter 1941, 99)

By engaging "in a constant striving to live up to" such heroes (Kelly 2003, 89), young citizens practice and imbibe specifically republican and/or democratic civic virtues. Nor is this confined to the early days of our republic, as the 1954 textbook *Civics for Americans* strikingly exemplifies. It quotes a naturalized citizen in a chapter on naturalization and the benefits of American citizenship:

> [T]his George Washington, who died long before I was born, was like a king in greatness, and he and I were Fellow Citizens. . . . It thrilled me to realize what sudden greatness had fallen on me; and at the same time it sobered me, as with a sense of responsibility I strove to conduct myself as befitted a Fellow Citizen. (Clark et al. 1954, 159)

There is a clear message here, reinforced throughout this textbook and others from the same time period, that good citizenship is a common responsibility resting on shared civic virtues; as our greatest citizens (such as Washington) did, so should we try to do in our own small ways. Dixon Wecter similarly remarks rather ruefully in his landmark work on American heroes that he and his schoolmates were constantly taught, "if we worked very hard and took infinite pains, and always did our duty, we might become little Washingtons." This is a two-sided sword, to be sure: "He is therefore a silent reproach to our shortcomings. Some of us, especially in boyhood, were inclined to resent the fact" (Wecter 1941, 130). I will discuss the risks of this approach, and consider how alternative uses of heroes and role models may ameliorate such resentment and potential attendant disengagement, in the final section of this essay.

Impart and Reinforce Common Civic Values and Norms

Closely related to the first goal of using heroes to provide models for civic emulation is that of establishing and promoting the civic values, norms, and virtues that are intended to tie the nation or civitas together. As I noted in the Introduction, each nation's heroes are often thought to provide a window into understanding the nation's soul: what it values and emulates, and how it conceives of itself—what it believes it stands for. Thus, Wecter lauds Washington, Franklin, Jefferson, Jackson, Lincoln, Robert E. Lee, Theodore Roosevelt, and others as those "from whom we have hewn our symbols of government, our ideas of what is most prizeworthy as 'American,'" linking them as tangible symbols of American values with "touchstones like the Declaration of Independence and the Constitution" (Wecter 1941, viii). As many authors have noted, this is in large part a constructed, even artificial process. Thus, Jackson symbolizes democratization and populism, not Native American genocide or anti-intellectualism, even though these may equally accurately capture both the man and some foundational American values. On the other side, the "heroification" (Loewen 1995, 19) process has similarly turned Martin Luther King into a symbol of America's ongoing 'dream' of equality and diversity, rather than a reminder of its persistent racism or militarism, against which King protested so mightily.[5] (See Kammen 1991 for an account of this process throughout US history.)

This process of national civic self-conceptualization and self-actualization through hero identification and elevation is made transparent when one looks at the treatment of national heroes in civics textbooks. Youth are explicitly instructed in the meaning they should ascribe to such heroes, and thus in the values they should ascribe to their country. Thus, *Civics for Citizens* (1974) instructs students that Mount Rushmore honors "four great Americans who were dedicated to the American ideal of freedom" (Dimond and Pflieger 1974, 7). In the same vein, *Magruder's American Government* (1953) shows a picture of students literally dwarfed by the statue of Thomas Jefferson at the Jefferson Memorial. The caption reads,

> These students in the Jefferson Memorial, Washington, D. C., find inspiration from one of our greatest patriots. Jefferson believed that all men were created equal, that men should make their governments, and that men should enjoy freedom of speech, of the press, and of religion. In his sixty years of public service, Jefferson stamped his personality and ideals indelibly upon our country. (McClenaghan 1953, 23)

In this case, the author drives home the point by not just telling the reader what Jefferson himself stood for, but further emphasizing that these ideals are "indelibly" stamped upon the country as well. Linking this use of hero identification with the purpose of inspiring emulation, the 1956 civics textbook *Youth Faces American Citizenship* similarly pictures Lincoln towering over visiting high school students, explaining, "These young men are rededicating themselves to the democratic ideals for which Lincoln stood" (Alilunas and Sayre 1956, 384). Here Lincoln's heroic figure provides both civic self-definition and a model for citizens' personal emulation.

Establish Touchstones for the Qualities Citizens Should Expect of Elected Officials and Other Civic Leaders

In addition to imparting the values that define the country in general, the identification and elevation of civic heroes can also serve to teach citizens the values and characteristics that ideally define their civic leaders in particular.

In this respect, civic heroes may not necessarily be models of emulation for all citizens. Rather, the implication is that such heroes are 'the kind of people' who should be running the country. Thus, the elevation of military heroes may serve to teach citizens that their elected leaders should also have served in the military, or at least demonstrate the virtues of strength, fearlessness, and discipline that military heroes often possess. Conversely, if young people are taught about heroes who fought injustice, bucked the system, worked to incorporate the disenfranchised, and so forth, they may similarly learn to look for civic leaders who possess these virtues or embody these ideals.

A corollary of this approach is the potential demeaning or civic exclusion of those who are not heroized. If certain kinds of people—women or non-whites, say—are *not* elevated as heroes, then the implicit (or even explicit) message is that such people are also not appropriate civic leaders. In response to a vast array of pressure groups, contemporary textbook publishers are now exquisitely sensitive to this concern about the exclusionary power of symbolism, and thus focus intensely on making sure that the heroes that students learn about are visibly diverse and multicultural. White men are now almost never featured consecutively in sidebars or photos in civics (or any other) textbooks; rather, every white man or other apparent 'mainstream' hero is followed by a visible ethnic or racial minority, woman, naturalized citizen, disabled person, or other 'multicultural' hero (see e.g., Davis et al. 2005; Hartley and Vincent 2005; McClenaghan 2003; Wolfson 2005; Glencoe/McGraw-Hill 2005). In this case, the aim is to provide multiple touchstones for civic leaders—touchstones for each racial and ethnic group, both genders, etc.—in order to inspire an inclusive conception of desirable civic leaders. (I come back to this issue of symbolic membership below.)

Teach Citizens Their Place by Contrasting Their Ordinariness with Heroes' Extraordinariness

At its extreme, this elevation of heroes as touchstones for civic leaders but not for 'ordinary' citizens can result in the antidemocratic lesson that ordinary citizens in fact should not be involved in governance or civic leadership at all. Thomas Carlyle expresses this conviction throughout *On Heroes, Hero-Worship, and the Heroic in History*.

> We come now to the last form of Heroism; that which we call Kingship. The Commander over Men; he to whose will our wills are to be subordinated, and loyally surrender themselves, and find their welfare in doing so, may be reckoned the most important of Great Men. He is practically the summary for us of *all* the various figures of Heroism; Priest, Teacher, whatsoever of earthly or of spiritual dignity we can fancy to reside in a man, embodies itself here, to *command* over us, to furnish us with constant practical teaching, to tell us for the day and hour what we are to *do*. (Carlyle 1893, 217)

Here, heroes are specifically granted powers and rights of civic leadership that ordinary human beings do not possess or deserve. Furthermore, ordinary human beings are not encouraged to develop heroic traits, to aspire to the virtues or powers possessed by "Great Men" such as Cromwell or Napoleon. According to this view, most people are not capable of leadership insofar as good leadership necessitates heroism, and we wouldn't want them to try—especially because society would be a shambles if we had more than a few heroic civic leaders in any generation. "Greatness is hard for common humanity to bear. . . . great men live dangerously. They introduce extremes into existence" (Schlesinger 1968, 342). Thus, in this approach heroes are taught as people to be admired and even feared, but definitely not to be emulated in aspiration or practice.

Insofar as civic leaders are considered to have qualitatively different virtues from ordinary citizens, another approach to civic education is simply to eliminate heroes from the curriculum at all. Joseph Moreau explains the perspective of a textbook author from 1885 thusly:

> The problem with colorful stories of past heroes, argued Alexander Johnston of Princeton, was that the 'mass of pupils' had little chance to emulate a John Smith or Pilgrim Father in contemporary, industrial America. They needed 'to learn from history the simple and homely duties of good citizenship.' (Moreau 2003, 50)

The practical implications of this approach may be found in the many 1950s civics textbooks that devoted full chapters to teaching the civic importance of having 'a pleasing personality,' being a 'good date,' and other such duties. This approach sidesteps the obviously antidemocratic implications of Carlyle's arguments while nonetheless maintaining a stark separation between the heroism of the elite and the more mundane virtues required of the rest of us.

Inspire Patriotism

A fifth purpose of identifying, elevating, and teaching about heroes can be to inspire patriotism. As Noah Webster argued, "Every child in America should be acquainted with his own country. . . . As soon as he opens his lips, he should rehearse the history of his own country; he should lisp the praise of liberty and of those illustrious heroes and statesmen who have wrought a revolution in her favor" (Noah Webster, "On the Education of Youth in America," quoted in Pangle and Pangle 2000, 32). This patriotism may sometimes require some historical reconstruction or even deception: "Although he had not admired Washington's leadership during the war, Rush thought it wise to tell less than the full truth about the founding fathers: 'Let the world admire our patriots and heroes. Their *supposed* talents and virtues . . . will serve the cause of patriotism and of our country'" (Tyack 2001, 337). Similarly, the accomplishments—both real and mythic—of such iconic heroes as Lewis and Clark, Douglas MacArthur, Harry Truman, Theodore Roosevelt, and the American cowboy, both reinforce America's 'can do' spirit (the function of imparting common civic values) and inspire love of the country that exemplifies such a characteristic. A variation on this approach is to inspire patriotism by highlighting the nation's history of nurturing and inspiring heroes: for example, by teaching that 'only in America' could heroic entrepreneurs such as Andrew Carnegie or Bill Gates achieve their dreams—and thus achieve the 'American dream' more broadly—or could heroes such as Helen Keller and Colin Powell rise from obscurity to greatness.

Unify the Country via Establishment of a Civil Religion

At the same time, 'mere' patriotism is just one stage along the continuum of civic purposes that heroes can be made to serve. Further along the continuum, civic heroes can be turned into "demigods" (Tyack 2001, 337), used to establish or burnish a civil religion that unites the country in a shared reverence of their deified patriots. This process has been especially apparent with George Washington, Abraham Lincoln, and Martin Luther King. "[H]ero-worship of the living Washington," for example, started as early as the 1770s and has continued virtually every decade since (Wecter 1941, 111; see also Chapter 6 *passim*). Consider *Legends of the American Revolution*, published in 1847, which

> told of a mystic who had heard the voice of God, 'I will send a deliverer to this land of the New World, who shall save my people from physical bondage, even as my Son saved them from the bondage of spiritual death!' This mystic came from Germany to the New World and one midnight consecrated Washington with holy oil, a crown of laurel, and a sword. (Wecter 194, 139)

Seventy-five years later, the civic impact of such deification can be seen in the report of a young immigrant girl: "'Never had I prayed . . . in such utter reverence and worship as I repeated the simple sentences of my child's story of the patriot. I gazed with adoration at the portraits of George and Martha Washington, till I could see them with my eyes shut'" (Tyack 2001, 356). Similarly, although it took longer for Lincoln to achieve demigod status,

> [i]n the twentieth century . . . Americans began to refashion the man of the people [Lincoln] along epic lines. Increasingly, they saw the Christ-like Man of Sorrows. They saw the Savior of the Union who takes upon himself the pain of his people. They saw the great moralist, the prophet of democracy, the Great Emancipator, the giant who changes the course of history. They saw the man that can never be reached: a man, for sure, but too good, and too big, to be treated as a man. (Schwartz 1990, 98)

Martin Luther King Jr. too, has attained an almost Christ-like stature in the United States. As Majora Carter recently commented in her introduction to a Martin Luther King Day radio special, "In my family, there was the Father, the Son, the Holy Ghost, and Dr. Martin Luther King, Jr." (Ostroushko 2009). Building on this, the standard narrative could be summarized, only a little facetiously, as follows: 'King lived and died for our sins. He wanted all people to live as brothers and to love each other. For some reason there was a lot of racism when King was alive. Through his work and especially his "I have a dream" speech, he taught people to love each other and not be racist anymore. A racist person then killed him. But his dream lives on, and now everybody gets along.' This myth was carried to a logical extreme a few years ago by the four-year-old son of a friend of mine. One day in late January (so a week or two after Martin Luther King Day), Hersh asked his teacher, "Who gave us nature?" Before his teacher could respond, Hersh burst out, "Martin Luther King gave us nature! Since he wanted us all to be kind and nice to each other, he gave us nature to help us remember how to be nice." As his teacher wryly remarked in an e-mail to his mom, "I thought this was wonderful, but reminded Hersh that while MLK did want all those things, nature was here before him" (Kanner 2007).

In all of these cases, Washington, Lincoln, and King are constructed as Christ-like heroes used to center a civic religion. As Wecter puts it, without irony (and probably appropriately so), "these heroes are . . . men who stand somehow for the essence of our faith, whose birthplaces and graves we make into shrines, and whose faces we carve upon mountains as our American way of writing poetry" (Wecter 1941, viii; see also Kammen 1991).

Unify the Country via Establishment and Reinforcement of Symbolic, Inclusive Membership

Another way to unify the country is by establishing and reinforcing an inclusive narrative in which all the nation's peoples (however defined) play a variety of heroic roles. I discussed above the potentially exclusionary characterization of civic leaders' necessary virtues—say, being white, a military veteran, or male—and I noted contemporary textbook authors' attempts in response to expand these often literal images of civic leadership in order to establish more inclusive ideals. A similarly self-conscious, symbolically inclusive approach to establishing and teaching civic heroes can also be deployed for the purposes of promoting a common national story in which all citizens are encouraged to see themselves and of which they are encouraged to feel a part. As Chicago mayor "Big Bill" Thompson put it in 1928, "All nationalities are entitled to a place in the sun, and our national heroes are the stars in the firmament of our patriotism" (Zimmerman 2002, 21). Although there have been sporadic challenges to this approach, historian Jonathan Zimmerman makes a persuasive case that this blandly unifying narrative essentially won out in textbooks throughout the 1980s and beyond. "Texts retained an emphasis on 'positive images' in history: every ethnic group could have its place in the textbook sun, so long as no textbook ever said a dark or critical word about its members. . . . Whites allowed new actors into the national story so long as the story stayed the same" (Zimmerman 2002, 128). The 2005 edition of *Civics: Government and Economics in Action* (Davis et al. 2005), a fairly typical middle- and high school civics textbook from this decade, demonstrates this logic. Although it doesn't feature 'heroes' as such, it does feature 15 "Citizen Profiles" ranging from Mickey Leland, James Madison, Carol Moseley Braun, and Louis Brandeis to Andrea Jung, Alice Rivlin, Thurgood Marshall, and Madeleine Albright. Each paragraph-long (five to seven sentence) profile—which invariably highlights the subject's nonwhite, non-Christian, or female status—is accompanied by a photo and followed by a question that reinforces the civic contribution made by that person to the country.

Combat Historical Fatalism

Public identification and elevation of heroes serve an entirely different set of civic purposes when they are used to demonstrate the importance of individual agency to civil society. These comprise the final three functions discussed in this part of the essay. First, if citizens can be taught to recognize heroes' power to "shape history" (Gibbon 2002, 23; see also James 1880), then they will realize that historical fatalism is foolish. History is not inevitable. Thus, citizens must assume some responsibility for shaping the future, too. "It takes a man of exceptional vision and strength and will—it takes, in short, a hero—to try to wrench history from what lesser men consider its preconceived path" (Schlesinger 1968, 350). When such 'lesser men' realize this, then they will themselves potentially refuse to "acquiesce[] in the drift of history" (Schlesinger 1968, 350) and assume civic responsibility themselves.

Motivate Citizens to Look for and Realize Greatness Within Themselves

Combating historical fatalism is an essential first step for inspiring citizens' assumption of even limited civic responsibility. A still-more ambitious goal is to inspire citizens to reach for the same level of greatness in assuming that responsibility as their heroes have achieved. "Great men enable us to rise to our own highest potentialities. They nerve lesser men to disregard the world and trust to their own deepest instinct" (Schlesinger 1968, 350). In a certain way, this takes us back to the very first civic function of heroes: to provide models for emulation. But that first goal was fairly modest. Citizens were expected to emulate their heroes only in specific ways (to be honest, for example, because George Washington was honest) and to a limited—to a human rather than heroic—degree. One may teach about the heroes of the past, however, in order to inspire and even create the heroes of tomorrow. As Ralph Waldo Emerson puts it, "Great men exist [and are taught about] so that there may be greater men" (Emerson 1907, 40). This function of teaching about heroes is to inspire citizens to seek out and achieve their own heroism, not necessarily in the same domain or with respect to the same virtues as the original hero made his or her mark, but in some way that enables "the higher self to prevail" (Gibbon 2002, xxi). Thus, someone who learns about Washington's heroic bravery may be inspired to reach for greatness inside of herself and become a great teacher, a remarkable sportswoman, or attain some other heroic standing, even if her achievement has nothing to do with bravery or politics (or honesty) as such. The Giraffe Heroes Project, which works extensively with young people and adults to "find new heroes, to tell their stories, and to help more people be heroic" (Giraffe Heroes Project 2008), clearly attempts to promote this civic function of identifying and elevating heroes. As they put it, "*Everyone* has what it takes to be a Giraffe"—their term for a hero who "sticks their neck out for the common good" (Giraffe Heroes Project 2008).

Symbolize Human Possibility

Finally, heroes can be used to expand our sense of what is possible for all of humanity. I discussed above the use of heroes in establishing touchstones for elected or other civic leaders; in this case, heroes are used to help citizens envision possibilities beyond those represented in their own lives or experiences. "Public heroes—or imperfect people of extraordinary achievement, courage, and greatness of soul whose reach is wider than our own—teach us to push beyond ourselves and our neighborhoods in our search for models of excellence. They enlarge our imagination, teach us to think big, and expand our sense of the possible" (Gibbon 2002, 13). This is obviously related to functions 8 and 9, but its purpose is not necessarily to inspire citizens to become their own heroes; rather, it is to inspire citizens to develop civic aspirations that go beyond the realm of the apparently possible and even realistic in order to set society on a better, more uplifting path.

Having taken the time to distinguish these ten civic functions of hero identification and education, I should reiterate that these rarely are so purely separated in practice. Consider, for example, a representative discussion of Rousseau's enthusiasm for heroes:

> [G]ood citizens . . . identify with great citizens from the past and with legislators. Citizens can be made to engage in a constant striving to live up to these great examples. As Rousseau says, 'From the effervescence excited by this shared emulation will be born that patriotic intoxication which alone can raise men above themselves, and without which

freedom is only a vain name and legislation only a chimera.' (Kelly 2003, 89–90)

In these few brief sentences, heroes are called upon to play at least three different civic functions: as models for emulation, sources of patriotism, and sources of unity that together help to construct a common civil society. Furthermore, Rousseau's formulation of the civic purposes of hero-worship seems to intimately connect all three functions, they are simultaneously and mutually reinforcing, as opposed to sequential or separable. The taxonomy of heroism's civic educative uses is thus admittedly more theoretical than empirical, and runs the risk of missing important interconnections. Nonetheless, I suggest that it is worth keeping in mind the many different—and at least in theory, distinguishable—civic functions that heroes can serve as we move into a consideration of whether each of these functions is in fact desirable or even possible in contemporary democratic societies.

USES OF HEROES IN CONTEMPORARY DEMOCRACIES

The Fall of Heroes and Rise of Role Models

It is no accident that most examples of civic education about heroes in Part I came from earlier times (eighteenth, nineteenth, and early to mid-twentieth centuries). There is strong evidence that the salience of heroes is severely limited in the contemporary United States, and thus that they no longer can (or do) fulfill many of the functions listed above. In an October 2000 Gallup Youth Survey, for example, young people were asked, "Do you have any heroes or heroines in the world today—men or women whom you personally greatly admire for their achievements and for their strong moral character?" Over a third of respondents (36 percent) answered no; they were unable to identify any hero or heroine whatsoever. The next largest group, comprising almost a quarter of young people (23 percent), selected a family member. After that, selection slowed to a relative trickle. In other words, barely 40 percent of young people were able to identify anyone beyond their own family whom they greatly admired for their achievements and character (Gallup and Lyons 2002).[6] Furthermore, even those non-familiars whom youth do claim to admire are diminishingly likely to be viewed as true heroes. Between 1979 and 1996, young people ages thirteen to seventeen were asked annually, "What one man/woman that you have heard or read about, living today in any part of the world, do you admire the most—not including relatives or personal friends?" Consider Table 8.1, which lists top ten admired men from 1979, 1986, and 1996 (Lyons 2008).

In contrast to the list from 1979, which includes a number of men to whom it is possible to ascribe heroism of some sort (although Gerald Ford?), it is hard to imagine that many teens in 1996 would have

Table 8.1   Top Ten Most Admired Men: 1979, 1986, and 1996

1979	1986	1996
Jimmy Carter	Ronald Reagan	Michael Jordan
Anwar Sadat	Jesse Jackson	Bill Clinton
Gerald Ford	Don Johnson	Brad Pitt
Menachem Begin	Pope John Paul II	Jesse Jackson
Richard Nixon	Desmond Tutu	Anfernee Hardaway
Muhammad Ali	Lee Iacocca	Emmitt Smith
Jerry Lewis	Bob Geldof/Prince (tie)	Ken Griffey Jr.
Pope John Paul II/ Gov. Jerry Brown (tie)	Tom Selleck	Cal Ripken Jr.
John Travolta	Rob Lowe/ Bruce Spring- steen (tie)	Michael Jackson
		Jim Carrey/ Shaquille O'Neal (tie)

defined most of the men they listed as 'heroes,' despite their potentially fervent admiration for them. Perhaps even more to the point, if they did in fact view Pitt, Hardaway, Smith, or Carrey (say) as heroes, that would suggest as much about the diminishment of the contemporary conception of heroism as about teens' propensity for selecting heroes in the first place.

Young people aren't operating in a vacuum, of course. Their contemporary disavowal of heroism arguably reflects a more general cultural shift. As I was researching the literature on heroes for this chapter, I was taken aback by the rash of articles starting in the late 1970s specifically titled "Where have all of the heroes gone?" Articles by this title have shown up in publications as diverse as the *New Statesman, Columbia Journalism Review, Newsweek, Control Engineering, Journal of Sport and Social Issues,* and *Journal of the American Osteopathic Association* (Axthelm 1979; Hanson 1996; Marr 1998; Silverman 2003; Truchard 2005; McDorman, et al. 2006). As far as I can tell from a fairly extensive electronic database search, there are few if any articles with such titles before the mid-1970s. I suggest that the sheer breadth of articles with this title signifies a common sentiment within American culture over the past thirty years. *Control Engineering* is not trying to present a new idea about the loss of heroism in contemporary life (or even in contemporary engineering); rather, it is tapping into a loss already collectively felt and acknowledged. Book titles have undergone a similar transformation. Consider the ambivalent *The Hero in Transition* (Browne and Fishwick 1983) and the despairing *Everybody Is Sitting on the Curb: How and Why America's Heroes Disappeared* (Edelstein

1996), in comparison to such previous studies of heroism as *The Hero, American Style* (Fishwick 1969) or Dixon Wecter's 1941 classic *The Hero in America: A Chronicle of Hero-Worship* (Wecter 1941). Along the same lines, in "Hero Worship in America," published in 1949, sociologist Orrin E. Klapp grapples with the challenge of explaining why there is so *much* hero worship (Klapp 1949). It is hard to imagine a sociologist identifying such a challenge today.

Admittedly, every age bemoans the loss of great heroes of previous ages and their replacement by apparently transient and superficial stars of the present. "[T]oday seems always less heroic than yesterday" (Wecter 1941, 489). Churchill himself regretfully noted in 1925, "The great emancipated nations seem to have become largely independent of famous guides and guardians. They no longer rely upon the Hero, the Commander, or the Teacher as they did in bygone rugged ages, or as the less advanced peoples do today." After asking, "Can modern communities do without great men? Can they dispense with hero-worship?" he commented in sorrow, "We miss our giants. We are sorry that their age is past" (Churchill 1925).

Churchill's regret, however, was rooted in heroes' replacement by measures, machines, and "'the common sense of most'" (Churchill 1925). He didn't bemoan generalized indifference or even antipathy toward heroes and heroism in general, the way many do today. Tyler Cowen remarks:

> The modern image of a leader is not Theodore Roosevelt charging up a hill, but rather Jimmy Carter fighting off a rabbit with a canoe paddle, Gerald Ford stumbling and bumping his head, or George Bush vomiting in the lap of the Japanese prime minister. Bill Clinton will be defined forever by his handling of the Monica Lewinsky affair. These images demystify power and produce a culture of disillusionment with politics and moral leadership. (Cowen 2000)

In recent decades, Cowen's comments accurately suggest, I think, that the conception of heroism—especially to the extent that it has historically been tied to leadership—has become diminished and even potentially debased. Heroes are no longer 'great men' and women straddling the world like a colossus. "Today," by contrast, "many Americans define heroes as decent people who sacrifice or try to make a difference. They name streets after local World War II veterans, parks after teachers, bridges after local politicians and philanthropists. . . . [T]hey democratize the word *hero* and jettison the Greek notion of the hero as superhuman and godlike" (Gibbon 2002, 11).

One potent contemporary example of this trend may be found in *CNN Heroes*, a "global initiative" that intentionally "showcase[s] examples of ordinary people who have accomplished extraordinary deeds" (CNN 2008). When I randomly checked CNN's links to "Heroes in the News" one afternoon (16 August 2008, 4:19 p.m.), every single link highlighted a person who had intervened in a crisis to save someone's life: "Missing toddler found safe," "Wheelchair-bound woman pulled from train's path," "Baby pulled from burning car," "Boy, 8, saves pal choking on rock," and so forth. This vision of heroism is totally divorced from any notion of societal change, greatness of character, or even intentionality. Perhaps even more to the point, this list hardly presents a model for civic emulation, unless we want young people to grow up quite literally to become ambulance chasers.[7]

None of this evidence suggests that admiration and even emulation of others is impossible or even unusual in contemporary American society— just that heroes are not the means by which such admiration and emulation are likely fostered. In place of outsized heroes, I believe that Americans have come to value life-sized role models. 'Role models,' as the concept was first defined in the 1950s—interestingly, just as conceptions of 'hero-worship' seem to have been drawing to a close (Addis 1996, 1381; see also Gibbon 2002, 12)—and continues to be used today, are people whom we admire and attempt to emulate. Heroes could in theory thus also be role models. But as an empirical psychological matter, at least in contemporary times, heroes do *not* serve as role models. Instead, role models are almost inevitably 'ordinary': they are people who seem generally similar to ourselves and whose differences from us tend to be along one particular dimension, rather than those who are truly extraordinary, especially across multiple dimensions (Addis 1996; see also Kemper 1968; Speizer 1981; Lockwood and Kunda 1997, 2000). It is their very ordinariness that inspires us to act differently and to emulate their achievements, not any overarching greatness of character, stature, or even impact.

Americans' shift from emulating (at least admiring) extraordinary heroes to emulating ordinary role models may help explain recent poll and survey results in which family members and friends have come to trump others in meriting mention as heroes or role models. Among adults, for example, the percentage of Gallup poll respondents identifying a family member or friend as their "most admired" living man has sextupled over the past sixty years; it has likewise doubled for most admired living woman.[8] Youth over the past twenty years have similarly embraced their family and close friends as being among the most admirable people. At the beginning of this section, I mentioned that one quarter of youth surveyed in 2000 identified a family member as their hero. This response was not anomalous. Studies of children, adolescents, and college students in the 1980s and 1990s consistently showed that young people more frequently selected their parents as heroes than anyone else (Averett 1985; Porpora 1996, 222; Pomper 2004, 22). In a 2002 study of young children, for example, 34 percent "named their parents as role models and heroes" and another 22 percent named friends and acquaintances (Anderson and Cavallaro 2002, 166); a 2003 study likewise showed that teenagers were most likely to identify their parents as their "most admired" living woman and man (Robison 2003; see also Yancy et al. 2002).[9]

Maria, a young woman whom I interviewed in Boston when she was a senior in high school, exemplifies this rejection of the distant, extraordinary hero in favor of the intimate, ordinary role model. In response to my questions, "Who do people try to teach you to take as role models? And who are your actual role models?" her reply speaks volumes:

> Of course, famous leaders. Martin Luther King, Malcolm X, people who have brought changes in our culture. But. . . . the one role model . . . that's like my hero or whatever you may call it, is my father. I didn't have the privilege for him to raise me as a child, as a baby or whatever. . . . My father was in jail. He served his time. He got out and the first thing he did was move from New York to Boston to start life. So I kind of got my father like 10 or 11 years old. And from then we've been growing as father and daughter. . . . You see my father now and you don't think that he had a hard life and that he did that stuff or whatever. Because he's left that behind and he started something new. And through his trial and error he succeeded through everything.

Maria is well aware of who she is supposed to view as a hero. But she is equally aware that these "famous leaders" do not directly inspire her in the way her father does. To some extent at least, it is her father's very weaknesses and struggles—matched by his slow but steady success "through everything"—that makes him a hero. Maria's attitude in this regard is absolutely typical of the young civic leaders (Maria was a representative on her neighborhood council) whom I interviewed in 2004 as a means of determining how and why some youth from historically disenfranchised backgrounds beat the "civic achievement gap" (Levinson 2007). Well over half of the youth civic leaders I talked with selected a formerly incarcerated family member as a role model or hero. Again, this was not because they were unaware of more traditional heroes. Rather, it was the personal relationship that was key, as Joel, a seventeen-year-old high school student in Boston, explained:

> Like all my teachers want me to look at Martin Luther King and Caesar Chavez. Martin Luther King. And I look at them and I don't see them as role models. You know?. . . . I mean, they were great leaders and all of that, but I don't mean, like, "Wow, that's a fine role model." You know, my role model is Jésus [the youth organizing leader at the nonprofit where Joel worked]. He has helped me so much. He's talked to me, you know. He's done things for me that I don't know if anybody would have ever done for me. And I'm so grateful for him. That's my role model right there. I look up to him.

I found identical results in a survey I conducted with approximately 100 young people in four communities. One of the survey questions asked them to complete the sentence, "My role model(s) is (are) . . ." Of those who answered, *93 percent* included at least one family member or friend and/or a religious figure such as God, Muhammad, or Jesus—someone with whom the students also seemed to feel a direct, personal relationship. Again, this is not because students were unaware of the more famous or extraordinary exemplars. They uniformly mentioned leaders such as Martin Luther King and others in listing four people "everybody from the United States has heard of." Rather, this data strongly reinforces the notion that as a practical matter, personal relationships totally trump abstract knowledge of distant heroes with respect to role model identification.

Are Democracies Better Off Without Heroes?

What are the civic implications in a democracy of this contemporary disavowal of extraordinary heroes in favor of ordinary role models? Not surprisingly, it's complicated. Some thinkers assert that the hero's fall from grace, and the role model's concomitant upswing, is actively good for a democracy. Four arguments support this contention. First, democracies are founded on a notion of equality—especially civic equality—that seems profoundly at odds with the public recognition and elevation of heroes.

> [T]he most important component in our unease about authority or greatness is surely democracy. Previous generations had democratic machinery and rhetoric: the outside scaffolding. We have gone further. We have a democratic culture: the spirit, the essence. . . . We find the notion of people being innately better or worse than we are frankly offensive. (Marr 1998, 26)

Marr's claim here seems to be about democratic psychology, but the point here can and should be made more broadly. To the extent that democracy is rule 'by the people,' we should not look for or expect significant distinctions between ourselves and our leaders. All citizens should be capable of democratic deliberation and participation. Citizens may well learn from and be inspired by fellow-citizen role models in this process because role models are in essence equal to oneself except for in defined particulars. It is antithetical to democratic egalitarianism, on the other hand, to identify 'heroes' whose achievements and strength of character ordinary citizens could never hope to match. As Christopher Kelly explains it,

> Liberal democrats tend to be suspicious of hero worship, fearing that it encourages inequality and dependency on those who are, or claim to be, superior. While they can be generous in their praise of heroic action, in their ordinary speech they frequently replace heroes with 'role models,' for whom the part played or the function fulfilled predominates over

intrinsic admirable qualities. It is easier to consider oneself as equal to one's role model than to one's hero. (Kelly 2003, 82–83)[10]

This preference for well-defined "functions" over personal virtue inspires Gerald Pomper's more radical, second argument that "Within the structures of a democracy, heroism is based on institutions, not personalities. . . . [D]emocratic heroes are ordinary men and women who ably perform their institutional responsibilities in times of crisis" (Pomper 2004, 4). According to this vision of democratic citizenship, the whole point is to create "roles [that] can be taken over by interchangeable equal individuals" (Kelly 1997, 348) within democratic institutions, while fostering each individual's skills and commitment to the democratic enterprise so that they inevitably perform at a high level, even at times of crisis. Democracy is premised on the value of the individual, including a belief in each individual's potential to contribute to the collective good. Along this line of reasoning, if democratic structures are designed correctly, citizens will almost automatically be enabled to contribute to the collective good through their ordinary actions. No extraordinary efforts of will would be required, or even be desired, because democratic institutions should be structured so as to anticipate and provide for a nation's needs through the everyday acts of its citizens, all of whom have the capacity to so contribute. "The basic premise of self-government is that the people themselves have enough character and collective wisdom to chose appropriate leaders and resolve their common problems. . . . Reliance on . . . heroes too easily leads to disdain for the staple of democracy, the ordinary citizen. . . . Human success will require common effort, not extraordinary intervention" (Pomper 2004, 5).[11]

Following on this, third, it is arguably profoundly dangerous for a country to put its faith in individuals' greatness with regard to civic leadership.

[W]e so often look for champions to protect us and preserve our society. . . . [W]e search for the charismatic leader who will easily solve the complex problems of modern life. This conventional view, however, has serious—and worrisome—implications for democratic politics. Demigods—people like Achilles—are few and far between. Relying on such heroes makes human welfare contingent on the exceptional intervention, often unreliable and always arbitrary, of these unique individuals. The successful resolution of crises then depends essentially on luck—on the chance that extraordinary people will be found to meet a crisis or that some person will undergo an ennobling transformation at the critical moment. (Pomper 2004)

In a way, this argument turns Schlesinger's claims about historical fatalism on their heads. Pomper agrees with Schlesinger that history's direction and outcomes are not inevitable. People—especially heroes—can make a profound difference in shaping the history of a nation. Pomper and Schlesinger part ways, however, on who should be expected—or accorded the right and responsibility—to make such changes. It is not the individual actor, acting almost as a legislator unto him or herself, who should be reshaping the destiny of a democracy. This would be antidemocratic in the extreme. As Sidney Hook warns, "If the hero is defined as an event-making individual who redetermines the course of history, it follows at once that a democratic community must be eternally on guard against him" (Hook 1943, 229). By contrast, the point of democratic governance is that all citizens should be empowered to work in concert to decide the direction of the nation and shape history. In addition, as a practical matter, it would be catastrophic for a nation's fate to depend on the heroism of a single, extraordinary individual. This is truly the path toward fatalism and historical impotence, for the reasons Pomper elucidates above.

Finally, a fourth argument against 'heroification' in a democracy is that the presentation especially of those in power as heroic can discourage citizens from exercising the level of scrutiny that is necessary for a well-functioning and just democracy. In his influential *Lies My Teacher Taught Me*, for example, James Loewen argues that history textbooks that seem inevitably to heroize the state are essentially "anticitizenship manuals—handbooks for acquiescence" (Loewen 1995, 216). Citizens in a democratic society should maintain a healthy skepticism about their leaders and the claims made on behalf of the state. If they do not, then they are effectively abandoning their governance and oversight role. But one does not treat heroes with healthy skepticism; to do so is effectively to deny their heroism. Thus, democracies may be better off without heroes—or at least, without the heroification of those in power.

Democracies Need Heroes

Even if all of the above arguments are true, there may well be other reasons to identify and honor heroes within contemporary democracies. Many of the civic functions of heroes enumerated above, for example, may remain desirable and even necessary in democratic states despite heroes' potentially antidemocratic implications in other respects. For example, even democracies—perhaps *especially* democracies—need to unify themselves around some common cause, identity, sense of history, idea, norms, or civil religion. As I discussed earlier, heroes have historically played a significant role in exemplifying, transmitting, symbolizing, and/or inspiring such unifying beliefs or characteristics (functions 2 and 5–7). Second, democratic leaders both need and deserve respect for doing their jobs. The diminishment or even negation of the heroic aspect of leadership arguably weakens those who have demonstrated the courage and commitment to take on responsibility, as well as discourages other good men and women from assuming the mantle of leadership when they know they will be granted little honor or respect for so doing. Andrew Marr eloquently exposes this tension:

The democratic culture shies away from the authority that gives democracy its focus, its story. We want, in our hearts, to have everyone on one level. That is the source of the pleasure when another big figure topples, boxer shorts round his legs. But the trouble is that effective representative democracy requires authority and respect—that willingness to look up to someone which we find increasingly hard to grant elected leaders. (Marr 1998, 26)

Relatedly, democracies as much as any system of governance—and possibly more than most—need to hold high expectations for their elected leaders and representatives (this was function 3 discussed in the first section). There was much talk in the 2000 and 2004 presidential elections about President Bush's appeal to the electorate as a 'regular guy' with whom they would enjoy sitting down and sharing a beer—unlike Al Gore and John Kerry, who few people at the time saw even as beer-drinking types, let alone as enjoyable bar stool company. In this context, Bush's poor grades in college, drunk-driving arrest, verbal miscues, and other peccadilloes made him more attractive to the electorate rather than less. "While the purpose of democracy was to give everyone a fair chance to rise, its method enabled rancorous men to invoke 'equality' as an excuse for keeping all down to their own level" (Schlesinger 1968, 343). But democracies are not well served by mediocrity (nor was it well served by Bush, as even most Republicans would agree), and they do not have to foster it. "[G]reat men have been chosen President. Democracy demonstrates a capability for heroic leadership quite as much as it does a tendency toward mediocrity," even if "the dislike of great men" is "a permanent potentiality in a democracy" (Schlesinger 1968, 344).

By 2008, in fact, the American electorate seemed to have overcome its infatuation with electing someone who seemed ordinary (Sarah Palin and "Joe the Plumber's" populism notwithstanding), perhaps recognizing that the country is better served by presidents who have extraordinary rather than merely run-of-the-mill skills and capacities. This recognition was arguably reflected in, and potentially even encouraged by, the candidates' emphasis on their own heroic qualities. John McCain's entire general election campaign was conducted on his basis of his status as a war hero and his heroism as a 'maverick.' Although Barack Obama's campaign did not argue directly that Obama himself was a hero, he was certainly treated as—and invested with the expectations of—a hero by a significant portion of the American electorate and even the global population. To the extent that these appeals to and invocations of heroism raised the electorate's expectations for their future president and led them to demand more rather than less from each candidate, that can only be to the good. There is no innate democratic virtue in mediocrity—and much to recommend greatness instead.

In addition, democracies depend on virtuous and vigorous citizens to remain healthy, legitimate, and effective. As I discussed above, heroes can be used to promote qualities of civic virtue, active civic engagement, and belief in and pursuit of excellence (functions 1 and 8–10). Continuing with some reflections on the 2008 presidential election, Obama quite transparently reflected his ascribed heroism back onto his acolytes, repeatedly claiming, "We are the ones we've been waiting for" (Obama 2008), and featuring at the top of every page of his Web site "I'm asking you to believe. Not just in my ability to bring about real change in Washington . . . I'm asking you to believe in yours" (Obama for America 2008). The tenor of these messages is to draw upon the implicit greatness ascribed to him by his followers (even the language of 'acolytes' and 'followers,' which comes so much more naturally in Obama's case than merely 'supporters' or 'voters,' emphasizes his heroic stature in some circles)—and to try to expand that attribution of greatness to include heretofore 'ordinary' citizens. Whether or not one agrees with Obama's beliefs, policy positions, or readiness for the presidency, it's hard to deny the power of these messages to energize and even potentially transform a democracy. Obama's candidacy also provided a tangible example of the way in which the perception of extraordinariness in another (i.e., in Obama) can both bring joy to those who revel in human possibility, and can push observers toward their "higher, better selves" (functions 9 and 10).

At the same time, one reason that people have been both suspicious of Obama himself and concerned about his message of citizens' being their own salvation (or at least their own change agents) is that both have been perceived as self-satisfied in a way that undercuts another potential civic function of heroes in a democracy: namely, to promote a healthy skepticism of oneself, and a recognition of one's own fallibility. As George W. Bush's presidency demonstrated as well as any, implacable self-confidence and refusal to doubt one's actions or judgments may have profoundly antidemocratic consequences. Recognition of others' greatness—including others' superiority even to ourselves—may be necessary to combat such hubristic self-satisfaction. Schlesinger, as usual, puts it pithily: "When we do not admire great men, then our instinct for admiration is likely to end by settling on ourselves. The one thing worse for democracy than hero worship is self worship" (Schlesinger 1968, 349). This is not to disavow the egalitarian concerns raised earlier; teaching citizens their (lowered) place in contrast to others' heroism (function 4) is clearly problematic from an egalitarian democratic perspective. But there is a democratic version of this attitude, by which the encouragement of humility, skepticism, and self-doubt can actually contribute to such democratic virtues as tolerance, willingness to deliberate with others, and acceptance of the burdens of judgment (Rawls 1971).

Most of the goals historically served by society's elevation and recognition of heroes thus may remain desirable in a democratic society, at least when pursued in moderate fashion and with non-overreaching aims. All could be pursued tyrannically, but none (except for the unreconstructed version of function 4, 'teaching citizens their place') need be so; I think that all others if suitably checked have a place in a democracy. It is worth raising expectations for our leaders and elected officials, for example, even though at the same time we do want young people, and citizens in general, in a democratic society to feel as if they have the capacity and opportunity to become civic leaders. This is the contrast between feeling as if we *could* be president and wanting a president to *be* the same as ourselves. It's a surprisingly complex position to make sense of. Returning to the rather frivolous but nonetheless politically potent example of beer drinking, I suggested above that our decision about who is better qualified to be president should not depend on whom we would feel comfortable having a beer with. At the same time, it is not unreasonable to expect that a presidential candidate know approximately what a beer (or a gallon of milk—consider Bush 41) costs, and it is also appropriate for a president to drink a beer—in other words, for a president to be human.[12]

Even if the public recognition and elevation of heroes is on balance desirable in a democracy, however, the evidence that I shared earlier suggests that heroes can no longer help us achieve all of these aims. Heroes may still be sufficiently comprehensible and salient to American citizens that they can fulfill some of the civic functions listed above. But they definitely cannot fulfill all. This brings us, therefore, to the final section of this essay, in which I explore the implications of heroes' theoretical civic uses and contemporary practical demise for civic education.

HEROES IN CONTEMPORARY CIVIC EDUCATION

The survey, interview, and other data presented above suggests that heroes—especially heroes such as civic leaders or activists, in contrast to movie stars or athletes—may no longer speak much to young people. But there is little in this data to suggest that the majority of young people are actively *opposed* to heroes, i.e., that teaching about heroes for a particular purpose would inevitably backfire. Furthermore, many extraordinary individuals are still *known* to young people, as the example of Martin Luther King Jr. demonstrated in the introduction to this chapter and in the interviews I discussed. Given this, I think that examples of extraordinary individuals (whether defined explicitly as 'heroes' or not) could effectively be used to promote civic aims that are based upon passive admiration and/or identity formation as opposed to active emulation. Specifically, it is possible that civic education about heroes could impart and reinforce common civic values and norms; establish touchstones for the qualities citizens should expect of elected officials and other civic leaders; inspire patriotism; unify the country via establishment and reinforcement of symbolic, inclusive membership; and symbolize human possibility. I do not think that any of these would come about easily, nor even that education about heroes is necessarily the best way to achieve these goals. But I also see no reason that teaching about heroes would be actively detrimental to these aims.

To the extent that we aim to inspire active *emulation*, however, then I think the evidence is quite clear that ordinary role models instead of extraordinary heroes should lie at the heart of civic education. There is already some empirical evidence of the promise of this approach. In their study of ten effective civic education programs, for example, Joseph Kahne and Joel Westheimer found that

> [S]everal students emphasized that exposure to 'ordinary' rather than 'famous' individuals often had the greatest impact. In contrast to the ubiquitous school programs that hold up Martin Luther King, Jr., as a hero to be respected (but not necessarily emulated), these programs offered role models who appeared to be ordinary people—not unlike the students. Encountering such people spurred students to imagine themselves as civic actors formulating and pursuing their own civic goals. (Kahne and Westheimer 2003, 64)

What would this look like in practice?

Based on my own teaching experience, I am inclined to think that there are four important steps to this process. First, educators need to select and introduce students to civically efficacious people who share some range of characteristics (racial, ethnic, cultural, religious, national origin, residence, and/or class related) with the students themselves in order to increase the chance that students will actually see them as role models—i.e., people mostly like themselves who inspire emulation. Second, students need to have the opportunity truly to get to know and feel a connection with these people, just as they feel intimately connected with the family members and friends they most often identify as their role models. Third, students need to learn *how* the ordinary, everyday actions taken by these people make significant differences to their communities. If they don't learn this, students have little to be inspired about or to think is worthy of emulation. Fourth, educators need to help students identify and practice the key skills deployed by these ordinary role models as a means of becoming efficacious, engaged civic and political actors themselves.

One year when I was teaching eighth grade, for example, we hosted Sam Yoon as a guest speaker. Yoon was then working for the Asian Community Development Corporation and running to be Boston's first Asian American city councilor. (He won.) After his presentation, students easily picked out such generic attributes as getting an education, caring about others, and working hard as keys to his success. But students' mouthing of these platitudes is hardly civically empowering—nor even a proof of learning, since students could equally easily have lauded such attributes before Yoon's presentation. Instead, therefore, I goaded students to examine the specifics of his efforts for social change: how he tried to use the media's interest in his personal story as the first Asian American candidate for citywide office in order to focus attention on the issues he cared about, such as affordable housing. Students were inspired to learn about how to communicate with the media, present themselves publicly, and use their own personal stories to direct others' attention to issues such as neighborhood violence and lack of job opportunities for youth. They developed valuable communication and presentation skills while incorporating their own backgrounds, interests, and concerns. The fact that students actually met and talked with Yoon, and that he lived nearby—one student saw him in a neighborhood diner a few days later, and another ran into him on the bus—helped keep them energized and fostered their sense that learning these skills might enable them to make a difference.

This active, relationship-oriented, and experiential approach contrasts significantly with the well-intentioned but, I think, fatally flawed approach to ordinary role models promoted in contemporary civics textbooks. Contemporary civics textbooks do an admirable job of at least gesturing toward the importance of ordinary role models. In reviewing five of the most popular civics books from this decade, I discovered they all placed significant emphasis on ordinary people doing great things, under the various headings of "Teens in Action" and "American Biographies" (Glencoe/ McGraw-Hill 2005), "The Power of One" (Wolfson 2005), "Young Citizens in Action" and "Biography" (Hartley and Vincent 2005), "Students Make a Difference: The Active Citizen" and "Citizen Profiles" (Davis et al. 2005), and "You Can Make a Difference" (McClenaghan 2003). Each of these textbooks promotes a much more active, engaged, and 'ordinary' vision of effective citizenship than did comparable civics books from the 1950s that I reviewed—including 1950s editions of some of these same textbooks—which had no such 'profiles' or resources. *Youth Faces American Citizenship* from 1956, by contrast, emphasizes the civic importance of developing a "pleasing personality" and a good smile, and teaches students how to be good dates (Alilunas and Sayre 1956).

Despite contemporary textbook publishers' evident good intentions, however, there are at least three enormous problems with a textbook-based, one-paragraph 'young citizens in action' approach. First, given standardized curriculum and especially standardized testing mandates, teachers have no incentive—in fact, they have a negative incentive—to use these textbook resources. By definition, 'ordinary,' unknown people will not be included in state curriculum frameworks or national content standards. When I taught eighth grade, therefore, I skipped over almost every one of the sidebars, insets, and pages emphasizing active citizenship because they did not fit into the curriculum calendar or district 'pacing guide.' It is hard to see how and why teachers might be led to make a different choice. This is a significant problem as well, of course, for teachers' more significant incorporation of ordinary role models into their classrooms and curricula as I describe above. But paradoxically, the greater effort, resources, and allocation of curricular time required to incorporate meaningful role models via experiential education may actually increase its potential for implementation in comparison to the relatively minor cost of reading a paragraph about 'teens in action.' In the latter case, no one in charge of developing state curriculum frameworks or finalizing the district pacing guide, say, would explicitly set aside time to incorporate these various examples of civic engagement. The assumption would be that these examples would naturally be woven in—but the curriculum is inevitably already so overstuffed, and assessments are frequently so high-stakes, that these sidebars become an obvious candidate for automatic elimination by the teacher. In the former case, by contrast, no one could or would assume that teachers will simply 'find the time.' If it is agreed that students should be learning about, developing relationships with, and practicing the skills or strategies of local, ordinary role models, then it would also be agreed that time must be set aside in the curriculum for teachers to help facilitate this. If time is not set aside, then it is clear to everyone that this is not a priority. If time is set aside, then teachers get the clear message that this is a priority and, with appropriate professional support, are more likely to do it.

A second and even more significant flaw with these paragraph-long snapshots of 'young people making a difference' in textbooks is that they are inevitably superficial, even *pro forma*. How much are students actually going to learn or get inspired by reading a paragraph about what some other teenager did? A single paragraph cannot teach students actual techniques or strategies for civic empowerment. In fact, four to five sentences cannot actually achieve *any* of the civic purposes discussed in the beginning of this chapter. They may be nicely symbolic of the importance of individual citizens' contributions to public life, but a snippet of this length cannot be anything more than symbolic.

Third, these references in textbooks to ordinary people whom no student actually knows utterly misunderstand the source and nature of role models. As we saw, role models are people with whom students feel a direct connection, usually because they know them personally. Four or five, even ten, sentences about a random teenager in a textbook are not going to promote the kind of personal identification and change in behavior that we hope for from young people who are inspired to emulate actual role models. Thus, the 'ordinary role model' approach when mediated by textbooks may end up being the worst of both worlds. Young people neither learn about extraordinary heroes who help them envision the expanse of human possibility, say, nor do they identify true role models (usually people they know personally, not just people like them such as random teenagers in a textbook) in order to learn to emulate them.

What can be done, then, in the context of a traditional, textbook-oriented, even coverage-driven civic education class that cannot or will not take on the more ambitious agenda I outlined above? In this case—and in fact, in every case, I believe—students should learn about collective action as an essential lever of power in civic life. Ordinary role models and even extraordinary heroes are rarely lone actors. Collective action by scores, hundreds, thousands, even millions of people frequently underlie the success of an apparently individual civic actor. Julian Bond makes this point in a compelling way with respect to Martin Luther King Jr.:

> Americans long for single, heroic leadership, the lone figure delivering salvation. King became that figure, but he came from a movement that was group-centered, representing democracy at its best. He did not march from Selma to Montgomery by himself. He did not speak to an empty field at the March on Washington. There were thousands marching with him and before him, and thousands more who one by one and two by two did the work that preceded the triumphal march. Black Americans did not just march to freedom; we worked our way to civil rights through the difficult business of organizing. Registering voters one by one. Building a solid organization, block by block. Building interracial coalitions, state by state. (Bond 1993)

In this respect, teaching about Martin Luther King Jr. *requires* that one simultaneously teach about the thousands of ordinary Americans who sustained the civil rights movement and actually ensured its victories. It is simply factually inaccurate—and civically disempowering—to teach in any other way.

This kind of curricular change could, at least in theory, be made fairly easily by reframing history and civics textbooks' civic narratives. Right now, they tend to focus relentlessly on the individual, neglecting the collective action lying at the heart of individuals' achievements. Sam Wineburg and Chauncey Monte-Sano thus complain with respect to Rosa Parks:

> Instead of a story about a mass-organizing movement—a narrative of empowerment and agency among ordinary people who in a single weekend printed 52,500 leaflets (enough, and then some, for every member of Montgomery's black community) and distributed them to churches while organizing phone trees and Monday morning car pools so that no one would have to walk to work—we meet the singular figure of Mrs. Parks. Together with King, she sets out on her civil rights walkabout, only to return to lead a passive and faceless people in their struggle for racial equality. (Wineburg and Monte-Sano 2008, 1201–1202)

This is a tragedy, but it is totally unnecessary. Textbooks could tell Rosa Parks' story as clearly, in the same amount of space, and much more accurately, by framing her actions as part of a "mass-organizing movement" of essentially ordinary people. Herb Kohl provides a model of how to do this in an essay that attempts to recover the collective action narrative by rewriting the story traditionally told about Rosa Parks' action.

The revised version is still about Rosa Parks, but it is also about the African American people of Montgomery, Alabama. It takes the usual, individualized version of the Rosa Parks tale and puts it in the context of a coherent, community-based social struggle. This does not diminish Rosa Parks in any way. It places her, however, in the midst of a consciously planned movement for social change. (Kohl 1995, 46)

Howard Zinn has similarly and famously done this for all of American history in his best-selling *People's History of the United States* (Zinn 1980). *The Covenant Curriculum: A Study of Black Democratic Action*, a recent civic curriculum initiative supported by Tavis Smiley and Cornell West, also promotes this historical civic understanding of the power of the collective. Assignment #2 in the curriculum, for example, states:

Black Democratic Action requires individual courage and collective organization. Therefore all of our work for human dignity and freedom must be informed by the extraordinary efforts of ordinary men and women who served and sacrificed for the precious ideals of democracy. You are charged to find and interview a person in your family or community who was a part of the black freedom movements of the 1960s and 1970s. (West and Glaude 2006)

In sum, I believe that extraordinary heroes and ordinary role models can be used in concert to promote the civic purposes listed in the beginning of this chapter. This is in part because they can each can find their own place and serve their own set of purposes in the curriculum, but even more because they can actually reinforce each other by helping young people (and in fact all citizens) come to understand that even the most profound civic changes, led by the greatest and most extraordinary of human beings, are usually brought about by the collective work of 'ordinary' people working together—of "men and women obscure in their labor," as Obama put it in his Inaugural Address (Obama 2009). Churchill commented about scientific heroes, "The throne is occupied; but by a throng" (Churchill 1925). I think this is terrific. The throne *should* be occupied by a throng—not just in science, but in all human endeavor—because it is in fact the throng that has the greatest capacity to bring about and sustain change in a democratic society. In this respect, as in so many others, it will be fascinating to see how President Obama and his team continue to mobilize and empower the 'throngs' who swept him into office. If the almost-daily e-mails I receive from David Plouffe are any indication—including the most recent ones urging me to attend a house meeting so supporters can "plan on how they can bring change to both Washington and their own communities" (Obama for America 2008)—this vision of cooperation and even codependence between an individual leader and the democratic masses may be encountering a renaissance. How this will affect civic education in schools, of course, is another conundrum indeed.

NOTES

1. I would like to thank Edward Copenhagen, Shari Dickstein, Leslee Friedman, Judith Keneman, Cynthia Levinson, Carla Lillvik, Linda Lyons, Jal Mehta, Meredith Mira, Justin Reich, Anna Rosefsky, and the members of the Penn Global Citizenship group for their considerable assistance with and contributions to this essay.
2. It is possible that Barack Obama's presidency will change this, but at this writing it is way too soon to know or tell.
3. I am passing over here whether our selective civic memory about his principles and practices is itself some cause for concern or even shame.
4. Daniel Boorstin wryly notes in this regard, "The universal lament of aging men in all epochs . . . is that greatness has become obsolete" (Boorstin 1968, 326).
5. As Sam Wineburg and Chauncey Monte-Sano put it, "We doubt that many high school students in an all-white classroom in Montana (or anywhere else) would recognize the King who told David Halberstam in 1967 'that the vast majority of white Americans are racists, either consciously or unconsciously'; the King who linked American racism to American militarism, calling both, along with economic exploitation, the 'triple evils' of American society; the King who characterized the bloodbath in Vietnam as a 'bitter, colossal contest for supremacy' with America as the 'supreme culprit'; or the King who in a speech two months before his assassination accused America of committing 'more war crimes almost than any nation in the world'" (Wineburg and Monte-Sano 2008, 1201).
6. Unfortunately, there's little way to get a longitudinal view of young people's attitudes toward heroes—at least with regard to their selection of a family member or other person known to themselves—since prior to 2000, the poll question specifically excluded family and friends from the list of possible answers: "What one man (woman) that you have heard or read about, alive today in any part of the world, do you admire the most, not including any of your relatives or personal friends?" Data is also unavailable on the percentage of youth who declined to name any person they admired prior to 2000.
7. Even this notion of heroism, which at least highlights the accomplishment of a heroic deed, seems to have become optional in contemporary usage. The fifteen-year-old "Harvard Heroes" program, whose purpose is to "spotlight[] exceptional staff members while emphasizing the excellence required to run an institution of Harvard's immense scale and complexity," recently 'honored' an editorial assistant "for her role as calendar editor for the *Harvard Gazette*" (Farrell 2008). I have no doubt that this woman does an excellent editing job. To designate her as a 'hero,' however, suggests an almost irretrievable debasement of the term.
8. In 1949, when the question was first asked and coded for this kind of response, only 1 percent of survey respondents named a family member or friend as the man that they "have heard or read about, living today, in any part of the world" whom they admired the most. Similarly, 3 percent of survey respondents named a family member or friend when asked about their most admired woman. These numbers stayed steady in 1955, the next year that results were broken down in this way. By 1966, however, the numbers started creeping up—3 percent for men and 5.6 percent for women—and they more than doubled again for men by 2006, when a full 9 percent of those identified were family or friends. Women have held steady at around 6 percent since the 1970s; I conjecture this is because of a shrinking gender gap with respect to recognition and publicity of public figures (original analysis of Gallup Organization 1949, 1955, 1966, 1977, 2006).

9. Although I am confining my discussion for the sake of clarity and brevity to the United States, there is ample evidence that young people in Europe also overwhelmingly select their parents, and then others directly known to them, when asked to identify heroes or role models (Bucher 1997; Bricheno and Thornton 2007).

10. It should be noted, though, that Kelly thinks that heroes arise in democracies nonetheless. "Democratic regimes have never lacked heroes. They have always found people who pledge their lives, fortunes, and sacred honor to establish governments based on democratic principles and people who give their last full measure of devotion to see that these governments endure" (Kelly 1997, 347).

11. Thomas Carlyle would be appalled, albeit unsurprised, by this utter rejection of heroes' desirability in a democratic society. He famously castigated "Democracy, which means despair of ever finding any Heroes to govern you, and contented putting up with the want of them" (Carlyle 1918, 249).

12. I will refrain here from entering the fraught whisky vs. beer vs. latte debates that arose during the 2008 Democratic presidential primary between the Clinton and Obama camps (Parsons and McCormick 2008).

BIBLIOGRAPHY

Addis, A. "Role Models and the Politics of Recognition." *University of Pennsylvania Law Review* 144, no. 4 (1996): 1377–1468.

Alilunas, L. J., and J. W. Sayre. *Youth Faces American Citizenship.* Chicago: J. B. Lippincott, 1956.

Anderson, K. J., and D. Cavallaro. "Parents of Pop Culture? Children's Heroes and Role Models." *Childhood Education* no. 78, 2002: 161–168.

Averett, J. "Facets: Today's Kids and Hero Worship, Who Can They Look Up To?" *The English Journal* 74, no. 5 (1985): 23.

Axthelm, P. "Where Have All the Heroes Gone?" *Newsweek*, August 1979.

Bond, J. "Remember The Man and The Hero, Not Just Half The Dream." *The Seattle Times*, 4 April 1993. http://seattletimes.nwsource.com/special/mlk/perspectives/reflections/bond.html (accessed 21 August 2008).

Boorstin, D. 1968. "From Hero to Celebrity: Human Pseudo-Event." In *Heroes and Anti-Heroes: A Reader in Depth*, ed. H. Lubin, 325–40. San Francisco: Chandler Publishing Company.

Bricheno, P., and M. Thornton. "Role Model, Hero, or Champion? Children's Views Concerning Role Models." *Educational Research* 49, no.4 (2007): 383–396.

Browne, R. B., and M. W. Fishwick. *The Hero in Transition.* Bowling Green, OH: Bowling Green University Press, 1983.

Bucher, A. A. "The Influence of Models in Forming Moral Identity." *International Journal of Educational Research* 27, no. 7 (1997): 619–627.

Carlyle, T. *On Heroes, Hero-Worship and the Heroic in History.* New York: Frederick A. Stokes, 1893.

———. 1918 [1843]. *Past and Present.* New York: Charles Scribner's Sons.

Churchill, W. *Mass Effects in Modern Life.* 1925. http://www.teachingamericanhistory.org/library/index.asp?documentprint=1032 (accessed 16 August 2008).

Clark, N. I., J. B. Edmonson, and A. Dondineau. *Civics for Americans.* New York: Macmillan, 1954.

CNN. *CNN Heroes: A Note to Educators.* CNN, 21 February 2008. http://www.cnn.com/2008/LIVING/studentnews/02/08/heroes.educator.note/index.html (accessed 16 August 2008).

Cowen, T. "The New Heroes and Role Models." *Reason*, May 2000. http://findar-ticles.com/p/articles/mi_m1568/is_1_32/ai_62162015/pg_1?tag=artBody;col1 (accessed 15 August 2008).

Davis, J. E., P. Fernlund, and P. Woll. *Civics: Government and Economics in Action*. 2005 ed. Upper Saddle River, NJ: Prentice Hall, 2005.

Dimond, S. E., and E. F. Pflieger. *Civics for Citizens: Annotated Edition*. Rev. ed. Philadelphia: J. B. Lippincott, 1974.

Edelstein, A. *Everybody Is Sitting on the Curb: How and Why America's Heroes Disappeared*. New York: Praeger Publishers, 1996.

Emerson, R. W. *Representative Men: Seven Lectures*. Leipzig: Bernhard Tauch-nitz, 1907.

Farrell, A. "Who Does Harvard Call a Hero?" *The Harvard Community Resource*, July 2008: 1, 4.

Fishwick, M. W. *The Hero, American Style*. New York: D. McKay, 1969.

Gallup Organization. *Survey by Gallup Organization, December 2–December 7, 1949*. iPoll Databank: The Roper Center for Public Opinion Research, Univer-sity of Connecticut, 1949. http://www.ropercenter.uconn.edu.ezp-prod1.hul. harvard.edu/ipoll.html (accessed 5 December 2008).

———. *Survey by Gallup Organization, December 8–December 13, 1955*. iPoll Databank: The Roper Center for Public Opinion Research, University of Con-necticut, 1955. http://www.ropercenter.uconn.edu.ezp-prod1.hul.harvard.edu/ ipoll.html (accessed 5 December 2008).

———. *Survey by Gallup Organization, December 8–December 13, 1966*. iPoll Databank: The Roper Center for Public Opinion Research, University of Con-necticut, 1966. http://www.ropercenter.uconn.edu.ezp-prod1.hul.harvard.edu/ ipoll.html (accessed 5 December 2008).

———. *Survey by Gallup Organization, December 9–December 12, 1977*. iPoll Databank: The Roper Center for Public Opinion Research, University of Con-necticut, 1977. http://www.ropercenter.uconn.edu.ezp-prod1.hul.harvard.edu/ ipoll.html (accessed 5 December 2008).

———. *Survey by Gallup Organization, December 11–December 14, 2006*. iPoll Databank: The Roper Center for Public Opinion Research, University of Con-necticut, 2006. http://www.ropercenter.uconn.edu.ezp-prod1.hul.harvard.edu/ ipoll.html (accessed 5 December 2008).

Gibbon, P. H. *A Call to Heroism: Renewing America's Vision of Greatness*. New York: Atlantic Monthly Press, 2002.

Giraffe Heroes Project. "Kids Page: Guided Tour Stop 1." Langley, WA: Giraffe Heroes Project, 2008. http://www.giraffe.org/guidedtour1_text.html (accessed 5 December 2008).

———. "Kids Page: Guided Tour Stop 2." Langley, WA: Giraffe Heroes Project, 2008. Available from http://www.giraffe.org/guidedtour2_text.html (accessed 5 December 2008).

Glencoe/McGraw-Hill. *Civics Today: Citizenship, Economics, and You*. New York: Glencoe, 2005.

Glicksberg, C. I. "The Tragic Hero." In *Heroes and Anti-Heroes: A Reader in Depth*, ed. H. Lubin, 356–66. Scranton, PA: Chandler Publishing, 1968.

Gomes, P. "Foreword." In *A Call to Heroism: Renewing America's Vision of Greatness*, by P. H. Gibbon, xi–xix. New York: Atlantic Monthly Press, 2002.

Hanson, C. "Where Have All the Heroes Gone?" *Columbia Journalism Review* 34, no. 6 (1996): 45–48.

Hartley, W. H., and W. S. Vincent. *Holt American Civics*. New York: Holt, Rine-hart and Winston, 2005.

Hook, S. *The Hero in History: A Study in Limitation and Possibility*. New York: John Day, 1943.

James, W. "Great Men, Great Thoughts and the Environment." *The Atlantic Monthly* 46, no. 276 (1880): 441–59.

Kahne, J., and J. Westheimer. "Teaching Democracy: What Schools Need to Do." *Phi Delta Kappan* 85, no. 1 (2003): 34–40, 57–66.

Kammen, M. G. *Mystic Chords of Memory: The Transformation of Tradition in American Culture.* 1st ed. New York: Knopf, 1991.

Kanner, E. Day care report re: MLK. Email from E. Kanner to M. Levinson. Boston, 7 March 2007.

Kelly, C. "Rousseau's Case For and Against Heroes." *Polity* 30, no. 2 (1997): 347–366.

———. *Rousseau as Author: Consecrating One's Life to the Truth.* Chicago: University of Chicago Press, 2003.

Kemper, T. D. "Reference Groups, Socialization, and Achievement." *American Sociological Review* no. 33 (1968): 31–45.

Klapp, O. E. "Hero Worship in America." *American Sociological Review* 14, no. 1 (1949): 53–62.

Kohl, H. *Should We Burn Babar? Essays on Children's Literature and the Power of Stories.* New York: The New Press, 1995.

Levinson, M. "The Civic Achievement Gap." CIRCLE Working Paper 51, Jonathan M. Tisch College of Citizenship and Public Service, Tufts University, Medford, MA, 2007. http://civicyouth.org/PopUps/WorkingPapers/WP51Levinson.pdf.

Lockwood, P., and Z. Kunda. "Superstars and Me: Predicting the Impact of Role Models on the Self." *Journal of Personality and Social Psychology* 73, no. 1 (1997): 91–103.

———. "Outstanding Role Models: Do They Inspire or Demoralize Us?" In *Psychological Perspectives on Self and Identity*, ed. A. Tesser, R. B. Felson, and J. M. Suls., 147–171. Washington, DC: American Psychological Association, 2000.

Loewen, J. W. *Lies My Teacher Told Me: Everything Your American History Textbook Got Wrong.* New York: The New Press, 1995.

Lyons, L. "No Heroes in the Beltway." *Gallup*, 30 July 2002. http://www.gallup.com/poll/6487/Heroes-Beltway.aspx (accessed 15 August 2008).

———. "Results for Teens, Ages 13–17, Most Admired Men + Women." Fax to M. Levinson. Princeton: August 21, 2008.

Marr, A. "Where Have All of the Heroes Gone?" *New Statesman*, 2 October 1998, 25–26.

McClenaghan, W. A. *Magruder's American Government.* Boston: Allyn and Bacon, 1953.

———. *Magruder's American Government.* Upper Saddle River, NJ: Prentice Hall, 2003.

McDorman, T. F., K. Casper, A. Logan, and S. McGinley. "Where Have All the Heroes Gone?" *Journal of Sport and Social Issues* 30, no. 2 (2006): 197–218.

Moreau, J. *Schoolbook Nation: Conflicts over American History Textbooks from the Civil War to the Present.* Ann Arbor: The University of Michigan Press, 2003.

Newport, F. "Martin Luther King Jr.: Revered More After Death Than Before." *Gallup News Service*, 16 July 2006. http://www.gallup.com/poll/20920/Martin-Luther-King-Jr-Revered-More-After-Death-Than-Before.aspx (accessed 18 August 2008).

Obama, Barack. 2008. "Remarks of Senator Barack Obama: Super Tuesday." Chicago. 5 February 2008. http://www.barackobama.com/2008/02/05/remarks_of_senator_barack_obam_46.php (accessed 8 December 2008).

———. "Inaugural Address." Washington, DC, 20 January 2009.

Obama for America. "Barack Obama and Joe Biden: The Change We Need." Obama for America, 2008. http://www.barackobama.com (accessed 7 December 2008).

————. "Barack Obama, Change We Need, Change Is Coming." Obama for America, 2008. http://my.barackobama.com/page/content/changeiscoming/ (accessed 10 December 2008).

Ostroushko, M., with E. Botein and B. Shapiro. "The Promised Land: Different Takes on the Legacy of Martin Luther King." In *The Promised Land*, ed. M. B. Kirchner. United States: Launch Minneapolis, 2009.

Pangle, L. S., and T. L. Pangle. "What the American Founders Have to Teach Us About Schooling for Democratic Citizenship." In *Rediscovering the Democratic Purposes of Education*, ed. L. M. McDonnell, P. M. Timpane, and R. Benjamin, 21–46. Lawrence: University Press of Kansas, 2000.

Parsons, C., and J. McCormick. "Blue-Collar Vote Tough for Obama: Group More Likely to Give Clinton Edge." *Chicago Tribune*, 10 February 2008.

Pomper, G. M. *Ordinary Heroes and American Democracy.* New Haven, CT: Yale University Press, 2004.

Porpora, D. V. "Personal Heroes, Religion, and Transcendental Metanarratives." *Sociological Forum* 11, no. 2 (1996): 209–229.

Rawls, J. *A Theory of Justice.* Cambridge, MA: Belknap Press of Harvard University Press, 1971.

Robison, J. "Teens Search for Role Models Close to Home." Gallup, 2003. http://www.gallup.com/poll/8584/Teens-Search-Role-Models-Close-Home.aspx (accessed 17 August 2008).

Schlesinger Jr., A. M. "The Decline of Heroes." In *Heroes and Anti-Heroes: A Reader in Depth*, ed. H. Lubin, 341–351. San Francisco: Chandler Publishing, 1968.

Schwartz, B. "The Reconstruction of Abraham Lincoln." In *Collective Remembering*, ed. D. Middleton and D. Edwards, 81–107. London: Sage, 1990.

Silverman, W. M. "Where Have All the Heroes Gone?" *Journal of the American Osteopathic Association* 103, no. 1 (2003): 27–28.

Speizer, J. J. "Role Models, Mentors, and Sponsors: The Elusive Concepts." *Signs* 6, no. 4 (1981): 692–712.

Truchard, J. "Where Have All the Heroes Gone?" *Control Engineering*, March 2005. http://www.controleng.com/article/CA509812.html (accessed 4 December 2008)

Tyack, D. "School for Citizens: The Politics of Civic Education from 1790 to 1990." In *E Pluribus Unum? Contemporary and Historical Perspectives on Immigrant Political Incorporation*, ed. G. Gerstle and J. Mollenkopf, 331–370. New York: Russell Sage Foundation, 2001.

Wecter, D. *The Hero in America: A Chronicle of Hero-Worship.* New York: Charles Scribner's Sons, 1941.

West, C., and E. S. Glaude Jr. *Standard Covenant Curriculum: A Study of Black Democratic Action.* Covenant with Black America, 2006. http://www.covenantwithblackamerica.com/resources/covenant_StandardCovenantCurriculum.doc (accessed 10 December 2008).

Wineburg, S., and C. Monte-Sano. "'Famous Americans': The Changing Pantheon of American Heroes." *Journal of American History* 94, no. 4 (2008): 1186–1202.

Wolfson, S. C. *Civics for Today: Participation and Citizenship.* Rev. ed. New York: Amsco School Publications, 2005.

Yancy, A., J. M. Siegel, and K. L. McDaniel. "Role Models, Ethnic Identity, and Health-Risk Behaviors in Urban Adolescents." *Archives in Pediatrics and Adolescent Medicine* 156, no. 1 (2002): 55–61.

Zimmerman, J. *Whose America? Culture Wars in the Public Schools.* Cambridge, MA: Harvard University Press, 2002.

Zinn, H. *A People's History of the United States.* New York: Harper & Row, 1980.

Part III
Moral and Religious Education

9 Privilege, Well-being, and Participation in Higher Education

Harry Brighouse and Paula McAvoy

An undergraduate degree from an elite university in a developed country provides access to membership of elites. The managers and leaders of national and international businesses, of government departments and national governments, of NGOs and of intergovernmental organizations are almost all drawn from the ranks of those who attended such universities. Many, if not, most, graduates of such universities can expect to command and consume far more resources than most of the world's population, and to have asymmetric power and authority over others, many of whom live in other countries and on other continents. In an economy that is already highly globalized, and in which skilled elites are geographically highly mobile, it is more likely than ever that they will spend some portion of their lives in other countries than those in which they were raised.

Membership of elites is not earned. Whether or not one can join the elite depends a great deal on luck. Whether one has the right kinds of parents, has engaged with schooling in the right way, where one is born, and whether one was born with the native talents that happen to be highly valued in the existing international market, all play a large role in determining one's prospects. With unearned privilege and asymmetric power come great responsibilities that are not always readily understood by those who bear them. Universities confer access to the privileges of elite membership. Do they, though, foster understanding of the accompanying responsibilities?

Until the 1960s American universities, and especially elite universities, took themselves to be in *loco parentis* and evinced a concern with the development of their students' characters. There was not a little of the noblesse oblige about this—in fact, there had long been a ready acknowledgement that higher education was a privilege, not a right, and that those who enjoyed it incurred obligations to others. There was also a strong element of paternalism; it was widely thought that adults in general, and college administrators and professors in particular, knew better what was good for students than the students themselves.

The 1960s saw an end to the role of *in loco parentis*. Regulations of dormitory life were relaxed, as was regulation of campus life generally, including of the curriculum. Most professors came to see their role as arm's-length from the students, to teach their subject without interfering with their personal lives. Similarly, universities backed off the role of character formation. Students go to college primarily to enhance their career prospects, and that motive is not questioned or undermined by the organization of campus life.

Recent years have seen modest moves back toward the more traditional approach to campus life. We welcome this, and would welcome less modest steps even more. The current chapter attempts to justify these modest moves on normative grounds. First we present an argument for a concern with character formation grounded in the claim that the traditional view that higher education was a privilege, not a right, was correct; and, we would add, that in the current era of globalized economic and political power, it is even more urgent to understand the responsibilities that accompany that privilege. Those who enjoy the benefits of higher education incur a debt to many of those who do not, and forming their character in a way that increases the probability that they will discharge that debt is a legitimate, and desirable, aim of higher educational institutions. Second, we present an argument that, independently of the privilege students enjoy, it is appropriate for college administrators to organize campus life paternalistically, to enhance the students' long-term prospects for well-being. Then we shall make some comments about what sort of actions and initiatives universities might undertake in the light of these arguments. Finally, we'll explore the rather obvious objection that our arguments are unduly paternalistic with respect to the students; that the reversion to some element of *in loco parentis* involves the university in too much parenting.

THE ARGUMENT FROM PRIVILEGE

> It is sordid and ungrateful . . . to receive an education at the public expense, and then devote it to purely private ends. (W. F. Allen 1890)

Higher education (HE) makes an important contribution to success, as measured in terms of lifetime expected incomes and access to interesting jobs. The precise amount of the wage premium attached to a degree is unclear: what is clear is that it is substantial. A recent Organization for Economic Cooperation and Development report (OECD) claims a premium in the UK of 17 percent (exceptionally high for OECD countries),[1] taking into account foregone earnings, costs of tuition, and tax rates (2002); and a Labour Force Survey study shows graduates ages twenty to twenty-four earning (gross) 25 percent more than those with A-level (and equivalent) qualifications.[2] Even if we assumed as low as a 10 percent all-things-considered premium, that is a substantial benefit, especially when combined with the relatively more interesting and autonomous jobs that are available to the HE graduate.[3] The premium attached to attending elite, as opposed to non-elite, institutions is almost certainly higher.

In the US the premium attached to completing higher education is even greater. Graduates with bachelor degrees can expect lifetime earnings 70 percent higher than high school graduates, and 100 percent higher than high school dropouts. Professional (further) degrees (such as MBAs, LLBs and MDs) yield lifetime earnings three times that of a high school graduate (see Day and Newberger 2002 for extensive data). These gross figures obscure considerable differences among kinds of degree and also among institutions. The premium is higher for science than for arts graduates, and it may be higher for graduates of elite than for graduates of low-prestige institutions. And variation itself, of course, varies over time and across countries.

Is this premium caused by an increased supply of human capital? Some of it must be. But a lot of it, we know, is about credentialism—universities playing the role that employers would otherwise have to play in preparing students for work, and playing another role of assuring social closure. Rapid increases in HE participation in wealthy democracies have always been driven by government action. Governments are under pressure from non-college-educated voters who see HE as a route to social mobility for their children and from college-educated voters who see it as a means of social closure.

Whatever the size of the premium, it is an artifice of the design of tax-transfer policy. As one would expect, the OECD estimates that HE has much a lower monetary benefit in those countries with more progressive tax-transfer policies. It is also an artifice of the private costs of higher education; if students had to pay the full cost of their tuition, that would make some inroads into the net monetary benefit. In principle it should be possible to design a tax-transfer regime in which the income maximizer was indifferent to, or even averse to, higher education. All this gives us a reason to be rather cautious in assuming that much of the premium is about increased human capital (though this is not to deny that human capital might be being increased while students are in college). Regardless, HE is highly segmented, and students, teachers, and employers are well aware of the purposes of the different segments. It is probably just as good if not better to attend UW-Madison at a low price as to attend Harvard at a high price, partly because UW–Madison at a low price enables you, if successful, to enter a graduate program at Harvard or somewhere similar. But attending UW Parkside is worse than Harvard at a high price, and this is widely understood. Similar segmentation occurs within the UK and other mass HE markets, and is well-enough understood in the culture, that it is able to play the sorting and social closure role that the Marxist conception assumes.

HE is required not only to enter or stay in the elite; it is required in order to have a reasonably secure sub-elite position. Once it has become standard for large numbers of people to use HE, employers are free to use the sorting effects of HE completion to screen potential employees. In terms of the skills, traits, and dispositions required, few jobs *intrinsically* require HE. But if HE is a general expectation, it makes sense for potential employers to allow governments and parents to bear the direct costs and potential employees the opportunity costs of education, and to disregard anyone who has not borne those costs—not only lawyers, accountants, journalists, chemists, and engineers, but also managers, technicians, nurses, and police officers. However, once employers use college completion as a gatekeeping mechanism, as they are bound to in an era of mass HE, this creates insuperable barriers for those who do not take up HE. To overstate the case, but not by much, there is a brief opportunity in one's late teens or early twenties, rejecting which makes it near impossible to advance beyond a certain level within the occupational structure; mass higher education rigidifies this fact. This is especially serious for those children whom school does not suit.

In sum, HE, and elite HE in particular, confers considerable private advantages to those who take it up. Those who take it up already generally come from the most advantaged sectors of society. Their advantages prima facie operate to the detriment of those who do not take up HE. What could justify a social institution, participation in which brings such a large private return, but the barriers to participation in which are substantial? It seems to us that there is, in fact, a very natural justification; that the private returns can be turned to the benefit of a larger public, and in particular to those who do not themselves participate. Requiring high standards for admissions to MD programs and allowing successful applicants to earn remarkably high wages as well as to enjoy an interesting and high-status position in society is justified if it produces effective doctors who serve others well. Similarly so for lawyers, businesspeople, agricultural consultants, and professors. Something like John Rawls's (1971) difference principle seems appropriate: society does right to allow some to get advantages that others do not get, if those advantages end up redounding to the benefit of the least advantaged.

But do the benefits of higher education redound to the benefit of the least advantaged? It all depends on two things: the structure of the economy, which includes the structure of the tax/benefit system and the regulatory framework within which the economy operates. An economy in which the CEO of a large company nets 10 times the (net) income of the average worker in that company appears to more closely meet the demands of the difference principle than one in which he nets 500 times the net income of the average worker. Regulation, or transfers, that reduce income inequalities while still permitting the incentives needed to spur production work to the benefit of the least advantaged. Tax cuts that essentially create rents for high-income workers who would have acted much the same way even at higher tax rates do not. The second factor concerns the motivations of those workers whose talents are best rewarded in the existing social environment, whatever that is. A society governed by a public service ethos in which those with marketable talents generally assume that, while they are permitted to pursue their own interests to some extent, they have considerable duties to the less advantaged generated by their own good fortune, is one in which we can predict that they are more likely to turn their productive talents to the use of those who are less advantaged. A brilliant surgeon might choose to earn 200k per annum working in a public facility rather than ten times that amount providing cosmetic surgery or heart surgery for the very wealthy. A brilliant mathematician might choose to teach mathematics on a public school teacher's income rather than work on Wall Street.

Universities are implicated in providing access to all sorts of socially constructed benefits. They are ill-placed to influence the structure of the economy. But they are well-placed to influence the structure of the motivations of the students they teach, to promote an ethos of public service, a sense of privilege and of what the duties are that accompany it. This, we think, is what they should do.

THE ARGUMENT FROM WELL-BEING

> In short, a curriculum is not complete which does not move the Eros, as well as the mind of the young, from where it is to where it might better be. (Schwab 1978)

Our second argument is more conservative in that it calls for a return to a former understanding of an 'educated self' that addresses the intellectual and moral development of the undergraduate. This is a response to the fractured environment of the modern research university in which faculty members are primarily focused on their own research and peer approval, leaving the undergraduate student body to devolve into what is often times a self-destructive, anti-intellectual, conformity-driven party culture.

It is difficult to know exactly how pervasive this behavior is on university campuses, and there are certainly many intellectually engaged students who make good decisions and are eager to learn. At the same time there is significant evidence that shows when the university takes a laissez-faire approach to the student ethos, they place 18-year-olds into a hedonistic crucible and are consequently creating well-positioned, but unhappy, people. In *Female Chauvinist Pigs*, Ariel Levy (2006) reports that the previously male "raunch" culture of sexual conquest has been embraced by young women who appear to delight in their own exploitation and unabashedly use men for sex. In *Unhooked*, Laura Sessions Stepp (2007) details how young women negotiate the 'hook-up culture' of high schools and colleges and argues that men and women who engage in this sex-without-dating behavior lie to themselves when they think there are no emotional consequences and are not, as other generations did, practicing how to be intimate and form lasting relationships. Donna Freitas of St. Michael's College in Vermont explains that:

Sexual promiscuity is the elephant in the dorm room: Every student knows that it's there one way or another—pressure, expectation, reality—but is either afraid to face the fact or too ashamed to admit that he fits the profile, or doesn't. If a student feels dissatisfied with the campus ethic of hedonism, he may well assume that something must be wrong with him because, after all, isn't unrestricted sexual freedom the collegiate version of the Promised Land? (Freitas 2005)

Further, undergraduates today are part of a pornography generation that has grown up with the Internet, and they have received untold number of e-mails inviting them into pornography sites. This, plus explicit cable television, has contributed to the normalization of sex as a commodity. The hook-up culture Stepp describes is, in fact, about using others to get what you want and divorcing sex from any emotion whatsoever. If the primary avenue for making friends and having a social outlet is to drink, have casual sex, and "work hard, play hard," then students are left with the unfortunate choice of conforming in order to develop a social network, or resist and choose, to some extent, isolation.[4]

One response to this situation might be to say that students are adults, and so long as they are acting within the rules and expectations of the university, then it is not the university's job to regulate private life. We agree that 'regulation' of private life is an inappropriate response, but disagree that the status of legal adulthood eliminates the university's obligation to pay attention to the social development of students. When university administrators think of exerting their influence on the behavior of undergraduates, the discussion is often focused on what type of rules should be imposed and how they should be enforced. Certainly, immediate safety concerns warrant some attention to the basic codes of conduct. However, by assigning egregious behavior problems to the administration and intellectual development to the faculty, the university fails in its properly understood aim, to develop the educated person. Further, by not responding seriously to the social needs of undergraduate students, the university enables the anti-intellectual forces of a hyperindividual, hypersexualized marketplace to become the major moral influence on campus.

In the modern research university we consider one to be educated when she has completed the minimum credits for a degree. In this university-as-credentialing-agency model the students' freedom of choice is of primary importance. In the general education curriculum, students are given tremendous latitude to select from a menu of courses, which are often unrelated and simply aim to expose students to a breadth of ideas and disciplines.[5] These courses hold mastery of the content as the primary aim, and do little to consciously cultivate a particular type of character. When the degree becomes about obtaining the credential, the student is severed mind and body. The institution cares about courses passed, professors are focused on the content of the class, and the private lives of students are mostly ignored so long as they do not violate basic behavior codes. The tenure structure of the modern research university cultivates this faculty–student divide by encouraging professors to focus their gaze on their research and senior colleagues. Mentoring undergraduates, especially pre-tenure, receives no institutional approval.

This understanding of what it means to be educated is much weaker than the ideal of the educated self imagined by philosophers of education. We are not able to provide a complete discussion of the debates within the field, but argue instead that most representations of what it means to be educated include the development of intellectual and moral capacities. Educated people know how to think ethically, practice good self-care, reflect before they act, and critically think about the messages they receive in the modern world. Most importantly, educated people want to act justly. They do not justify their behavior for their own advantage and instead weigh their desires against ethical principles. Mastery of particular disciplines, of course, plays a role in developing the educated person, but the content is not separate from the moral aim, and rigorous study ought to engage students in discussion of the good and virtuous life.[6] This is not a call for a complete return to the nineteenth-century liberal arts curriculum, but a return to the idea that universities ought to reunite the mind of the student with her lived experiences and fuse right behavior with good thinking.

This understanding of the aim of a university education does not allow the institution to take a hands-off approach to the student culture. In fact, a university is obligated to consciously cultivate a climate that supports the development of the type of character we have described. To understand this obligation, the university must first accept that a student culture will develop whether or not the university interferes with it. If we are correct that a laissez-faire approach invites Budweiser and Bacardi to establish the culture through T-shirt giveaways at local bars and advertisements to spring break foam parties in Mexico, even if a minority of students participate, the party culture becomes high-profile behavior and the image of a 'normal' undergraduate experience. Some undergraduates enroll and are eager to participate in this culture, others are drawn in later, and still others hope to hold on to more traditional values. By allowing the values of the alcohol and pornography industry to dominate, the university makes it more difficult for traditional and middle-of-the-road students to flourish at the university. For those wanting to participate fully in the 'unrestricted freedom' of university life, the university supports the development of a character that is antithetical to its aims. Just as a business is held responsible for creating a safe work environment and cannot argue that, so long as employees are getting their work done, it is not the management's responsibility to monitor how they are treating each other, so too must the university cultivate a culture that supports the development of healthy, educated individuals.

Some readers may think that the environment we have described is not a bad environment, all things considered, or that we have mischaracterized it. One might think that the hook-up culture embodies a healthy balancing of sexual immediacy and deferred intimacy, given the interests students have in establishing long-term careers. Or one might think that we, and the journalists who write about it, exaggerate the hedonism and sexualization of campus culture.

The portrayal of campus life we have given is, we realize, incomplete. Some campuses exert considerable control over the cultural mores, partly through selecting students, and partly by enforcing strongly paternalistic rules. Even large public university campuses have very diverse student populations; movements like the Campus Crusade for Christ and the smaller left-wing political organizations provide countervailing influences to the corporate sponsorship of pornography and alcohol, and numerous students are able to construct intellectually and emotionally healthy microenvironments. But we think that the portrayal we have given captures some of the changeable reality of campus life. And we think that reality is deeply unhealthy for most though not all of the students involved in it.

If you disagree, you will find the substance of this part of our argument uninteresting. But you might still find the more fundamental argument interesting. The more fundamental argument is that the university should take considerable steps to shape students' attitudes and choices in ways that are likely to serve their well-being in the long term. If you think there is no need to do that because their choices already serve that interest, you should ask yourself whether, and to what extent, it would be legitimate for the university to exercise such power in the less happy circumstance in which prevailing environment is unhealthy.

WHAT IS TO BE DONE?

One way to respond to this argument would be to conceive of two kinds of programs: those that promote service and those that promote well-being and character. Another approach is more Deweyian and views these character attributes (service and well-being) as interconnected qualities of the educated self. Consequently, the best policies will work to develop both of these dispositions, not through rule making, but through the purposeful development of the curriculum and culture of the university.

One common theme arising out of our two arguments is the value of promoting cross-age interaction. The large university creates for the students a very unusual environment, one in which most of their daily interactions, and almost all of their intimate interactions, are with other people in the eighteen- to twenty-three-year-old age range. They are thus intensely exposed to the influences of others in that age group and the influences that those others mediate. No workplace, no family, and hardly any other social environment has this feature (even retirement homes tend to have a wider spread of ages, and probably of life experiences, than the undergraduate classes on most elite college campuses). A central aim is to expand and diversify the range of influences on the formation of the students' characters and attitudes. To that end, universities could design academic programs so that students interact with the same professor and with a cohort of students throughout their undergraduate careers. They might also create, as several smaller universities have done, faculty residences attached to undergraduate residences and encourage more faculty interaction in the lives of undergraduate.[7] This type of programming is fairly common within small liberal arts colleges, but is quite rare in larger research institutions. College halls and their faculty mentors might also become 'communities of service' in which, as part of their graduation requirements, residents are charged with identifying a local, national, or global problem and executing a program for change.[8] Encouraging faculty–student interaction beyond the classroom should have two outcomes. First, the student culture would be infused with adult role models who, we hope, have a greater understanding of well-being and could help counter the anti-intellectualism within the peer group. Second, as the faculty became more aware of the issues and concerns of their students, they could take this information into the classroom to, as Schwab suggests, move students "from where [they are] to where [they] might better be" (1978).

Universities might also restructure the general education curriculum to be less about the delivery of information in discrete courses, and more about engaging students in contemporary ethical and social problems—especially problems of interest to young adults. In 'foundational studies,' students would select interdisciplinary course clusters that focus on a particular issue.[9] One example might be a cluster called Love in the Modern World in which students would enroll in a psychology course on social relationships, a literature course that examines the origins and representations of romantic love, a sociology course on families, and a religious studies course focused on how different belief systems view spiritual and interpersonal love. In addition, the students in the cluster might have a discussion group in which they would read several journalistic accounts of the undergraduate hook-up culture and discuss how the information in the courses do and do not intersect. Or, clusters could have community components in which students might observe family court, work at a rape hotline, or organize a poetry reading on campus. Ideally, these cluster courses would be designed around questions that would help students think about how they ought to live as adults in the modern world in addition to introducing them to a variety of disciplinary lenses. Within these clusters students would have more interaction with each other and would build relationships within classrooms. In addition, given that professors know that these students are also working with three of their colleagues, when academic or behavioral issues arise, they might be able to address the problems as a group, rather than be left to deal with them alone.

Such policies reshape how the university views its obligations to students, but also obviously have implications for the role of the professor. We have already identified that one factor contributing to the laissez-faire ethos is that tenure requirements lure the focus of junior faculty away from engaging in student life. In large research universities it is easy for a student to go an entire four years with barely a personal word with a professor; and for many students it is difficult to engage with professors at all. Professors see research as their main job, teaching as something to be devolved to graduate students, and engagement with students on matters of personal life and career advice as no part of their job at all. Some of the measures above (for example, arranging academic schedules to make it more likely that professors encounter the same students several times in the course of their undergraduate careers) would make teaching more rewarding. We would also advocate measures such as release from administrative burdens to make space for more personal interactions with students, and tenure rewards for getting involved in, for example, the resident hall initiatives. We believe that daily and close interaction with people who have relatively stable lives, whose values are diverse, and many of whose values and ways of living are discordant with those promoted by the cultural forms with which the students have the most direct contact, would inject an alternative—and broadly speaking, healthy—influence into their lives.

There are also policies outside of the university that interfere with creating the type of character we describe. In most of the United States the drinking age is twenty-one, a fact that puts the university in the role of enforcing prohibition, rather than modeling moderation. With a drinking age of nineteen, a resident hall could create a policy that allows students to have drinks in the common area, but disallow drinking games and alcohol at parties.[10] In an environment in which more adults were interacting with students, the university could consciously create a culture of moderation and adult, rather than *Animal House*, drinking habits.[11] American universities could do more to advocate for a drinking policy that would be more conducive to the well-being of their student bodies. To help universities cultivate a character of public service, a national loan forgiveness policy for students who choose particular career paths would, at least, remove some of the disincentives for students who would leave school carrying debt. More helpful yet would be a national policy that would give all graduates who worked for five years in the public or nonprofit sectors a $15,000 stipend that would help offset the opportunity cost for choosing a service career. We are not in a position to fully argue for these national- or state-level policies, but hope that they illustrate the kind of policymaking that would contribute to reshaping the educational aims of a research university.

These suggestions have a common aim of using the university to (1) facilitate healthy, intellectual interaction between students; (2) provide students with more adult mentoring; and (3) encourage students to puzzle about how they ought to live in the world. Further, we argue that the university must take an active hand in molding the ethos of student life by actively resisting the culture of hedonism and self-interest promoted by popular culture targeted at young adults. Just as universities have taken action (although there is certainly room for improvement) to create an ethos of cultural tolerance on campus, so must they actively cultivate a climate that nurture students' well-being and their sense of obligation to serve those who enjoy fewer advantages than they do throughout their lives.

SHOULD THE UNIVERSITY ACT IN LOCO PARENTIS TO ADULTS?

Our analysis and proposals give rise to a very natural objection: that we are endorsing a level of paternalism that is unacceptable. Most students in universities are adults; they are legally eligible to drive, to vote, to marry, to join the armed forces, to choose whether or not to undergo higher education, and to do almost all the other things that adults do,[12] so they should be permitted to make their own judgments about how to live their lives. The institutions they attend have no business trying to shape or constrain their choices, except insofar as they must obey the law. This kind of reasoning was used in the 1960s and 1970s by students trying to break down the institution of *in loco parentis*; it could be used now to oppose the kinds of measures that we have suggested, and one of our arguments—the well-being argument—for them.

We believe that we can meet the objection.

Before explaining how, it is worth seeing exactly what the objection touches in our argument. Our argument from privilege is not paternalistic. The argument from privilege does not motivate the proposed reforms by appeal to the good of the students themselves, but by appeal to the good of others—those less-advantaged people to whom the students have stringent duties of justice. The idea is that the students are enjoying an unearned and artificially constructed advantage, and that advantaged is justified only if it redounds to the benefit of others who are less advantaged. The argument from privilege justifies reforms on the grounds that they make it more likely that the unearned benefits will, in fact, redound to the benefit of the less advantaged and will therefore more likely be justified. There is nothing paternalistic, or wrong, about placing conditions on receipt of such a benefit, especially when the recipient is in a position to refuse the whole package.

But our argument from well-being is indeed motivated by a concern for the students themselves, so *is* open to the charge of paternalism.

We have four responses. First, let's assume the premise of the objection, which is that eighteen-year-olds are truly adults with fully developed capacities for making good judgments about how to live their lives. Then, they have an easy option for avoiding the paternalistic measures we propose: they can choose not to go to college. Most eighteen-year-olds, in fact, do not go to college but instead enter workplaces in which their daily lives at work are far more stringently regulated than that of most students, but in which their private lives are left to their own management. The paternalistic measures we are proposing are optional. Think, by comparison, of the way that a military shapes the dispositions and characters of its recruits; or the way that the emergency services train recruits. There is an explicit goal of developing certain kinds of character traits—this is part of the game. It is possible to dispute that the military develops undesirable traits, but when the military consists solely of true volunteers, it is hard to make the case that they have some complaint against their characters being shaped. So the charge that there is something wrong with the paternalism we propose is weakened by the fact that students volunteer for the environment we are proposing.

Second though, we doubt the premise that in our social environment, eighteen-year-olds—in fact, eighteen- to twenty-two-year-olds—are for the most part fully formed adults who know their own good better than anyone else does. Rather, most (though certainly not all) of them are still persons in formation. This is not to say that in all social environments people of this age are still minors. In another social environment, in which children are encouraged to take responsibility for their own lives and those of others by their early teens, it might well be that at eighteen most people are close to as mature as they are going to become. But in our environment, where at eighteen very few children have substantial experience of being responsible for themselves or others, they are at a stage where they have to experiment with how to live and get to know themselves separately from their parents. Of course, the reason they haven't matured is because they have not had to take responsibility for themselves or others, so it would be inappropriate to maintain exactly the level of monitoring and regulation that the good parent maintains. But our proposals do not embody that level of monitoring and regulation. It might be wrong to prohibit sexual activity and alcohol consumption, and even to enforce reasonable sleeping hours, but it is not, we think, wrong to intervene in the environment in ways that fall short of prohibiting self-destructive behavior, but encourage other kinds of behavior and careful reflection.

Part of what worries the anti-paternalist objector to our argument is probably the observation that we want an institution to devise and enforce rules concerning behavior, rather than the advice about living that underlies the rules. Think about an idealized apprenticeship relationship, in which the apprentice works closely with the artisan to whom he is apprenticed. Not only does he closely observe the job being done and gradually learn how to do it, but if he turns up late or tired or hung over, his overseer enquires why this is and advises the apprentice on how to manage his life in order to succeed in work. The anti-paternalist, presumably, has no problem with this kindly advice. But in most universities, most students will not have a close enough relationship with any particular adult for such advice to be usefully offered, or for it to be taken in good faith. One aspect of our proposals is to alter this fact by creating a presumption among faculty that they have some responsibility for advising students on life management, both through impersonal and very occasional class-level discussion, and through personal encounters with students.[13] For good or ill (and we suspect it is for ill), the only way that most students will be influenced by this advice is through the establishment and maintenance of rules.

This leads to the third point. Education, if successful, is intrinsically a paternalistic process. The point of the student entering into a relationship with the teacher is that the teacher either knows what the student does not and is skilled at imparting that knowledge, or he knows how to facilitate in the student the development of skills and knowledge that, in fact, neither of them yet has. The relationship is one in which manipulation is permissible, even when the student is an adult, as long as the manipulation is guided by the interests of the student and at least when the student enters the relationship voluntarily. A teacher may deliberately withhold information from the student in order to make possible the student's discovery of the information herself; or he may withhold praise from very good work in order to trigger the further effort that produces excellence; or conversely, he may praise less-than-excellent work in order to prompt the same effort. Age makes no difference here: a thirty-year-old teacher is charged with the same duties to a forty-five-year-old student as to an eighteen-year-old (though may, indeed, find it more difficult to carry them out).

The fourth point is just that there is no nonpaternalistic default. Universities bring large numbers of young people together into an environment that is created by the university's administrators and its long-term employees. The university administrators have to take responsibility for the environment their actions structure. In most elite universities most of the students are aged eighteen to twenty-two because universities choose to admit people of that age; they choose what factors to weigh and how much relative weight to give them in admissions. In other words, they choose for each student the main peer influences that student will experience. Most of the students live on or close to campus and spend most of their daily life among other students (roughly their age). Universities, like the rest of us, know that most of these students are newly away from their main personal adult influences, and that the central impersonal adult influences that they share are mediated by commercial popular culture. Universities decide whether to build student residences with single rooms, double rooms, or triple rooms; they decide whether to make them coeducational or not, how close to place them to commercial districts, whether to require students to live in them; and whether to run academic programming within them. Universities decide to hold large lecture classes of 500 or more students, whether to ensure that all students have at least one small class with a tenure-track or tenured professor in their freshman year, and what mix of academic classes to require. Universities know that these decisions will have effects on the quality of life of the students themselves, and whatever they do they have to hold themselves responsible for those effects that are foreseeable. If there were a default, generated by some natural necessity for rounding up together same-age students into a single place and making them live together in a certain kind of environment, then university officials and professors could take refuge in that fact to disclaim responsibility for the effects. But that is just not the case. If they know that a particular environment is bad for those they have enticed to the university, resort to some anti-paternalist principle is not a good-faith defense.

CONCLUSION

Universities probably did well to abandon some of the more extreme aspects of *in loco parentis*. But our sense is that they have gone too far. As institutions that facilitate access to unearned advantage, they have a duty to influence the beneficiaries of that advantage to be motivated so that the benefits redound to the advantage of others who are less advantaged. As institutions that bring together large numbers of young people who will inevitably be exposed to one another's influence and the influence of corporations that have no interest in their well-being, universities have a duty of care for those young people. Our sense, based only on experience and conversation, is that numerous university administrators think hard, and try to act, on the motives and in the ways that we recommend. We equally worry that they meet resistance from many faculty who have a far more laissez-faire attitude toward the students in their charge. Our aim in this chapter has been to strengthen the resolve of said administrators and undermine the position of said faculty members by showing that the laissez-faire attitude is wrongheaded.[14]

NOTES

1. OECD, *Education at a Glance 2002* (Paris: OECD, 2002), Chapter A: "The Output of Educational Institutions and the Impact of Learning."
2. *Graduate Market Trends*, Spring 2001.
3. J. Borland et al. estimate the return to HE in Australia as AU$300,000 (earnings over a working lifetime) and $90,000 (net monetary benefit). US and UK returns in text.
4. "Work hard, play hard" is the unofficial motto of students at Duke University (Sessions Stepp 2006).
5. The primacy of the value of choice is in part a result of student movements in the 1960s that challenged the traditional Western canon and rightly demanded the inclusion of minority voices into the university curriculum. In fact, this movement has left us with what is arguably the only clear moral message supported by the university, which is the cultivation of multicultural toleration—a message that comes through the curriculum and student organizations and is promoted, to some extent, in student life through diversity training programs. This is not to say that universities are free of racism.

Instead, the promotion of 'tolerance' is an example of institutional support for the idea that an educated person ought to be culturally sensitive.

6. This description of the 'educated person' is largely drawn from John Dewey's *Democracy and Education* (1944) and R.S. Peters' *Ethics and Education* (1966).

7. To offer one example, Washington University in St. Louis has a Faculty Associates Program in which a faculty member works with a resident advisor to create community and act as a mentor for the floor. Associates receive a modest stipend with which they plan events and activities. In addition, the university is working to create faculty housing attached to residence halls, a policy that brings family living onto campus. Thanks to Mary Elliott, Assistant Director of Residential Life at Washington University, for alerting us to this example.

8. Ideally, these would move students beyond 'charitable' activities such as canned food drives, and instead put students in contact with organizations working for more systematic change. For example, a hall might have a human rights theme and be charged with educating the campus by bringing in speakers, organizing fundraisers for international rights organizations, and traveling together on a campaign with a group like Global Exchange (http://www.globalexchange.org/index.html).

9. A similar program is being used at University of Wisconsin–Madison as an optional freshman seminar called Freshman Interest Groups or FIGS. In these, a lead professor is chosen who identifies a theme and teaches one seminar course and then selects two other courses, roughly on the same theme, that the same group of students must take concurrently.

10. Thanks again to Mary Elliott for pointing out this possibility.

11. The current drinking age causes students to head to house parties in their first few years of school, where research has shown they are more likely than they are at public drinking locations to find illicit drugs and to play drinking games that increase overall alcohol consumption (Clapp et al. 2006).

12. Drinking alcohol is one striking exception in most states in the US.

13. For example, Brighouse recently taught a freshman class for the first time. One of the students was regularly sleeping in class, another was regularly a couple of minutes late. He spoke to both of them about their problems and offered relevant advice. The late student was never late again; the sleeping student improved (slightly). But both subsequently said appreciatively that no other professor had mentioned their respective problems, despite their manifesting them in every class.

14. We're grateful to numerous undergraduate students for conversations that helped us to shape and moderate our views and arguments—to name a few, Jessica Pung, Emma Milbhauer, Elise Volkman, Wasim Salman, and Dustin McMahon. Thanks also to Lindsey Chambers for incisive comments on an early draft, and to an audience at the Philosophy of Education Society of Great Britain annual conference. Due to the sensitive nature of our argument, we are more than usually obliged to relieve all those thanked of any responsibility for the substantive claims and arguments of the chapter.

BIBLIOGRAPHY

Allen, W. F. "Practical Education." In *Essays and Monographs by William Francis Allen*, 136–150. Memorial volume ed. Boston: G.H. Ellis, 1890.

Borland, J., P. Dawkins, D. Johnson, and R. Williams. *Returns to Investment in Higher Education Program Report No. 1: Report to the Vice Chancellor, the University of Melbourne*. Melbourne, AU: Melbourne Institute of Applied Economic and Social Research, 2000. http://www.melbourneinstitute.com/research/micro/rihe.pdf (accessed 22 June 2008).

Clapp, J., M. Reed, M. Holmes, J. Lange, and R. Voas. "Drunk in Public, Drunk in Private: The Relationship Between College Students, Drinking Environments and Alcohol Consumption." *American Journal of Drug & Alcohol Abuse* 32, no. 2 (2006): 275–285.

Day, J., and E. Newburger. *The Big Payoff: Educational Attainment and Synthetic Estimates of Work-Life Earnings*. Washington, DC: US Census Bureau, 2002.

Dewey, J. *Democracy and Education: An Introduction to the Philosophy of Education*. New York: The Free Press, 1944.

Freitas, D. "Taste: Excess and longing." *Wall Street Journal*, 20 May 2005, Eastern edition. Document ID: 842296811, retrieved from http://wallstreetjournal.com (accessed 17 December 2007)

Levy, A. *Female Chauvinist Pigs: Women and the Rise of Raunch Culture*. New York: The Free Press, 2006.

Organisation for Economic Co-operation and Development. *Education at a Glance 2002: OECD Indicators*. Paris: Organisation for Economic Co-operation and Development, 2002.

Peters, R. S. *Ethics and Education*. London: Allen and Unwin,1966.

Rawls, J. *A Theory of Justice* Cambridge, MA: Harvard University Press, 1971.

Schwab, J. "Eros and Education." In *Science, Curriculum, and Liberal education*, eds. I. Westbury and N. Wilkof, 105–132. Chicago: University of Chicago Press, 1978.

Sessions Stepp, L. *Unhooked*. New York: Riverhead Hardcover, 2007.

10 In Defense of Multiculturalism

Mark Halstead

THE PROBLEM: HOW TO RESPOND TO CULTURAL DIFFERENCE

When many Muslims around the world took offense at the publication of cartoons in the Danish newspaper *Jyllands-Posten* and elsewhere depicting the Prophet Muhammad as a terrorist and began to protest vigorously against them (Modood 2006), the incident highlighted not only the gulf of misunderstanding and fear that still exists between different cultures (in this case, between Islam and the West), but also the difficulty of finding an appropriate response to cultural difference. This chapter argues that in spite of recent devastating critiques of multiculturalism, it remains a philosophically sound concept and is in fact the approach to cultural difference that holds out most hope for the future. The chapter begins by considering contemporary claims by journalists and politicians about the 'death' of multiculturalism before turning to a closer examination of the actual arguments and debates. The chapter concludes with a brief examination of the implications for education. In the discussion, examples are drawn mainly from Muslims in the UK, for three reasons. First, the impact of cultural diversity in the British context is seen most clearly in the case of the Muslims because they are less likely than other groups to be integrated in terms of religious practices, language, food, dress, intermarriage, or core values. Secondly, it is Muslims more than any other minority group who are implicated in and affected by recent changes in attitudes to multiculturalism—so much so that some commentators find it hard to be sure "whether it is 'multiculturalism' or 'Muslims' and 'Islam' that is being questioned" (Allen 2007, 127). Thirdly, the situation of Muslims in the UK is closely watched in other Western countries with significant cultural minorities, including the Netherlands, Germany, and Denmark, and thus any arguments developed are likely to be of international interest.

The initial response to the cartoons among most westerners was one of bewilderment at the Muslim reaction: how can people take such offense at a joke? From a Western perspective, even if one found the cartoons distasteful or offensive, one would acknowledge the cartoonists' right to freedom of expression and respond with tolerance. The principles involved are thus the same as those in the *Satanic Verses* affair (Akhtar 1989; Ahsan and Kidwai 1991). But the bewilderment was just as strong on the other side, with the Muslim protestors calling the cartoons both blasphemous and provocative because it was clear that the cartoonists knew that Islam forbids any depictions of the Prophet Muhammad, let alone one that shows him as a terrorist. Muslims thus interpreted the affair as a failure to respect their most sacred beliefs, the very foundation of their distinctive way of life. The gulf between Muslim and non-Muslim perceptions was picked up and exaggerated by the Western media, which both reflects and shapes public opinion.

The problem of how to respond to cultural difference is also illustrated by the growing practice among Muslim women in Britain and elsewhere in the West of wearing the *niqab* (veil) in public places. After former British Foreign Secretary Jack Straw wrote an article expressing his dislike of the veil and his intention to ask any constituents wearing one to remove it when they spoke to him (Straw 2006), a massive debate ensued. Some participants in the debate considered it disrespectful to Muslim women and damaging to good community relations to try to tell them what to wear; but many welcomed the invitation to express their opinions, and some newspapers took the opportunity to express anti-Muslim or racist sentiments. At an individual level, many westerners feel uncomfortable with the veil at least partly because they are used to communication that combines speech and body language (such as smiling and frowning), and the veil makes the latter form of communication impossible. More fundamentally, many see the veil as an obstacle to integration and to women's participation on equal terms in society. It is often assumed that women are forced by men to wear it. Even more extreme responses included claims that women wearing veils are "frightening and intimidating" (Woolas 2006), that they are trying to impose Islamic law on British society, and that the veil is an "invitation to rape" (Lévy 2006, 35). Muslim explanations are often ignored; namely, that it is a symbol of commitment to Allah by putting his will first, particularly in relation to the requirement of modesty and not flaunting one's sexuality. The veil may also be a symbol of identity and of resistance to expectations of assimilation into "corrupt" Western values (Gereluk 2008). There seems to be little support among non-Muslims for the right to wear the veil, and policymakers frequently seem to be looking for excuses to ban it. This happened in the case of Aishah Azmi who was sacked as a teaching assistant in Dewsbury for refusing to remove her niqab when men were present, and in the case of defense lawyer Shabnam Mughal who was taken off an immigration appeal case after refusing the judge's request to remove her niqab in court. The reasons given for seeking to ban or discourage the wearing of the veil in public include difficulty in communication, safety issues, security issues (because there have been claims that male criminals have donned the niqab or the *burqa* to escape detection and arrest), and protecting women from oppression—though, ironically, if it is the Muslim women themselves who choose to wear the veil, as generally seems to be the case, then this protection of women's freedoms itself becomes oppressive.

In both the Danish cartoons affair and the extended debate about the veil, a common strand of underlying thinking is 'Why can't *they* be more like *us*?' This of course ignores the fact that *they* are part of *us*, if by 'us' we mean British citizens. Among the many strengths of multiculturalism are that it highlights the moral **duty** citizens have to tolerate differences in fellow citizens, so long as the differences do not lead to public harm; and also that it draws attention to the danger of alienation or conflict if a particular minority feels itself oppressed or not treated with the same respect as other citizens. Multiculturalism insists on giving a voice to all the different cultures represented in a country and ensuring that members of different cultural groups are treated with equal respect. We therefore need to distinguish between private and public reactions to cultural difference. Private reactions may include emotional responses such as bewilderment and resentment alongside other, more morally considered responses such as benevolence, respect, and concern. Clearly, not everyone is persuaded by the multicultural agenda. Public reactions, on the other hand, can be seen in the policies adopted by the government or by public institutions such as the BBC, where there is an expectation that these will be rationally justifiable and broadly in line with the fundamental liberal values of society. This means in effect that policies will be multicultural, or at least it did so until the start of the new century. How far things have changed in the last nine years will be discussed in the next section.

So far, multiculturalism has been treated as if it were a single way of responding to cultural difference, but in fact it is a broader term encompassing at least three different possible responses. The first, which I shall call 'strong multiculturalism,' requires respect for all cultural differences except those that demonstrably harm the public interest or result in serious physical abuse. It allows minority groups, if they wish, to live their lives in accordance with their own beliefs and traditions, virtually untouched by contact with the values of the broader society (so long as there is peaceful coexistence among the different faiths and traditions), and it allows them to pass these on in an undiluted form to future generations. It thus accepts that religious or other deeply held cultural beliefs and practices can trump other, more rational considerations or the practices of the majority culture in any decision about how minorities should live their lives. In Lustgarten's words, cultural minorities should have "unrestricted freedom to follow their own customs and religious practices, be governed by their personal law and receive education in their language and cultural tradition" (1983, 101). The key point is that they should never be forced into a position where they have to act against their own fundamental beliefs (for example, by being provided with food in schools or hospitals that their religion forbids them to eat). Strong multiculturalism usually includes the claim that the state has the duty to support the minority cultures of law-abiding citizens, for example, by granting holidays on religious festivals, encouraging minority languages, allowing time for prayer at work, accepting Muslim dress codes, providing facilities for single-sex swimming in public swimming pools, allowing mosques to broadcast the call to prayer, and so on. Some people associate strong multiculturalism with an obligation to celebrate diversity, but in fact this is not a necessary condition. We cannot expect Muslims to celebrate the fact that westerners are insulting their prophet any more than we can expect supporters of free speech to accept the banning of certain cartoons simply because they cause offense to some people. These freedoms are tolerated, but not necessarily celebrated.

The second, which I shall call 'weak multiculturalism,' accepts a more limited form of cultural diversity but at the same time emphasizes community cohesion. On the one hand, it accepts that minority groups should be recognized and represented in any common institutional structures and decision-making processes of the broader society, but on the other, it requires a strong commitment on the part of all citizens to the shared values of the broader society. The roots of weak multiculturalism are found in the *Swann Report* (DES 1985), which describes a "genuinely pluralist society" as "both socially cohesive and culturally diverse" (8, 316–317). According to this report, members of minority groups should be free to maintain their distinctive cultures and lifestyles, at least in areas of life "where no single way can justifiably be presented as universally appropriate" (ibid., 4). But this freedom is subject to two major constraints: First, priority must be given to taking on "the shared values of the wider pluralist society," for without these there would be the danger that society would fragment along ethnic or religious lines; and second, the group's authority and control over the individual is constrained by the requirement of "free choice for individuals" (ibid., 6). It is clear from the report that the roots of contemporary thinking about community cohesion (which lies at the heart of weak multiculturalism) go back many years. The aim is that all groups should feel sufficiently comfortable with local and national policies that they are prepared to resolve any remaining issues or disagreements through discussion and negotiation rather than through conflict or violence. The approach therefore presupposes certain liberal values, particularly democracy, negotiation, individual freedom, and equality.

The third is 'minimal' or 'tokenistic multiculturalism,' which makes only small concessions to cultural minorities and which may indeed become a cover for assimilationism. For example, specific minority cultural practices including culinary and musical ones may be tolerated or welcomed, but few if any concessions are made to the distinctive beliefs and values of cultural minorities (especially those that are comparative newcomers to the West), and they are expected to conform to the majority culture. This is seen as in their own best interests as well as in the interests of the broader society. If they choose not to, they are themselves responsible for any unpleasant consequences. This view is associated with the politics of the Right, but even liberals have argued that if the life offered to the young in minority religions or immigrant communities is too impoverished, then "assimilationist policies may well be the only humane course, even if implemented by force of law" (Raz 1986, 423–424).

The difference between these three versions of multiculturalism can be illustrated by reference to the veil. The first would allow Muslim communities to police their own members and require women to wear the veil if the community considered this a religious duty. The second would permit the wearing of the veil, but only if it were a matter of autonomous individual choice. The third would refuse Muslim women the freedom to wear the veil in public because such cultural or religious symbols are divisive and might fan the flames of conflict. It is argued in the next section that in recent years the first of these versions of multiculturalism has been discredited as an acceptable response in the eyes of many people, and that though the second remains official policy, what we are seeing in practice is a significant slide in the attitudes of the broader population from the second to the third version. This slide is seen more in the metaphors and emotive language used in the popular press to describe multiculturalism than in any philosophically coherent discussion of the topic (Halstead 2007). Indeed, it is argued here that the third version is philosophically, politically, and morally unsound. Assimilation takes for granted the superiority of Western moral values and can be seen as a disguised form of cultural domination (Halstead 1988, 145–147).

THE CONTEXT: THE DRIFT AWAY FROM MULTICULTURALISM

There is a long-standing tradition of opposition to multiculturalism in some quarters of the UK that is mainly associated with right-wing politics. For example, in his retirement speech as Secretary of State for Education in 1986, Sir Keith Joseph strongly criticized multicultural education and called for schools to "transmit British culture" (Halstead 1988, 281). In this speech he was echoing the views of the Bradford head-teacher Ray Honeyford, who was forced into early retirement the same year because of his resistance to local multicultural policies. What is different since the turn of the new century, however, is the coincidence of a stronger emphasis on national identity and community cohesion with a perceived threat to the West from Islamic extremism, with multiculturalism being blamed for providing the context in which extremism can thrive. The emphasis on national identity is seen, for example, in the "Life in the UK" test that must be taken by all those seeking to settle permanently in the UK or apply for British citizenship, and in a series of speeches on Britishness by the Prime Minister; for example, in a speech in 2007, he claimed that Britain is defined "not by ethnicity but . . . by common values and shared interests," that Britain needs "a stronger sense of patriotic purpose" and that "what was wrong about multiculturalism was not the recognition of diversity but that it over-emphasized separateness at the cost of unity" (Brown 2007). Concern has been expressed that recent rises in net immigration (the net increase in 2007 was 237,000) have led to lower levels of community cohesion in the areas most affected (HCCLGC 2008). The perceived threat from Islamic extremism resulting from what Allen calls "urgent and historical events" (namely 9/11, Bali, Madrid, 7/7, and Mumbai), and the responses in terms of the "war on terror" (Allen 2007, 125–126; cf. Modood 2005) have resulted in a new definition of the global situation in the form of a vicious circle. Islamic extremism is defined as a major threat in the world, therefore Muslims in the West are treated with greater suspicion and in turn become alienated by what they perceive as unjust and inequitable treatment, and in the end some may become more sympathetic to extremism. This is commonly described as the 'legacy of multiculturalism' (Carmichael 2007). Johnston (2008) argues that multiculturalism has metamorphosed from an expression of "Britain's characteristic toleration of other people's ways, religions, cuisines, languages and dress" into a "political creed that held that ethnic minority groups should be allowed to do what they liked" and that this new creed has allowed Islamic extremists to separate themselves from the rest of British society, with murderous results.

In 2004 Trevor Phillips said that multiculturalism was effectively moribund as a political ideal because it emphasized difference rather than shared British values (Baldwin 2004) and the following year in a speech to the Manchester Council for Community Relations claimed that Britain was "sleepwalking" toward segregation (Phillips 2005). Such remarks captured the popular imagination, coming as they did from the mouth of someone who as chair of the Equality and Human Rights Commission is in some sense a spokesperson for Blacks in the UK, and there followed numerous newspaper articles and television programs on the theme of the 'death of multiculturalism.' However, an immediate problem with this phrase is clear: multiculturalism has two distinct dimensions. The first is to do with recognizing rather than ignoring the distinctive cultural identities of British citizens from minority backgrounds and with acknowledging their right to cherish, preserve, or modify those identities as they choose while enjoying the privileges and exercising the responsibilities of British citizenship. The second is to do with harmonious coexistence among the different groups that make up British society, and this involves welcoming diversity, encouraging cross-cultural understanding between groups, ensuring institutional justice and participation for all groups, and eradicating inequality and discrimination. Phillips was criticizing only one of these dimensions, because he was worried that it could result in some groups leading self-contained lives in isolation from the broader society, but the slide to include both dimensions has been an easy one.

Some British newspapers proceeded to test the bounds of acceptability with a regular crop of front-page headlines presenting negative images of Muslims, and the use of increasingly intemperate language in articles about multiculturalism. For example, Melanie Phillips depicted multiculturalism as "enforcing a doctrine of state-mandated virtue to promote racial, ethnic and cultural difference and stamp out majority values" and spoke of a continuum in Islam "that links peaceful, law-abiding but nevertheless intensely ideological Muslims at one end and murderous jihadists at the other" (Ashley 2006, 8; cf. Phillips 2006). Julie Burchill earlier expressed similar sentiments: "Call me a filthy racist—go on, you know you want to—but we have reason to be suspicious of Islam" (2001). Politicians and Christian leaders such as Archbishop John Sentamu and Bishop Nazir Ali have also expressed open opposition to multiculturalism. In a speech in 2006 the Labor cabinet minister Ruth Kelly appeared to signal the end of multiculturalism as an official policy. In 2008, the Conservative leader David Cameron attacked multiculturalism for creating a "cultural apartheid" (Watt 2008, 9). Substantial sections of society are becoming increasingly hostile to Muslims and other minority communities and see multiculturalism as a threat to the traditional British way of life. In his Manchester speech Trevor Phillips noted that most white Britons could not name a single nonwhite friend (Phillips 2005). Perhaps David Harrison is right when he claims that "a consensus has emerged that the multiculturalism experiment was necessary, but that its time is over" (2008).

One result of this new climate has been a drift toward more discriminatory policies and practice toward Muslims, including discrimination in recruitment, employment, and the workplace; Islamophobic attacks on individuals and mosques; bureaucratic delays in responding to Muslim requests for planning applications for mosques or schools, or for cultural sensitivity in hospitals and healthcare generally; and disproportionate targeting under antiterrorist legislation. Such things not only have a disruptive effect on the daily lives of ordinary Muslims in Britain, but can also cause deep-seated resentment (Richardson 2004). Modood's point in relation to the Danish cartoons has wider application: "From the Muslim side, the underlying causes of their current anger are a deep sense that they are not respected, that they and their most cherished feelings are 'fair game'" (2006, 2). As he notes, the combination of "inferior protective legislation, socio-economic marginality, cultural disdain, draconian security surveillance, the occupation of Palestine, and the international 'war on terror'" (ibid.) makes life in Britain an uncomfortable experience for many Muslims.

The questions arise as to how far these trends result from a gut response of what I have elsewhere called "cultural racism" (Halstead 1988, 145ff.), and how far they are underpinned by a coherent framework of philosophically justifiable values and arguments. The next section identifies the main arguments that are put forward against multiculturalism and subjects them to closer analysis.

THE DEBATE ABOUT MULTICULTURALISM: ARGUMENT AND COUNTERARGUMENT

Among the polemic, invective, innuendo, myth-making, and mischief-making noted in the last section, three significant arguments against multiculturalism can be identified. The first is that it undermines social cohesion and can result in the self-segregation of minority communities. By encouraging different attitudes and values to thrive, it is socially divisive and fosters fragmentation. What is needed to counter this divisiveness is more integration and more emphasis on the shared values of the broader society. The second argument is that because it supports group rights and group identities, multiculturalism pays inadequate attention to individual needs and individual autonomy and fails to provide an escape route for individuals from pressures to conform to group expectations. Multicultur-alism is also said to involve an essentialist approach to religious, cultural, and ethnic identity, and because many minority cultures have traditionally involved beliefs and practices that are discriminatory against women (or other groups, such as gays) there is a danger that multiculturalism's sup-port for the right of minority cultures to maintain their traditional values and practices might harm women—or at least fail to support their right to escape oppression and determine their own future (cf. Okin 1999). The third argument is that by allowing traditional beliefs and practices to be uncriti-cally maintained, multiculturalism provides a context in which extremist attitudes can flourish within Western nations, and "impressionable young men" (to use Philip Johnston's term, 2008) from minority groups can be exploited. None of these arguments is purely philosophical, but it is worth considering rather more closely how they relate to the dominant values of liberal democratic societies.

Divisiveness

With regard to the first argument, it is important to note that neither hold-ing different personal or cultural values nor making different institutional provision for distinctive sub-groups in society is necessarily socially divi-sive. Difference is not the same as divisiveness. On the contrary, difference is healthy in a democracy, and democratic values and practices assume the existence of difference. The key issue is whether the differences exist in a context of mutual respect. Recognition of difference can be a positive thing both for minorities and for the broader society: for minorities because it symbolizes respect and the freedom to follow one's own worldview, and therefore it generates feelings of loyalty to the state that recognizes such rights; and for the broader society because it is enriching, encourages democratic debate, and facilitates autonomous choice. However, there are some situations when difference *can* lead to divisiveness. For example, if the adherents of one faith maintain that their lifestyle is the only one that is morally acceptable and that all other faiths are a waste of time, this can undermine the respect for other groups that is essential to the flourishing of liberal democracies and encourage a sense of identity based on opposi-tion to, rather than positive interaction with, the broader society. This can lead to ghettoization and a breakdown of social cohesion (Halstead and

McLaughlin 2005, 64–65). However, it would be a mistake to assume that every situation in which communities are ghettoized and live 'parallel lives' is the result of self-segregation. For example, if the majority responds to minority groups with prejudice, discrimination, and social exclusion, then this will cause alienation and withdrawal. Often, talk of 'self-segregation' proves to be a way of blaming victims for something that is not initiated by them. Some empirical examples may help to clarify the point. The Muslim ghettos in many inner cities in the UK came about as mainly a result of white flight rather than the desire of Muslims to set up self-contained residential districts, and so the fact that Muslims are now trying to make the best of the situation by creating institutions within the ghetto to meet their cultural needs does not make this a case of self-segregation. Indeed, to condemn black or Muslim institutions as 'self-segregated' but not white or Christian ones, as the *Swann Report* does, appears discriminatory (DES 1985, 515). Nor is it reasonable to blame Muslim schools for not meeting the level of 25 percent non-Muslim admissions as recommended in the *Cantle Report* (Community Cohesion Review Team 2001); their admission policies normally welcome non-Muslim students, but the problem is the lack of applicants.

In a similar vein, Anthony O'Hear writes of "concentrations of Muslims who show little inclination to integrate with the host society" (2006, 97), thus putting the blame firmly on the shoulders of the Muslims themselves. If what I wrote in the previous paragraph is correct, however, there is first a need for the 'host' society to eradicate racist and Islamophobic attitudes and practices, and then to introduce a set of policies based on trust, tolerance, acceptance, respect, and a commitment to pluralism; Muslim groups can be blamed for self-segregation only when such positive policies are already in place. If this seems an impossible dream in the current social and political climate, we should remember that the establishment of the first state-funded Muslim schools in the UK, which occurred barely ten years ago, had highly important symbolic value in Muslim eyes (although it affected only one percent of the Muslim children in the country) in terms of recognition, trust, and respect. If this climate of respect can be restored (though this is unlikely to be achieved by forcing minorities to adopt an artificial, static, middle-class notion of Britishness), then perhaps Muslims will cease to be too fearful to engage in democratic discussions with non-Muslim groups about how to achieve an appropriate balance between integration and cultural maintenance, or to put it another way, a balance between shared and legitimately distinctive values. What many Muslims want is economic and political integration, plus Islamic personal and social values (Halstead 1986, 16). Economic and political integration implies a set of shared values, but these must be genuinely shared (or at least agreed upon in democratic discussion), not imposed by the broader society, or else they will be seen as another example of cultural domination. Examples of such shared values include a basic social morality without which no form of social life would be possible and the acceptance of a common system of law and democratic government. Islamic personal and social values are what give meaning and structure to the lives of individual Muslims. They are not static; indeed, they will evolve in their own sometimes unexpected ways (cf. Stratton 2006) and may exemplify unusual blends of the traditional and the new, which only a situation of genuine cultural pluralism can deal with.

Group Control

The second argument against multiculturalism relates to the tensions that can exist between group identity and individual rights and needs, especially when group identity is defined in a rigid and uncompromising way. As noted in the first section of this chapter, stronger forms of multiculturalism accept the right of groups not only to live their lives in accordance with their own beliefs and traditions, virtually untouched by contact with the values of the broader society, but also to pass these on in an undiluted form to future generations. There are two problems with allowing groups this level of freedom. First, if there are injustices within the traditional culture, such as forced marriage and honor killings, these are more likely to be perpetuated under a system of strong multiculturalism. Okin (1999) rightly notes that many of these injustices disproportionately affect women. Second, if groups are free to uncritically socialize the next generation into their own values and practices, the consequent cultural encapsulation may become oppressive, especially to those individuals who feel they have no realistic chance to exit their community (cf. Okin 2003). Such problems as these have led some to question the right of groups to preserve their identity in this way (cf. Sen 2006) and to argue (in line with much traditional liberal thinking) that individual rights must trump group rights. As Crittenden points out, "in classical liberal theory there was no commitment to intermediate groups as essential constituents of a corporate society. The fundamental units are individuals and the state. The former make up an aggregate whose collective will is expressed by the state" (1982, 13). In line with this view, the recently introduced citizenship courses in the UK encourage young people to think of their primary identity in terms of membership of a state ('British') rather than a faith ('Muslim'), and a common educational experience for all children is widely supported (perhaps justified in terms of children's rights) irrespective of their religious or cultural background. A corollary of this view is the claim that "the responsibility for the adaptations and adjustments involved in settling in a new country lies entirely with those who have come here to settle" (Honeyford 1982). An even more extreme response would be to try to exclude anything to do with cultural values and cultural identity from the school curriculum altogether.

But these responses in turn are not without their problems. Education cannot take place in a cultural vacuum (Merry 2007, 72ff.), and it is unrealistic to expect that schools should play no part in identity formation.

If schools are not conscious of their part in the process, they will still be engaged in it unconsciously. So it may be better to make explicit the cultural values and assumptions that underpin the school's ethos and teaching. However, once it becomes apparent that certain forms of primary identity (such as nationality) are being privileged at the expense of others (such as religion), this may be perceived as oppressive by those groups whose identity is determined solely or mainly by religion—Sen calls it their "singular affiliation" (2006, 20)   thus causing resentment and undermining commitment to the very citizenship that is being promoted. A further problem is that children and young people may end up with a confused identity just when they most need cultural coherence, stability, and continuity. The phrase 'between two cultures' has often been used to describe the predicament of such children, though the phrase itself is ambiguous. It may refer to (a) being in the process of crossing over from one culture to another, (b) floundering or drowning away from the safety of either culture, or (c) seeking out or creating a middle path (Halstead 1994, 317–320). The first of these, I have argued, is oppressive unless voluntary; I shall discuss the second shortly under the heading 'Extremism;' but for now I shall turn to the third and argue that a careful study of identity theory and identity formation (cf. Merry 2007, 75–76) can lead to a more moderate solution to the problem of group identity and individual rights.

First, it is clear that multiculturalism does not require an essentialist approach to cultural identity. There is considerable diversity among Muslims anyway, in terms of levels of commitment and practice (ibid, 95–96), though doubtless certain beliefs and practices can be identified as providing a fall-back position that most Muslims agree on as central to their religion. But change over time is normal, indeed inevitable. For example, Muslims are not immune to fashions—in clothes, music, entertainment, living styles, even personalized number plates (Stratton 2006). A more serious change is that second and third generation British Muslims often have a much deeper knowledge of the *Qur'an* and the *hadith* than their parents, who may have a more traditional, ethnically oriented form of religious practice. This is likely to result in a sharp decline in traditional practices such as first cousin marriage, forced marriage, and female circumcision because these have no basis in Islamic teaching. There is clearly scope now for younger Muslims to make a bigger contribution to British society, and it is ironic that this stage has been reached at a time of unprecedented anti-Muslim sentiment. There is a growing recognition that a strong cultural identity can also be a route to the development of personal autonomy (Merry 2007, 75; McLaughlin 2008, 189ff.). I have argued elsewhere that education should combine three elements: education for democratic citizenship, education for a specific cultural attachment, and education for cross-cultural understanding (Halstead 2003, 288ff.). The last of these seeks to encourage mutual understanding, tolerance, respect between groups with different cultural values, rational deliberation about cultural difference, and an awareness of the difficulty of trying to live with difference. This might be understood as a precondition to autonomy by making children aware of alternatives. It could also provide a catalyst for change and development as a result of interaction between groups, and a safety valve for those who find the culture of their parents and community too suffocating and need an exit strategy. A commitment to multiculturalism thus requires respect for different cultures, but not an uncritical acceptance of all cultural practices. As Bikhu Parekh points out, multiculturalism does not imply that all cultures

> are equally rich and deserve equal respect, that each of them is good for its members, or that all cultural differences deserve to be valued. All it means is that no culture is wholly worthless, that it deserves at least some respect because of what it means to its members and the creative energy it displays, that no culture is perfect and has a right to impose itself on others, and that cultures are best changed from within. (Parekh 2006, 337)

Extremism

The third argument against multiculturalism links it to extremism, or at least involves the claim that multiculturalism provides a context in which extremist attitudes can develop freely. The concern here is not so much that multiculturalism may allow the development of fundamentalist attitudes toward women or homosexuals, for example, or the indoctrination of young people into beliefs such as creationism that lack scientific credibility (though such beliefs may indeed lead to an undermining of the democratic values of the broader society, particularly freedom of expression), but that multiculturalism involves misplaced tolerance that is not sufficiently rigorous in challenging the sort of extremist violence that endangers civil liberty and security. Extremist violence has escalated in many parts of the world since the start of the twenty-first century, and can be seen in the UK in the mainly Muslim riots in the northern cities of Bradford, Oldham, and Burnley in 2000 and 2001, as well as in the 7/7 terrorist attacks. Multiculturalism, it is claimed, because of its support for diversity of all kinds and its insistence on treating all cultures equally irrespective of their merits, has allowed the UK to become a 'breeding ground for terrorism.' I shall argue (avoiding the emotive language) that it is not multiculturalism but political injustice and economic exploitation in Western policies toward the Muslim world that has led to a growth of 'extremism' among some Muslims in the West (and indeed worldwide), and that the answer is not to abandon multicultural values and adopt a more hard-line approach, but to encourage greater respect and cross-cultural understanding and thus peaceful coexistence and cooperation. From an educational perspective, this includes helping young Muslims in the West to develop a strong self-identity and treating them fairly and justly, and from a political perspective it involves not adopting unjustifiable aggressive policies toward Muslim states. This kind of multicultural approach, in my view, holds most promise for ensuring that young Muslims in the West will grow up into tolerant, balanced, and responsible citizens with much to offer the broader society.

'Extremism,' like knowledge generally, is defined by those in power. The current dominant definition is based on the belief that the West needs to protect itself from an axis of evil, made up of countries like Iran that support terrorism and subcultural movements like al Qa'ida in countries that don't openly support terrorism. However, this does not adequately explain why some terrorists were born and brought up in the UK or other Western countries. An alternative explanation is that even the worst terrorist atrocities such as 9/11 should be understood not as proactive acts of evil, but as a form of protest full of lethal symbolism, a *re*-action to what is perceived as continuing injustice from America and its allies. The question then is how to react to the reaction. It is clear that an escalation of violence and injustice will lead to an increase in sympathy toward those engaged in active resistance to what is seen as continuing unjustified aggression. The answer is not to try to crush all signs of resistance through military power; nor to offer financial incentives to Muslim organizations defined as 'moderate' (i.e., pro-Western); nor to put in place leaders who support the West even though they do not carry their people with them; nor to give free rein to a racist press, and thus encourage popular prejudice and discrimination against Muslims. Extremism is nurtured by violent opposition, just as it is marginalized by respect and understanding. This is where multiculturalism has a role to play, in encouraging greater acceptance and cross-cultural understanding toward Islam and Muslims, as a way of moving toward mutual recognition and cooperation. Extremism is most likely to develop among Muslims in the West if they have no sense of democratic belonging or inclusion and if they feel alienated as a result of continuing persecution, oppression, discrimination, and injustice.

This section has implied that far from undermining universal liberal values, as D'Souza (1991) and Barry (2001) suggest, multiculturalism has actually grown out of core liberal principles such as justice, equality, rights, freedom, tolerance, and respect for persons and that it is best understood as a liberal response to the increased number of people from diverse cultural backgrounds living in Western states (cf. Dhillon and Halstead 2003, 146). It has sometimes been claimed that multiculturalism operates on the second-best principle: if Muslims, for example, are not prepared to fully participate in the life of the broader society, it may be better to grant them certain rights and make certain accommodations that will encourage partial participation rather than have them withdraw into complete isolationism. However, there are good grounds for arguing that multiculturalism is much more than this. Parekh, for example, presents an upbeat case for multiculturalism, arguing that cultural diversity is both inescapable and desirable and that it encourages mutually beneficial dialogue between different cultures, so long as they treat each other with equal respect. He recognizes that all citizens of a multicultural society need a common sense of belonging, but argues that this can be achieved only if the state offers a "just recognition" to all its constituent communities as well as a "just share of economic and political power" (2006, 343).

THE IMPLICATIONS FOR EDUCATION

These can be sketched in fairly briefly because they follow on naturally from what has been said above, and in any case a number of educational issues have already been touched on. Educational policy is currently being constructed to fit in with the new post-multicultural agenda, and this involves a greater emphasis on surveillance in schools and universities than has existed in the past. At the level of higher education, the new policies may include monitoring student Islamic societies, banning certain groups such as Hizb ut-Tahrir from university campuses, and watching Muslims at universities for signs of extremism (DIUS 2008). At the school level, they include the banning of a student from wearing the *jilbab* to school (Dyer 2006); the new guidance issued to schools on the detection of extremism (DCSF 2008); and the requirement that all schools, including all faith schools, promote community cohesion, understood partly as having a "common sense of identity" and a "common vision and sense of belonging" (DCSF 2007, 1, 3). It is clear that what is happening here is that the new ways of thinking about extremism and terrorism are being introduced directly into schools and generating new requirements relating both to curriculum and to educational ethos. Diversity is perceived as potentially dangerous in educational contexts just as in society at large, as it is a route through which extremism can take hold.

However, if the analysis of the 'death of multiculturalism' discourse earlier in this chapter is correct, then this emphasis on mistrust, surveillance, and monocultural values may be the worst possible way to achieve a cooperative and harmonious society and the most likely way to generate a sense of alienation. If they are to offer a positive experience to all children equally, schools must provide an education that recognizes rather than ignores the cultural identity of children from minority groups and the distinct needs that arise from that identity; or at least, parents must have the option to send their children to separate (but not divisive) schools that give equal emphasis to the religious and cultural values of the parents and the political and economic values of the broader society. This is precisely what multicultural education offers, with its double emphasis on (a) respecting minorities, caring for their cultural needs, and making sure they are not subject to cultural domination or discrimination or put in a position where they are required to act against their fundamental values, and (b) meeting the needs of all children by preparing them for life in a multicultural society (cf. Dhillon and Halstead 2003). There are three main arguments for multicultural education. First, it provides a better-quality education that involves broadening the mind, expanding horizons, being open to new possibilities, and learning particular values such as respect and tolerance. Second, it is more democratic, egalitarian, and respectful toward children from minority groups than monocultural education. Third, it is better for society at large, as it is more likely to result in social cohesion than policies based on compulsion. A minority group's commitment to its host society will be much stronger if it feels trusted and respected enough to be given the same choices and privileges as members of the majority group (in terms of whether or not to send their children to a faith school, for example). A country that can allow minority faiths the freedom to establish their own faith schools is a country that is comfortable with its own cultural diversity and one that is determined to treat all its citizens with justice and respect.

BIBLIOGRAPHY

Ahsan, M. M., and Kidwai, A. R. *Sacrilege Versus Civility: Muslim Perspectives on "The Satanic Verses" Affair.* Leicester: Islamic Foundation, 1991.

Akhtar, S. *Be Careful With Muhammad: The Salman Rushdie Affair.* London: Bellew Publishing, 1989.

Allen, C. "'Down with Multiculturalism, Book-Burning and Fatwas': The Discourse of the 'Death' of Multiculturalism." *Culture and Religion* 8, no. 2 (2007): 125–138.

Ashley, J. "The Multicultural Menace, Anti-Semitism and Me." *The Guardian*, 16 June 2006.

Baldwin, T. "I Want an Integrated Society With a Difference." *The Times*, 3 April 2004.

Barry, B. "The Muddles of Multiculturalism." *New Left Review*, 8, 2001: 49–71.

Brown, G. "We Need a United Kingdom." *Daily Telegraph*, 13 January 2007.

Burchill, J. "Some People Will Believe Anything." *The Guardian*, 18 August 2001.

Carmichael, W. "The Death of Multiculturalism." BillCarmichael.20six.co.uk., 2007. http://billcarmichael.20six.co.uk/billcarmichael/art/4378306 (accessed 3 September 2008).

Community Cohesion Review Team. *Community Cohesion: Report of the Independent Review Team Chaired by Ted Cantle.* London: Home Office, 2001.

Crittenden, B. *Cultural Pluralism and Common Curriculum.* Carlton: Melbourne University Press, 1982.

Department for Children, Schools and Families (DCSF). *Learning Together to be Safe: A Toolkit to Help Schools to Contribute to the Prevention of Violent Extremism.* Nottingham: DCSF, 2008.

———. *Guidance on the Duty to Promote Community Cohesion.* Nottingham: DCSF, 2007.

Department for Education and Science (DES). *Education for All (the Swann report).* London: HMSO, 1985.

Department for Innovation, Universities and Skills (DIUS). *Promoting Good Campus Relations, Fostering Shared Values and Preventing Violent Extremism in Universities and Higher Education Colleges.* London: DIUS, 2008.

Dhillon, P. A., and J. M. Halstead. "Multicultural education." In *The Blackwell Guide to Philosophy of Education*, eds N. Blake, P. Smeyers, R. Smith, and P. Standish, 146–61. Oxford: Blackwell Publishing, 2003 .

D'Souza, D. *Illiberal Education: The Politics of Race and Sex on Campus.* New York: The Free Press, 1991.

Dyer, C. "Muslim Girl Loses Lords Fight Over Jilbab." *The Guardian,* 23 March 2006.

Gereluk, D. *Symbolic Clothing in Schools.* London: Continuum, 2008.

Halstead, J. M. *The Case for Muslim Voluntary-aided Schools: Some Philosophical Reflections.* Cambridge: Islamic Academy, 1986.

———. *Education, Justice and Cultural Diversity.* London: Falmer Press, 1988.

———. "Between two cultures? Muslim children in a western liberal society." *Children and Society* 8, no. 4 (1994): 312–26.

———. "Schooling and Cultural Maintenance for Religious Minorities in the Liberal State." In *Citizenship and Education in Liberal-Democratic Societies: Teaching for Cosmopolitan Values and Collective Identities,* eds. K. McDonough and W. Feinberg, 273–295. New York: Oxford University Press, 2003.

———. "Multicultural metaphors." In *Education in the Era of Globalization,* eds. K. Roth and I. Gur-Ze'ev, 147–60. Dordrecht: Springer, 2007.

Halstead, J. M., and T. H. McLaughlin. "Are Faith Schools Divisive?" In *Faith schools: Consensus or Conflict?* eds. R. Gardner, J. Cairns, and D. Lawton, 61–73. London: RoutledgeFalmer, 2005.

Harrison, D. "After 'No-go' Bishop, Multiculturalism Debated." *Daily Telegraph,* 4 February 2008.

Honeyford, R. "Multiracial Myths." *The Times Educational Supplement,* 19 November 1982.

House of Commons Communities and Local Government Committee (HCCLGC). *Community Cohesion and Migration.* London: Stationery Office, 2008.

Johnston, P. "Multiculturalism is Breeding Intolerance." *Daily Telegraph,* 7 January 2008.

Lévy, B-H. Interview reported in J. Frazer "the pop philosopher unveiled," *The Jewish Chronicle,* 13 October 2006.

Lustgarten, L. S. "Liberty in a Culturally Plural Society." In *Of Liberty,* ed. A. Phillips Griffiths, 91–107. Cambridge: Cambridge University Press, 1983.

McLaughlin, T. H. *Liberalism, Education and Schooling.* Eds. D. Carr, J. M. Halstead, and R. Pring. Exeter: Imprint Academic, 2008.

Merry, M. *Culture, Identity and Islamic Schooling.* New York: Palgrave Macmillan, 2007.

Modood, T. "Remaking Multiculturalism After 7/7." OpenDemocracy.net, 2005. http://www.opendemocracy.net (accessed 16 March 2006).

———. "The Liberal Dilemma: Integration or Vilification?" OpenDemocracy.net, 2006. http://www.opendemocracy.net (accessed 16 March 2006).

O'Hear, A. *Plato's Children: The State We Are In.* London: Gibson Square, 2006.

Okin, S. M. *Is Multiculturalism Bad for Women?* Princeton, NJ: Princeton University Press, 1999.

———. "'Mistresses of Their Own Destiny': Group Rights, Gender and Realistic Rights of Exit." In *Citizenship and Education in Liberal-Democratic Societies: Teaching for Cosmopolitan Values and Collective Identities,* eds. K. McDonough and W. Feinberg, 325–350. New York: Oxford University Press, 2003.

Parekh, B. *Rethinking Multiculturalism: Cultural Diversity and Political Theory.* 2nd ed. Basingstoke: Palgrave Macmillan, 2006.

Phillips, M. *Londonistan: How Britain is Creating a Terror State Within.* London: Gibson Square, 2006.

Phillips, T. "After 7/7: Sleepwalking to Segregation." Speech given to the Manchester Council for Community Relations, Commission for Racial Equality, London, 22 September 2005.

Raz, J. *The Morality of Freedom*. Oxford: Clarendon Press, 1986.

Richardson, R., ed. *Islamophobia: Issues, Challenges and Action*. Stoke-on-Trent: Trentham Books, 2004.

Sen, A. *Identity and Violence: The Illusion of Destiny*. London: Allen Lane, 2006.

Stratton, A. *Muhajababes: Meet the New Middle East—Cool, Sexy and Devout*. London: Constable, 2006.

Straw, J. "I Want to Unveil My Views on an Important Issue." *Lancashire Evening Telegraph*, 5 October 2006.

Watt, N. "Cultural Sensitivity Putting Rights at Risk, Warns Cameron." *The Guardian*, 27 February 2008.

Woolas, P. "Muslim Women Who Wear the Veil Can be Frightening and Intimidating." *Sunday Mirror*, 8 October 2006.

11 Children's Autonomy and Symbolic Clothing in Schools
Help or Hindrance?

Dianne Gereluk

INTRODUCTION

Political, religious, and social symbolic clothing in schools has come under great scrutiny, particularly by the media and the general public. Most notably, France's legislation banning all 'ostentatious' religious symbols in schools took a bold stance in protecting its civic republican tradition in schools, despite not having established uniform policies in schools (Bowen 2007). Schools in England have come under greater pressure to address various religious requests to provide alternative uniforms to accommodate various religious symbolic clothing (DCSF 2007). American schools are grappling with how to create a cohesive and safe school environment when certain political and social symbolic clothing may challenge, disrupt, or cause offense to other students and the greater local community (Brunswa 2004). An increasing number of legal cases in the United States have ruled in favor of school authorities having more discretion to ban various symbolic clothing (Gereluk 2008).

In these (and numerous other) instances, banning symbolic clothing provokes an interesting dilemma about whether such bans undermine the theoretical ideals of fostering liberal aims in education, in particular, protecting and fostering children's future autonomy. Proponents of banning symbolic clothing and those in opposition both lay claim to protecting children's autonomy within the boundaries of the school gates. I consider both of these claims of autonomy by applying Rawls' principles of capacity for a conception of the good and a capacity for a sense of justice, and consider whether autonomy is impeded by the permissibility or banning of symbolic clothing.

Before moving on to this theoretical discussion, it is important to lay out what constitutes symbolic clothing. A possible interpretation is that all clothing is symbolic to a certain extent. What one wears, whether consciously or subconsciously, partially constitutes part of an individual's identity. While I do not completely disagree with the position that all clothing to a varying extent helps to form an individual's identity, I start from the assumption that 'symbolic' clothing must go beyond a mere fashion statement or preference, and must have a deliberate communicable intent that signifies that person's identity. I further suggest that broadly speaking there are three large categories of symbolic clothing: religious, political, and social. However, such categories need not be separate from one another, and symbolic clothing often may cross over in such a way that in many cases distinctions between the three categories may not exist. "The Islamic doctrine of *tawhid*, for example, suggests that politics, like everything else, exists only beneath the broad umbrella of religion" (Greulich 2008, xii). Given this premise, let us turn to the issue of autonomy and how it is applicable to the permissibility of symbolic clothing in schools.

SYMBOLIC CLOTHING AND THE PROTECTION OF CHILDREN'S AUTONOMY

Underpinning Rawls' notion of autonomy are two higher-order interests— those of a capacity for a conception of the good and a capacity for a sense of justice. In this section, I wish to consider whether a capacity for a conception of the good may provide guidance regarding the extent to which children should be allowed to wear symbolic clothing in schools. The capacity for a conception of the good entails having the capacity "to have, to revise, and rationally to pursue a conception of the good" (Rawls 2001, 19). Let us consider this principle within the context of symbolic clothing.

The first part of guaranteeing a capacity for a conception of the good entails that individuals must have sufficient opportunities to partake in activities that they find worthwhile and important to them. Wearing symbolic clothing may be valuable to individuals, particularly if the clothing is not just an accessory but is integral to their belief system. The five Ks of Sikhism highlights this point in that the physical symbols are not just an outward sign of one's faith, but are part of the customs and rituals that show one's devotion and commitment to the religion. The second suggests that individuals need not have a fixed conception of themselves, but "form and develop as they mature, and may change more or less radically over the course of life" (Rawls 1993, 20). Schools may provide children with various opportunities to be exposed to and understand different ways of life. The protections of both having the ability to pursue and to revise one's conception is integral to Rawls' notion of autonomy.

Given these principles within a capacity for a conception of the good, two drastically different positions can be drawn on the basis of protecting children's autonomy. On the one hand, the curtailment of symbolic clothing may be viewed as a way of protecting the future autonomy of children. Children will be influenced largely by the way that they are raised within the private sphere of their family and local community. Children should have an opportunity to shed their private conceptions to explore alternative lifestyles. On the other, the curtailment of symbolic clothing may be considered in direct violation of protecting children's conception of the good. Children require opportunities to develop their identity, and one important way is identifying themselves through their clothing. Is it possible to reconcile these two opposing positions regarding the permissibility of symbolic clothing?

A justifiable concern is whether children that are inducted into a particular belief system will be able to consider, explore, and revise their conceptions, particularly if the belief system is entrenched in various customs and rituals such as in the case of symbolic clothing. Harry Brighouse argues:

> Autonomy-facilitation requires a modicum of discontinuity between the child's home experience and her school experience, so that the opportunities provided by the home (and the public culture) are supplemented, rather than replicated, in the school. (Brighouse 2006, 23)

If parents belong to a particular religious affiliation of which their associations and shared sense of belonging is tied to symbolic clothing, it may be very difficult for children to resist the influences of their parents and community in not wearing the stated piece of clothing. Being born into an Amish community, for instance, will inevitably result in that child being inducted into symbolic clothing that is associated with that particular religious community. With very little exception, children will adhere to the customs and rituals that are a part of their parents' and community's beliefs, and if that particular community has symbolic clothing attached as part of their customs, then children inevitably will follow the customs.

If children have relatively little to no say regarding symbolic clothing, should schools provide a 'safe haven' that allows no symbolic clothing? The notion of *laïcité*—the separation of church and state in France— seems to argue such a point (Gereluk 2006, 2008). The notion of equal exclusion is prioritized in the French education system whereby all individuals are to shed their private associations at the school gates. The school is hoped to promote civic republican ideals that can be fostered without the hindrance or constraint of individuals' private identities. The aim is that children will be better-placed to consider and explore alternative perspectives and life choices without the encumbrance of their private familial and communal ties.

While the belief that schools should attempt to foster children's future autonomy is a desirable liberal aim and worthy of pursuit, it is difficult to see how well schools can achieve this aim by banning symbolic clothing in the hopes of creating a neutral space. Three potential problems exist with this position. The first is whether individuals are able to shed their private conceptions by removing their symbolic clothing. If the symbolic clothing is part of their belief structure—particularly if it is an integral part of their rituals and customs—removing the piece of clothing will either cause them great distress by compromising their identity or will not change their fundamental views about their viewpoints. The potential repercussion is that by taking a hard stance in the hopes of exposing children to different ways of living, schools potentially create a situation whereby they become more resilient and defiant in considering alternative lifestyles.

The second weakness is that by banning symbolic clothing in schools educators may potentially miss a substantive opportunity to openly discuss different perspectives. In effect, having children wear symbolic clothing may provide the impetus for significant teaching opportunities in direct and meaningful ways for children. Diversity and respect do not become theoretical abstractions, but become pressing issues that are experienced in the daily lives of students and staff.

The final concern, as I have argued elsewhere (Gereluk 2005), is whether schools can really create a neutral space. The ideal of laïcité in France highlights the practical problems of attempting to create such a 'neutral' environment. It may be the case that schools can limit or exclude certain curricular texts in the hopes of providing a neutral space, but in so doing, it creates a default position in what it excludes. Consider two examples: removing all religious texts in France, and removing the teaching of evolution in some American states. In both instances, by removing the particular texts, one creates another default perspective: in France, that of either secularism or the underpinning of the Catholic tradition, and in the United States, that of Christianity, or more accurately, Christian fundamentalism. Withdrawing contested issues in the curricula sends clear messages of what is privileged by the absence of its content. What is not said becomes an increasingly important factor. Removing evolution from the curriculum on the grounds that equal weight must be given to the different perspectives of how humans came to be sends a strong message that more weight must be given to religious perspectives. Attempting to create neutrality within the school walls may have the opposite effect of highlighting the absence of that which schools are trying to equalize.

Even if one claims that schools can be educative and neutral safe-havens for students to thrive, the way in which schools are structured make them less-than-neutral spaces. Most schools in Western countries are structured around the Christian calendar, which provides certain advantages to those who are of the Christian faith. Schools are closed on Sundays in France, rather than on another day of the week (for example, Saturday, which is the day of Sabbath). School holidays that coincide with Christian festivities will naturally favor students who share Christian beliefs. The historical vestiges of how children are taught may have strong Protestant or Catholic undertones. The subtle, hidden forms of the curriculum are pervasive in schools and it is virtually impossible to make a school 'value free' despite one's efforts. Selectivity about how children are taught, what is taught, and when it is taught are all laden with implicit and explicit values, making the school the least likely institution for being a neutral space. This line of argument is not compelling given the impossibility of a school to become neutral.

If the aim is to foster autonomy by banning symbolic clothing in schools, the likely effects are that at minimum, this will be ineffective because individuals do not simply 'shed' their identities at the door, particularly if the clothing is integral to their sense of identity. It is more likely that banning symbolic clothing in schools in the hopes that children will be more able to explore new cultures and lifestyles will only make them more defensive about their own associations, rather than able to explore new ways of life in an open and challenging way. And finally, schools will simply do a poor job of providing a 'neutral' space given the impossibility of such a task.

Let us move on to the argument that favors allowing symbolic clothing with the hopes of increasing children's future autonomy. This line of reasoning suggests that facilitating and developing children's future autonomy rests with allowing children to have increasing levels of informed decisions about how they wish to lead their life, which may or may not include what they wear. Children may view clothing as a significant part of their identity in how they wish to define themselves. This is particularly the case in adolescence, when much of their identity may be constituted by what they wear. Sports apparel, drama or music clubs, political and social symbols are often used by individuals to show their affiliations and allegiances. Given that clothing is an identifier of an individual's preferences, one might argue that allowing students to wear symbolic clothing may assist in developing children's future autonomy.

Allowing children to decide about the clothing that they wear based on reasons of autonomy, however, seems unconvincing as well in most instances. While individuals' autonomy might be influenced in the way that an individual dresses to express and associate themselves to things that they value, that does not seem to be an important enough reason to allow children to wear symbolic clothing in schools. And in most cases, the majority of students will be influenced by consumer-driven, designer label clothing targeted to children by the fashion industry.

> [T]he US embraces a conception of freedom that is highly individualistic and tightly connected to the free market. Consequently, a walk through the "shopping mall" of the typical American high school allows one to immediately identify groups as "the preppies", "the stoners" , "the jocks", "the gangbangers" and the "techies"—And back-to-school shopping is as important to an American summer as is the 4th of July. (McAvoy 2008, 1)

The pressure to purchase and gain status through the clothing children wear is arguably not based on informed critical decisions, but is a result of external peer pressure driven by a consumer culture. Children will have sufficient opportunities beyond school hours in which they can express and identify themselves in the ways that they dress. The opportunity is not closed to students forever, but may be limited to times when they are not in school. Autonomy does not rely on children's ability to express themselves by what they wear. Critical judgment and a capacity to understand, exercise, and deliberate in meaningful ways during school hours will do more to build autonomy in children than allowing them to decide what they can or cannot wear. In the second instance, schools may again provide a place where children do not have to succumb to the pressures of consumerism, and can instead focus on arguably more meaningful experiences that will improve their future autonomy. "If the symbolic clothing is non-essential, but forms a part of someone's identity, it is difficult to argue, despite the clothing helping to develop one's sense of individuality and autonomy, that this is a fundamental part of becoming an autonomous individual in schools" (Gereluk 2008, 127). Other, arguably more meaningful ways to develop children's autonomy exist beyond the often superficial realm of clothing.

That being said, allowing symbolic clothing may help facilitate children's future autonomy not because children get to choose what they wish to wear, but by the potentially educative opportunities that symbolic clothing may provide by exposing children to differences found in their school community. A heterogeneous student demographic (and one that is visibly different by the various symbolic clothing) may provide more opportunities for discussion and debate rather than a homogeneous one. For instance, the presence of a hijab in a largely white student school may create a dialogue between classmates about why one wears the hijab. The discussion about alternative lifestyles does not become an abstract theoretical discussion, but an integral aspect of the lives of fellow classmates. Despite parents' inabilities or reservations about limiting their children's exposure to alternative lifestyles, schools provide children with opportunities to be exposed to and participate in different meaningful experiences. And while schools will not level this out, providing a school system that attends to a number of different experiences will reduce such inequalities.

Conversely, the potential withdrawal of students who may wear symbolic clothing creates a narrower homogenous student demographic within the school boundaries. Attempts to ban symbolic clothing has often created situations whereby families feel compelled to withdraw their children from the school in order not to compromise their faith. This has negative consequences for the children who may be withdrawn from the school, and consequently, these children will have less exposure to other students. It also has a negative consequence for those students who remain in the school and who are not exposed to a more heterogeneous student body. Banning symbolic clothing may limit the opportunities for both sets of children to have the opportunity both within and beyond the school to meet and share different perspectives among friends and acquaintances.

The argument that schools can protect children's future autonomy by creating a neutral place to explore different ways of life seems untenable. The opposing argument that children's autonomy is developed by their freedom of expression through clothing seems unconvincing. However, exposure to different forms of symbolic clothing in one's daily school life may enhance the potential opportunities for students and staff to create a meaningful dialogue that is present in children's lives. A capacity for a conception of the good offers some guidance for the permissibility of symbolic clothing. The strength of this argument does not rest in simply allowing children to make decisions about their clothing. Rather, the weight of protecting a capacity for the conception of the good is fostered by creating an atmosphere that allows for children to be exposed to different backgrounds and perspectives. Such integration seems integral to facilitating autonomy in meaningful ways.

A CAPACITY FOR A SENSE OF JUSTICE

Rawls' principle of a capacity of a sense of justice is arguably applicable to symbolic clothing in certain contexts. A capacity for a sense of justice includes the "capacity to understand, to apply, and to act from (and not merely in accordance with) the principles of political justice that specify the fair terms of social cooperation" (Rawls 2001, 18–19). This entails ensuring that individuals are informed about rules and regulations that will have a direct impact on their lives; having substantive opportunities to participate in public matters if they so choose; encouraging a critical threshold of citizens to participate in the public sphere of a society in order that the political community does not disintegrate; and providing protective mechanisms, should individuals wish to re-enter public deliberation. If the overarching stability of a political community requires these factors to be fostered and protected, then schools may be one institution to cultivate such dispositions in children.

Symbolic clothing has not only been worn as an outward expression as part of one's identity, it also has been used as a sign of political resistance, civil disobedience, or solidarity. Simply put, students have used symbolic clothing to make a political comment about society. An important landmark American case, *Tinker v. Des Moines Independent School District*, highlights the use of symbolic clothing as a sign of political protest.[1] In 1965, three students were expelled for wearing black armbands to school to protest the Vietnam War. Having heard of the protest a few days earlier, the school adopted a policy stating that any student wearing the black armband would be asked to remove it, and failing that, would be suspended from school until they agreed to conform to the new policy. The initial court ruling was decided in favor of the school, noting that the school's discretion to ban the armband was a safeguard intended "to prevent disturbance of school discipline" (258 F. Supp. 971, 1966). The verdict was later overturned by the United States Supreme Court stating that student expression should be protected unless the behavior would "materially and substantially interfere with the requirements of appropriate discipline in the operation of the school" (*Tinker*, 1969). This landmark case proclaimed that "students do not shed their constitutional rights to freedom of speech or expression at the schoolhouse gate" (ibid.).

The *Tinker* case demonstrated that schools should be tolerant of issues of symbolic clothing in protecting students' free speech unless one could show that it would substantially interfere with the daily operation of the school. Yet more recently, this landmark case has been challenged with more discretion increasingly being given to school authorities in the United States. Timothy Gies, an American student, was expelled for wearing various political symbols on T-shirts including a peace sign, an anarchy symbol, an upside down American flag, and an antiwar quote from Albert Einstein (ACLU 2004). Gies was expelled on the basis that his T-shirts might become disruptive to the school by causing offense to his fellow classmates and those in the local community.

The rise in Muslim girls wearing the hijab has increased significantly in France as a sign of solidarity and political resistance to the banning of ostentatious religious symbols (Gereluk 2008). In 1989 three girls were expelled from a French state school. The school allowed the girls to cover their hair and neck but not their faces on the school grounds, and required they take it off once they entered the school. The girls refused and were barred until they would comply. After three months of standoff between the girls and the school, the girls gave in, and then ten days later rescinded their promise to abide by the ban. The debate became much more contested when four girls were barred from another school for wearing the hijab in 1993. This time, however, approximately seven hundred girls joined in support of the four girls, wearing the hijab as a sign of solidarity.

More recently, many American high schools and campuses have allowed students to hold Day of Silence protests to draw greater attention to the problem of bullying and harassment regarding one's sexual orientation. This initiative was set up by the Gay, Lesbian and Straight Education Network (GLSEN). Students dress in a variety of ways ranging from having their mouths taped shut to wearing political T-shirts about the event. The message is clear and communicable, and the clothes worn are clearly meant to raise awareness. Since 1996, the event has gained in numbers and status across the United States. Paula McAvoy (2008) points out that in raising political awareness toward greater tolerance for sexual orientation and gender expression through the Day of Silence event, students opposed to the event have begun a counterprotest. Protest T-shirts have been worn on the same day with such slogans as "Straight pride" or "Love the sinner, hate the sin." Participating schools are now reconsidering their stance to allow the Day of Silence given the potential instability with counterprotests among students.

The examples of the black armbands, antiwar T-shirts, the hijab, and Day of Silence protests all point to signs of political resistance and protest within the school walls. It is clear that schools have a duty to ensure the safety of their students and to minimize disruption that may inhibit the daily running and educational aims of the school. However, it is difficult to predict what pieces of symbolic clothing may cause such a disturbance that would in turn lead to massive unrest, as well as to volatility among the student body. Schools will naturally be inclined to take a cautious stance against this. On the one hand, schools wish to provide a safe and stable school environment. On the other, in attempting to do so, schools may take an overzealous approach to banning any piece of clothing that may be deemed inappropriate.

A distinction between symbolic clothing that is 'offensive' and that which is 'oppressive' is helpful here.[2] While symbolic clothing may be offensive, this is a relative notion depending on the nature of the offense, the extent and duration of the offense, and the number of individuals who may be offended. The notion of offense proves unhelpful in determining whether a school has strong grounds to ban symbolic clothing given the potential disruption. Those pieces of symbolic clothing that are considered offensive and that may disrupt the daily routine of school life may still be permissible under my principles. Symbolic clothing that is oppressive, however, is impermissible because of the intent to cause undo emotional or physical harm or repression to others. The political messages to which I allude are a case in point. All four examples, to one degree or another, incite some level of disruption or raise the level of debate in a public sphere. The students were explicit in making a political statement, and strife between students who disagree with the statement is a possible consequence. Symbolic clothing that is oppressive to others seems entirely justifiable to ban in schools— in this case, the counterprotest T-shirts. Symbolic clothing such as gang wear, the Confederate flag, and KKK symbols clearly send an explicit message to those who are not part of that group to intentionally suppress or harm others. The potential for disruption and unrest is evident, and the oppressive symbolic clothing causes undo physical or mental harm. Clearly, schools are fully justified in banning all forms of symbolic clothing that fall within this category.

If one of the underpinning principles of a liberal aim is to cultivate a capacity for a sense of justice, then allowing students to make political statements through their clothing may be one meaningful way in which students can learn to develop this disposition. Amy Gutmann (1987) argues that developing civic virtues in children is not a mere ideal or preference, but is vital if we are to preserve and foster democratic sovereignty. Schools have the ability to provide a political education that could teach all children the civic virtues necessary to participate and shape the political structure and stability of society as future adults and citizens.

Schools are integral to preserving the political culture, which is necessary for a liberal democracy to thrive. Understanding and participating in a political culture is not something one just comes to know, it encompasses certain habits, skills, and dispositions that each individual must be inducted into in a meaningful way. Eamonn Callan makes this point when he states that public institutions play a vital role in the way that they induct individuals into the larger political sphere:

> . . . it is a shared way of public life constituted by a constellation of attitudes, habits, and abilities that people acquire as they grow up. These include a lively interest in the question of what life is truly and not just seemingly good, as well as a willingness both to share one's own answer with others and to heed the many opposing answers they might give; and active commitment to the good of the polity, as well as confidence and competence in judgment regarding how that good should be advanced; a respect for fellow citizens and a sense of common fate with them that goes beyond the tribalisms of ethnicity and religion and is yet alive to the significance these will have in many people's lives. (Callan 1997, 3)

It requires a logical and coherent political education, deliberately considered and developed in children—not through mere osmosis or exposure, but through active and deliberate thought processes and engagement about civic virtues and the political structures in society. Viewed in this light, the place of symbolic clothing in schools may provide opportunities for meaningful discussion about public life that closely ties in with the students' private conceptions and views. It is an educational opportunity for teachers (and schools) to critically debate, provide open discussion about, and even model how individuals should participate, exercise, and understand the dispositions that should parallel the larger political public sphere.

If educators are sincere about developing a capacity for a sense of justice, then surely this does not occur through passive, abstract learning. Limiting discussion or removing potentially contentious issues that may cause offense, unrest, or instability seems antithetical to fostering the dispositions of a capacity for a sense of justice. Learning how to contend with substantive issues, such as symbolic clothing, that are present and real in children's day-to-day lives is something schools should address and confront rather than shy away from. The tendency of schools to avoid controversy does little to develop the dispositions required for individuals to actively engage in the larger public sphere. Allowing children to wear symbolic clothing presents opportunities for students to learn how to critically discuss and reflect upon their own values and the values of others. To be a good citizen also requires inculcating a notion of respect—again, for oneself and for others. And learning how to critically and rationally debate the merits and complexities inherent in symbolic clothing is central to the skills and habits that should be a part of learning to develop a sense of justice.

WHEN DOES SYMBOLIC CLOTHING GO BEYOND
THE PERMISSIBLE BOUNDARIES OF SCHOOLS?

It would be foolhardy to suggest that all symbolic clothing warrants the same protections and thus permissibility in schools within the principles of autonomy and justice. As I have argued elsewhere (Gereluk 2008), three criteria are helpful in banning some forms of symbolic clothing:

(1) whether the clothing creates significant health and safety concerns
(2) whether the clothing is oppressive to oneself or to others
(3) whether the clothing significantly hinders the educational aims of the school

It seems reasonable to suggest that it is justifiable to ban clothing that may cause significant health or safety concerns for the individual or for others. The onus, however, must be on the school to show how wearing the symbolic clothing would cause a significant risk to the student or to others. Attempts have been made, for instance, to suggest that the hijab could be a safety risk due to the safety pins that girls may use to pin the head covering in place. Yet this seems foolish for a couple of reasons. First, alternative adjustments can be made to ensure that the pins are not used during classes where there might be a potential risk, such as during physical education. For example, using an elastic band for the hijab instead of straight pins alleviates the potential safety risk.

A Canadian Supreme Court judgment in the case *Multani v. Commission scolaire Marguerite-Bourgeoys*[3] ruled out the safety concerns posed when a Sikh boy brought a *kirpan* (ceremonial dagger) to school. The kirpan was deemed by the school board to be a significant threat to the safety of other students in schools. Yet in a unanimous decision by the Supreme Court of Canada the judges stated that the threat of the kirpan is parallel to other everyday objects found in schools such as scissors, hockey sticks, and other objects that if used inappropriately would cause a potential safety risk to other students. Given that the kirpan is a dull object, is never used as a weapon by the Sikhs, and would be wrapped in a cloth and sewn inside the boy's trousers, the Supreme Court felt that the threat to other students was minimal. The onus is on schools to have strong grounds to ban symbolic clothing based on this criterion lest it be used as a rationalization for banning symbolic clothing rather than on significant and potential threats to the safety of students.

The second criterion—that of oppression—is based on the idea that symbolic clothing that causes undue and sustained physical or mental harm or suppresses an individual's future opportunities goes beyond the acceptable parameters of symbolic clothing. If the aim of schools is to protect children's autonomy, and significant evidence can be found that the symbolic clothing is oppressive, then banning the clothing seems appropriate. The criterion of oppression provides protections not only to those that are oppressed by wearing the symbolic clothing, but to others who may be oppressed by the message that the symbol may represent. In the former instance, symbolic clothing that oppresses individuals by the wearing of that particular accessory seems justifiable to ban. In the latter, symbolic clothing that has a clear intent to oppress and is used to show aggression or hostility to others is similarly intolerable.

The Day of Silence protest may be less clear cut in determining whether to:

(1) allow the event with the counterprotesters;
(2) allow the event, but ban the counterprotest T-shirts; or
(3) simply ban the event in its entirety.

When such an event is endorsed by the school, it might be reasonable to argue that all students should have the ability to express their viewpoints—for or against—even if it creates potential unrest or instability. I argue that the criterion of oppression, however, becomes a key distinction in banning the counterprotest T-shirts. The counterprotest T-shirts not only express a viewpoint that is counter, but their direct motive is to oppress and hinder the views and opportunities and is targeted at a particular group of individuals due to their sexual orientation or gender expression. Using this criterion, schools can justifiably ban the counterprotest T-shirts that are oppressive while still endorsing the Day of Silence event.

The final reason often cited to ban symbolic clothing is that the clothing may significantly inhibit the educational aims of the school. Similar to the first criterion, the burden is on the school to show how the clothing may seriously impinge on the educational aims of the school. Instances of symbolic clothing that fall in this category seem far and few between. The *niqab*, (a Muslim head dressing that reveals only the eyes) presents significant physical and social obstacles to that individual, and arguably goes beyond the permissible boundaries of what should be allowed in schools. Commonly, schools may justify banning symbolic clothing because it may impede the ability of certain students to partake in physical education classes. Two considerations seem important here. First, one must consider whether accommodations could be made to the symbolic clothing that would not compromise the individual's beliefs, and still allow the student to carry out the activities. Changing the hijab so that girls could wear a head covering with elastic rather than safety pins is one such small accommodation that allows the girls to partake in physical education and fulfill the educational mandate.

Second, if an accommodation cannot be met, one must consider whether there are other comparable activities in which the student could partake so that the educational mandate need not be compromised. Clearly, not all students need to fulfill *every* activity. For instance, not all students in every school will be exposed to swimming, horseback riding, or martial arts. Rather, what seems to be important is that students are exposed to a number of physical activities. Deciding that minimum threshold of activities is near impossible. It may be the case that students who receive little exposure to varied activities at home and in the community will require more activities within the school environment. Yet, if educational aims can be broadly met through a range of activities a student may engage in while wearing the particular piece of symbolic clothing, then schools should be hard pressed to ban it for its potential limitations on *some* activities.

CONCLUSION

Symbolic clothing offers some interesting opportunities for children and schools in developing Rawls' two higher-order interests: a capacity for a conception of the good, and a capacity for a sense of justice. In most cases, allowing children to decide what they wish to wear does not substantially develop or secure these two interests. Symbolic clothing differs in that the clothing goes beyond a mere fashion statement or preference and has a deliberate communicable intent, often associated with political, social, or religious beliefs (or a combination of the three). The inherent associations that the symbolic clothing has to these larger belief structures provides a greater and more substantive level of diversity that is visible and present among children and adults.

An attempt to foster autonomy by creating a level of 'discontinuity' between the school and home life, as Brighouse (2006) argues, may have unintended consequences either by increasing a political resilience or a withdrawal by those groups of individuals about whom we may have particular reservations regarding their future autonomy. Similarly, attempting to dispel any potential disruption or unrest in the school may also suppress an educational opportunity for students to develop a capacity for a sense of justice through symbolic clothing and the issues that arise from it. Symbolic clothing may offer opportunities for schools to find ways in which to provide meaningful opportunities for engagement that will help to facilitate children's autonomy and develop civic virtues.

NOTES

1. *Tinker v. Des Moines Independent School District*, 393 U.S. 503 (1969).
2. See Gereluk 2008, 110–118 for a detailed argument of the distinction between symbolic clothing that is offensive and oppressive.
3. *Multani v. Commission scolaire Marguerite-Bourgeoys*, [2006] 1 S.C.R. 256, 2006 SCC 6.

BIBLIOGRAPHY

American Civil Liberties Union (ACLU). "Judge Rules in Favour of Michigan Students' Right to Wear Anti-war T-shirt to School." *Free Speech*, 3 October 2003.

http://www.aclu.org/FreeSpeech/FreeSpeech.cfm?ID=13913&c=87 (accessed 5 November 2005).

BBC. "Cross Row Stokes Christian Anger." Bbc.co.uk, 15 October 2006. news. bbc.co.uk/1/hi/uk/6051486.stm (accessed 15 April 2008).

Bowen, J. *Why the French Don't Like Headscarves: Islam, the State and Public Space.* Princeton and Oxford. Princeton University Press, 2007.

Brighouse, H. *On Education.* London, New York: Routledge, 2006.

Brunswa, D. *The School Uniform Movement and What it Tells Us about American Education: A Symbolic Crusade.* Landam, MD: Scarecrow Education, 2004.

Callan, E. *Creating Citizens: Political Education and Liberal Democracy.* Oxford: Clarendon Press, 1997.

Department for Children, Schools and Families (DCSF). *DCSF guidance to schools on school uniform and related policies.* London: DCSF, 2007. http://www.dcsf. gov.uk/consultations/index.cfm?action=conResults&consultationId=1468& external=no&menu=3 (accessed 12 October 2007)

Gereluk, D. "Should Muslim Headscarves be Banned in French Schools?" *Theory and Research in Education* 3, no. 3(2005): 259–271.

———. *Education and Community.* London: Continuum, 2006.

———. *Symbolic Clothing in Schools.* London: Continuum, 2008.

Gutmann, A. *Democratic Education.* Princeton, NJ: Princeton University Press, 1987.

McAvoy, P. *Symbolic Clothing in Schools: Author Meets Critics.* Panel symposium, Cambridge, MA, 12 April 2008.

Rawls, J. *Political Liberalism.* New York: Columbia University Press, 1993.

———. *Justice as Fairness: A Restatement,* ed. Erin Kelly. London: Belknap Press of Harvard University Press, 2001.

12 Global Religious Education

Peter Simpson

INTRODUCTION

Global religious education is the hope of the world. Only through religion and education therein can people hope to attain in this life (not to mention the next) freedom, happiness, and peace. This thesis will not be accepted by most political or social thinkers, and in particular not by liberal ones; it commits, or at least is alleged to, the sins of uniting religion to politics and of denying people the right not to be religious. Actually, it commits neither sin. But, be that as it may, the opposition to it by liberals is self-serving, and their alternative form of government commits worse 'sins.' I will explain these two points in the first two sections that follow. I will then in the final two sections argue for my thesis about religious education.

LIBERAL OPPOSITION TO RELIGION IN POLITICS

Liberals base their opposition to the thesis in question on the ground that religion is not a publicly enforceable truth. But that religion is not such a truth is itself a claim that is either true or false. If it is false then why follow it, and why lay it down as the condition of decent politics? If it is true, then to form the basis of public life it must be a public truth deserving of being taught and implemented as public doctrine. Liberals, therefore, must do what they accuse the religious of doing, namely uniting politics to doctrine and denying people the right to reject the doctrine.[1]

Liberals, at least in recent years, have come to recognize this inconsistency. They have tried, therefore, to change their position in order to avoid it. The liberalism that is inconsistent, they say, is comprehensive or 'metaphysical' liberalism. The liberalism that is not inconsistent, and that can and should be made the basis of sound politics, is not comprehensive but 'political.' Political liberalism differs from metaphysical liberalism in that it does not make any grand assertions about some comprehensive vision of the ultimate goal of life, nor does it base its claim to rule on such assertions. Its claim to rule is that it alone can reconcile and harmonize all the conflicting comprehensive visions, including especially religious ones, and end war and oppression. It does this by resting its claim to rule on what is politically common to all religions and comprehensive visions, namely 'an overlapping consensus.' This consensus consists of political principles that everyone can endorse, even if on different grounds, and that can serve as the basis of a free and peaceful life together. Such a consensus, because it is not itself a comprehensive vision but is endorsable by all comprehensive visions, can be made the basis of political life without requiring, as those visions do, the forced imposition or suppression of any controversial doctrine.

This reply misses the point of the original criticism, and the version of liberalism it proposes no more escapes the charge of inconsistency than the one it replaces. The original criticism is that liberalism is inconsistent, not because it is a system of politics based, like religious systems, on a comprehensive vision of the good, but because it is a system of politics at all. Any system of politics must espouse some views while rejecting others and impose some policies while forbidding others. Liberalism itself espouses the view that comprehensive views of the good should not form the basis of public life, and it imposes the policy that such views should be forbidden from determining policy. So liberalism does forcibly impose one doctrine, namely this doctrine of liberalism itself (even if this be only 'political' liberalism). Indeed, it cannot fail to do so if it is going to be a working system of politics. No system of politics could function as a form of public life if it excluded nothing and imposed nothing. Liberals effectively admit this fact when they call for the suppression of this or of that (as of religion in state schools). They should therefore also admit that this makes their position no better or more tolerant than that of their opponents.

One cannot sensibly retort that liberalism is more tolerant in its basic idea than other systems, for no system in its basic idea is more tolerant than any other. Every prevailing system excludes incompatible ideas from public dominance because not to do this is to give up being the prevailing system. So when challenged, liberalism too only allows freedom and tolerance to liberals, that is, to people who agree with liberalism about what should dominate in community and about what the consensus should and should not include.[2]

Nor can one sensibly say that liberalism is more tolerant because it tolerates more things, for that is first not a recommendation and second not true. Other systems tolerate things that liberalism thinks intolerable (such as racism, sexism, and the like); and those systems are not better for being thus more tolerant. There is no necessary merit in a system that tolerates more evil things.

Nor again can one sensibly say, in response to this, that liberalism is better because unlike the other systems, it tolerates all things that one may choose to do that do not interfere with what others choose to do (it only refuses to tolerate things which do interfere, like racism and sexism), for this begs the question. To adopt such an understanding of what is to count as tolerable is to understand toleration as liberalism understands it. So to say that liberalism is better because it is in this way more tolerant is to say that liberalism is better because it is liberalism. Any system at all can prove itself better like this.

CONSEQUENCE OF LIBERAL POLITICS

What is distinctive of liberalism, and especially in its more recent 'political' form, is its secularism or its denial of an independent political role to religion. Religion may exist in liberal systems but only as a private belief and practice and not as a public one. This privatization of religion, however, has proved to have grim practical results.

The prime such result is what we now call the state. Political power and organization has, of course, always existed in human life but not, until modern times, in the distinctive form that is the state. By 'the state' I mean, following Max Weber, that organization of political power which takes to itself a monopoly of coercion, that is, of the use of force to impose obedience to laws and policies. Let me quote:

> Today the relation between the state and violence is an especially intimate one. In the past, the most varied institutions . . . have known the use of physical force as quite normal. Today, however, we have to say that a state is a human community that (successfully) claims the *monopoly of the legitimate use of physical force* within a given territory . . .[3]

What Weber brings to our attention here is the difference between what existed before and what exists now. Before the modern emergence of the state, no institutional structure had a monopoly of coercive enforcement. The power to coerce was not concentrated at any one point but was suffused through the mass of the population. The nearest approach to the state in premodern times (though Weber does not mention this) was tyranny, where one man did possess something close to a monopoly of coercion over everyone in a given area. That was typically why it was called a tyranny: instead of all the citizens sharing control, only one or a very few did. Even kingships were not tyrannies in this sense because kings ruled through powers of coercion diffused in the general mass.

One sign of the accuracy of Weber's definition is the absence of organized police forces in the premodern world. The police force is the institutional locus of the state's ordinary coercive power and holds a place analogous to that held in the past by the armed guard of the tyrant. The functions we now depute exclusively to the police were performed previously by the citizens, who relied on themselves and their relatives and friends for the enforcement of rights and for defense and protection. Another sign is the professional armies that exist in our modern states. What we call a professional army used to be called a standing army, and standing armies were considered a threat to peace and liberty. They constituted a permanent power of violence in the hands of the rulers that the rulers could use to impose on the people whatever they wished and whenever they wished it. Liberty and peace were to be secured, not by such permanent forces of coercion, but by occasional armies composed of the people themselves, which rulers could only muster at such times and for such purposes as the people might approve of and willingly pay for, and which, when the time and purpose passed, naturally disbanded themselves.

The emergence of the state was made possible in large part by the advance of secularism and liberalism, by which I mean by the suppression of religion as a political power. The evidence is twofold: the state of nature doctrine invented by Thomas Hobbes and the Protestant Reformation.

The State of Nature Doctrine

This doctrine has two features that deserve special notice: it treats human beings as isolated units, and it treats political power as indivisibly single.

In the state of nature doctrine, people are thought of as moved by individual goods that divide and bring them into conflict. Individuals as such could happily unite if the goods they pursued were joint goods that required joint pursuit and joint possession. They would not unite, but they would live in peace, if the goods they pursued were not mutually exclusive. They would unavoidably come into conflict if one individual cannot pursue his goods without preventing other individuals pursuing theirs. Human goods would, in this case, divide and set at odds; they would not unite. Such is what happens in the state of nature, whether immediately, as in Hobbes' version, or progressively, as in Locke's and Rousseau's, or by idealized construction, as in Kant's and Rawls'.[4] Attached to this idea of the divisive character of human goods is also the idea of the equality of all individuals. That all human beings, qua human, are equal is an old idea. What is new in the state of nature doctrine is that the desires of all human beings are equal too. Earlier doctrines taught that some goods were intrinsically superior and that those who pursued these goods were superior in character (though not in nature) to those who did not. This inequality of character naturally carried over into inequality of social and political status. Such inequality can find no justification in the state of nature doctrine. What replaces it is liberalism. For if, first, goods do not unite but divide people, and if, second, all desires are equal, then the solution for keeping a peace that is equal for all is that each only pursue his goods to the extent and in the way that all others can also pursue theirs.

There is another way of keeping peace. One individual could dominate everyone else and pursue his goods at their expense. This solution is the very unequal peace of the tyrant. In practice there can be no such tyrant; he is only possible in idea. No mere man could manage to be sufficiently strong and clever to keep everyone else in subjection. But while an all-powerful tyrant is impossible, an all-powerful tyranny is not. In fact, as Hobbes saw, such a tyranny is necessary. For liberalism is intrinsically unstable. It requires people to refrain from doing what, by nature, they most want to do, namely pursue to the full their individual goods. Admittedly, anyone who attempted to do this would come into conflict with those around him and frustrate himself as much as them. But the temptation to do what one really wants must always be strong, and so, because the fear of the war of all against all is not enough to deter everyone all the time (or to deter the strong and clever much of the time), it needs to be backed up by the fear of the state. The state fulfills the role of the all-powerful tyrant and imposes, by brute force, liberal tolerance on chronically intolerant individuals.

The state as so conceived is the state of Weber's definition. No state could do the job required if there were other powers of coercion around that could rightly oppose it, for that would just perpetuate the war of nature that the state was set up to stop. The state must, by necessity as well as by the right of liberal doctrine, be a single, comprehensive power that brooks no rival. In particular it must brook no religious rival. The state can allow religions to exist, but only on two conditions: that they give up any claim to their own coercive power and that they accept the principles of liberal tolerance, especially as regards other religions. Otherwise the state must, in the name of liberal peace, suppress religion as ruthlessly as it suppresses any other opponent.

The state has to take to itself, therefore, a supremacy not just of power but also of teaching. It must impose on all religions the overriding belief of liberal tolerance and must forbid them the right to teach any doctrine that is incompatible with its own doctrine of liberalism. The state cannot, therefore, be neutral between religions. For it could be neutral while also being on a par with religions. But, to do its job, the state has to be superior to religions. It must dictate to them, if they are to be tolerated, both what they may publicly do and what they may publicly teach. For instance, it cannot tolerate a religion whose practices and teachings deny the authority claimed by the rulers or the rights accorded by them to other state-sanctioned religions. Yet all religions have to do this from time to time because it is of the essence of what a religion is that it have authority to interpret the will of the gods to men, especially about the proper forms of worship and about resistance to impious rulers. The state, therefore, in order to retain its monopoly of control, must take to itself a role and an authority that in all previous ages had been denied to everyone except priests.

The Protestant Reformation

Prior to this famous revolution, the religious authorities held a power equal and sometimes superior to that of the political authorities. The political authorities could not conduct the ordinary business of ruling, to say nothing of the extraordinary business of waging war, without the sanction of the priests and the performance of the due prayers and sacrifices. We are nowadays inclined to say that in the premodern world there was no separation of church and state. But this is inaccurate. In premodern times there *was* a separation of the religious from the political power. For both powers were *powers*, that is, sources of control within and over people's lives. Moreover, these powers were independent of each other, or if conflict arose, the religious power took precedence. For, after all, if there are gods, men are dependent on them and not they on men. The gods can be influenced by men through prayers and sacrifices, but they cannot be ruled by men. In the end, men's lives and fortunes are dependent on the will of the gods. Woe betide any merely human or political power, therefore, that would defy the gods or ignore their earthly ministers.

Such convictions are found not only in the pagan world of the Greeks and Romans (whereof their poetry and their histories bear eloquent witness), and not only in the pagan world of other ancient peoples, but also in the theistic world of the Jews, the Christians, and the Muslims. The Old and New Testaments and the Qur'an, together with the postscriptural histories of all three religions, bear as eloquent witness here as do the pagan writings. It is medieval Christendom, however, that probably gives us the most articulated version of the theory. The independence of the two powers and their duty of mutual support became crystallized in Pope Gelasius' famous doctrine of the two swords,[5] where what is to be noticed is less that the swords were *two* than that they were both *swords*. The spiritual power had as much its own coercive laws as did the temporal, and each fought to prevent its own force and authority from being absorbed by the other. Because they were two, neither could have, let alone claim to have, a monopoly of coercion. Indeed, neither had a monopoly within its own sphere, for the feudal system checked the power of the kings through the nobles and the power of these through the peasants, while the doctrine of apostolic succession endowed the bishops with an authority that neither derived from the pope nor depended for its continuance on his sufferance.

This state of affairs could only end, and a monopoly of coercion could only be secured by the political power, when the idea that religion and the gods were superior to politics and to human rule ceased to have so tight a hold over men's minds. In Europe the first step in this process was taken with the Protestant revolt against Rome. That revolt was not just a revolt against priests as the authoritative teachers of religion but also, of necessity, a revolt against the Church as an independent power in men's lives. Protestants only succeeded at the time in escaping the power of Rome and of the emperor, and only continued to succeed thereafter, because they made alliance with rival political powers and won from them both protection and support. This de facto dependence of the religious on the political power became, as was perhaps inevitable in light of the struggle that had existed between them up to that point, an absorption of the religious power into the political. No coercive power at all was left on the religious side, and the political power took over the monopoly of it. At the end of the religious wars that the Protestant revolt precipitated a key stage was reached when, first by the Peace of Augsburg in 1555 and then by the Peace of Westphalia in 1648, the principle was adopted of *cuius regio eius religio* or "whose the region his the religion." It meant that whoever held the political power in a given territory was to determine also what religion that territory should follow. A neater expression of the doctrine that the state has control over religion would be hard to find.

The main ingredient in this growth of monopolistic power was what can only be called the apotheosis of the state. Religion, even pagan religion, prevented such apotheosis because it taught the subordination of all human things to the divine. This subordination prevented men from believing that anything human could be the best or most powerful thing to which total obedience might be due. But, with the abolition of religion as a center of power and authority independent of the state, such belief became actual. It found striking expression in the remark of Hegel that the state (not the Church) is "the march of God in the world".[6] To believe that oxen or other beasts are gods, or even that the sun and moon and stars are, as the pagans did, was indeed foolish, but at least it kept alive the truth that the divine must be other than man and not under his control. An extreme of folly is only reached when, as in Hegel's remark, man and the works of man are identified with the divine.

So much should serve to falsify the alleged separation of church and state in the modern world. One does not separate the religious and the political merely by denying political power to religion or merely by denying ruling status to priests. One does so by denying divine power to the political. But to endow the political with what was previously reserved to religion is not separation of church and state; it is absorption of the church by the state. In medieval Christendom (as also in other religious civilizations) there was a true separation of the political and the religious powers, for both possessed control and authority and each could resist the other. But that was because there was no state, or no monopoly of coercive power, in medieval Christendom.[7]

One might argue in response to this that the state having a monopoly of coercion is a good thing. It puts a stop to war and oppression. But this claim is false in both its parts. The liberal state is only nonoppressive in the sense of oppression that liberalism itself defines. This is a frivolous way to discuss oppression. Few systems are oppressive by their own definition of oppression. If the absence of oppression is to be a way to judge between systems, we need a definition of oppression that does not beg the question from the start.[8]

The monopolistic state has not served to stop war either. It has created a war unparalleled in human history for death and destruction, namely total war. The world wars of the twentieth century are the supreme examples. Where the political power is only one among several powers, and where this political power is diffused through many different orders of society, a total mobilization of society for war is impossible.[9] No power has the monopoly of control over society to bring about a total mobilization of it, and that all the separate powers should agree to cooperate for this purpose, or to do so for long, cannot be credited. The diffusion of power, not the concentration of it into the state, would alone prevent total war.

One cannot even say that it was the totalitarian and not the liberal version of the state that caused total war. In the world wars of the twentieth century that were fought between liberal and totalitarian states, the liberal states caused at least as much death and destruction as the totalitarian ones, and these liberal states also pursued war when the totalitarian ones would have preferred peace. The Kaiser in 1914 may have wanted to extend the German victory over France from 1870, but he did not want to attack Britain or the United States. Hitler too, while he wanted to conquer the Slavic peoples to the East (and at least to neutralize France), did not want to fight Britain or the US. Mussolini did not want to fight them either. The German and Italian dictators wanted their own empire, but alongside and not against those of Britain and the US.[10] That Britain and the US fought, and for total enemy capitulation too, was the decision of these liberal states.[11] And if it be said they had to fight to save liberalism, this only shows that liberal states will fight for themselves and what they believe in like every other political system. So how is liberalism better as regards war then, since all systems will fight when they think they must? The only difference seems to be that liberalism will fight total wars while most of these other systems will not be able to, and that is an argument against liberalism and the state, not for them.

It is hard to see how humanity has gained from any of this.

RELIGION VERSUS THE STATE

In order to be rid of the monopolistic state, we do not have to return to the world of pagan Greece and Rome or to the world of medieval Christendom. There are many good things about the modern age, not least our advances in science and technology, that it would be ridiculous as well as churlish to give up. Some sort of mixing of the new and the old is required.

First, as a result of the above argument, we must recognize that the modern idea of the separation of church and state is but propaganda designed, consciously or not, to prevent the dismantling of the state's monopoly of coercion. Religion must therefore be brought back as a distinct force and motivation strong enough to defeat the state. For if people are to overcome the state's subjection of them and their lives to its all-embracing control, they must have somewhere to stand independently of it. To achieve that they must cease to believe, or to be tempted into believing, that the state is superior to the priest and has authority to determine what is and is not tolerable in religion. The best way to achieve this is, in turn, that they should believe that there is another god that stands above all human things as lord and judge. The belief in a divine judge is not only rational (and so fit to persuade the learned) but also the instinctive belief of mankind. The number of men who can really live as atheists, even in the face of imminent death, is vanishingly small. Certainly they are few enough to be able, for the most part, to be left to their own devices. The vast majority of mankind will always believe in some god or other. The important thing is that they believe in a god that stands above all human things and especially above the state or the political power. Hence the need for widespread belief in and teaching of the existence of such a god.

The teaching should not be in the hands of the state. The state is necessarily hostile to these beliefs (they derogate from its own power), and would, if it had to tolerate them as a public force, twist them to its own purposes. No teaching at all should, therefore, be in the hands of the state. Religious education could not be effective unless it suffused the whole educational process. State education, because of what the state is, is necessarily nonreligious if not antireligious. But non-state education, to be real, cannot just be lessons taught in private classrooms. It must find support and reinforcement throughout people's lives, which it will not do as long as the state is possessed of extensive control over people's material and personal existence. Internal checks, such as one finds in the US Constitution, are not enough. Such checks can and do exist alongside monopolistic power. There must be external checks coming from within society; or society must have a real separation from and independence of the state.

Religion, as already indicated, is the most powerful of these checks, but its power extends further. While the state should not be providing all the supports it now does, yet this cannot mean that no comparable supports should take their place. People are individually weak and dependent on others for almost everything in life. The key point is that they should not have to depend on the state, and on its distant and impersonal (and therefore eminently idealizable and divinizable) welfare structures and functionaries. Let them depend instead on those immediately known to them, their families, whom because of personal closeness they cannot divinize but whom they can love. The family is not just parents and children but also grandparents and grandchildren, uncles and aunts and cousins, as well as close friends. The family has historically been the most powerful source of independence from political control. It has got its strength too mainly from religion, since this has given the family its first roots and has surrounded it, and the rights and duties of parents, with the awe and sanction of the gods. Further, the family provides, when not corrupted, the means and substance of common life requisite for firm and lasting friendships, for mutual loyalty and trust, for sustained joint action, for the inventions of thought and art. It provides too the haven where there will always be a welcome, and the last resting place where the dead may be honored, remembered, and supplicated. Other associations can generate similar bonds, from those forged at school to those forged in common physical or intellectual endeavors. The friendships that such unions create form fixed centers of action independent of the state and uncontrollable by it.

That is why the more complete the state, the more hostile it has proved itself to be to such things, and in particular to the family where they all begin and to which they all somehow relate. The state cannot be all-powerful if there are powers among men that do not depend on it. The liberal state has acted in many ways to undermine the family and the independence of the family. The state control of schools takes from parents the right to decide how their children are to be educated. It also requires high rates of taxation that deprive parents of the freedom of choosing how to spend their own money. Similar high rates of taxation are required for the provision of public welfare, whose bureaucratic inefficiencies and invasions of family privacy must be endured by all except the very rich. The free availability, even the active promotion, of abortion and artificial means of contraception are also not without deleterious effects on the stability and health of family life. To say that all these things are key elements of individual freedom, which only killjoys or the indifferent could oppose, betrays neither thought nor honesty. Free sex is not part of freedom, unless yielding to the passions is freedom. Nor is freedom having one's money taken by others to determine how it is spent. Freedom is when one can make one's own decisions for oneself and one's family, and when one does so by following reason, not passion.

The destruction of the family, and of the religion that supports it, is the best way also to destroy the bands of comradeship, since the latter so often and so naturally finds its roots and supports in the former. The destruction is complete when to all this is added the ideology of individualism, born of liberalism's state of nature doctrine, wherein each person is considered a separate unit, endowed as a separate unit with his own individual rights and beholden to none in his choices, provided he not interfere with the choices of others. A doctrine more calculated to divide people than this doctrine of rights and of mutual noninterference is hard to imagine. A doctrine more calculated to reduce people to slavery is hard to imagine too. If the good, as liberalism teaches, is what appeals to each and what each has the right to follow, then not only will most people follow their passions most of the time, but also an all-powerful coercive state will need to be always on hand to stop those passions driving people into violent conflict. The result is that people are made into slaves and the state into a tyrant.

Such a condition is not freedom nor happiness nor peace, at least not a happiness or peace worthy of man.

ALTERNATIVE SOLUTION

The solution is to be found, as it has always been found, in traditional religion. By traditional religion I mean religion that teaches the existence of a transcendent God who cares for, as He will also finally judge, the creatures whom He has made. But a distinction must be drawn between religion's moral teachings and its speculative ones.

By speculative teachings I mean teachings about the nature of God and his creative activity. The Christian teaching that God is a Trinity is such a teaching, as is also the Jewish teaching that God spoke the world into existence in six days, the Muslim teaching that Mohammad is the last prophet of God, or the pagan teaching that things were created by the sexual congress of the first gods. These speculative teachings are often incompatible with each other (unless interpreted allegorically), but the moral teachings they are associated with are not. Nor do these moral teachings so depend on the speculative that if the latter are rejected so must the former. They are, moreover, largely the same while the speculative ones much differ. The speculative are also optional, even sometimes within the same religious community, and can safely be left unenforced (except by excommunication if necessary). The moral are not optional and can safely be required.

The moral teachings are twofold. The first, already mentioned, concerns the existence of a suprahuman power that is guardian of right, avenger of wrong, and final judge of the deeds of men. The second concerns the principles of right and wrong or how men ought to behave, in which alone (and not in the pursuit of the passions of liberalism's state of nature) happiness is to be found. Despite surface differences these principles are basically the same. The well-known Ten Commandments, inherited from the Jews, are a neat summary of them. For although the first three commandments about God and the Sabbath are not, as such, the same for all, they are nevertheless so in what they say about the need to pay divine honor, through determinate acts on determinate occasions, to the Supreme Being. All these commandments, while universal as regards their immediate content, admit of much particularity of interpretation and application as one descends to the details of concrete actions. In such interpretation and application differences between peoples and religions increasingly appear. But the same is true of all principles and laws, even those in force in liberal states. Men's actions, despite a general sameness, vary infinitely in particular details, and require for correct judgment the prudence born of age and experience. Yet even here the conviction is universal that there is a correct judgment to be made and that particular actions, like general ones, are in themselves right or wrong and not merely in relation to opinion or passion or interest.

Implicit in these commandments are the habits to be developed through and for keeping them, commonly called virtues. These virtues, like the commandments and principles, are also essentially the same and universally acknowledged. Their opposites, the corresponding vices, are no less universally recognized and no less universally condemned.

Religions agree in these doctrines. Even those who profess no religion agree in them. While it is true that people sometimes act against the moral laws and virtues, and while it is also true that none is free of the temptation so to act, few are brazen enough to believe, or to say they believe, that the laws are wrong and the virtues detestable. Those who are thus brazen make themselves hated and feared by everyone else, even by each other. Who would not hate and fear someone who cares not for the life or property of others? Such a one is ready to kill or rob whomever he meets and has made himself the enemy of mankind.

The moral doctrines form a consensus shared by everyone, religious and nonreligious, which one might well call an overlapping consensus. It embraces everyone despite their differences in other matters, the religious ones in particular. In order to understand and explicate this consensus there is no need of the lengthy disquisitions or controversial thought experiments beloved of professional academics. The principles of Right (as summarized in particular in the Ten Commandments) are this overlapping consensus, which has existed explicitly in this form within Christian, Jewish, and Islamic civilizations from the beginnings of each, and has existed implicitly and in effect in every other civilization and religion (however limited the range of others to whom it has at times been applied[12]). There is no need to hunt about for it in hidden places. It is right there in the actual knowledge and practice of everyone's ordinary and daily life.

That this consensus overlaps all religions and is separable from the speculative doctrines proper to each does not mean that it is separable from all religious beliefs and behaviors. Because the moral doctrines divide into a set of principles of right and wrong on the one hand and a belief in a transcendent guardian of these principles on the other, and because the latter involves religious convictions, religion is integral to the moral doctrines. Still, the precise relation that holds between these two elements needs explication.

First, note that the principles have a certain immediate self-evidence that makes them logically independent of the conviction about a divine judge. They retain their truth and universality even in the absence of this further conviction. That is why the nonreligious can hold to them no less than the religious. The moral principles do not logically need to be derived from nor to receive confirmation in any prior truths, whether religious or not. They can and do stand in and by themselves.[13]

Second, note that these principles can be used to judge religions and actions undertaken in the name of religions. Those who claim religious sanction for murder or theft or deceit can be judged criminal, for instance, and the religion which gives them such sanction can be judged corrupt. Or the principles can be used to show that those who think their religion counsels action against the principles have misunderstood or corrupted their religion. One can argue on these grounds that al-Qaeda's support of terrorism is a corruption of Islam, and Muslims have so argued. Another case is Bartolomé de Las Casas who condemned, in the name of their shared religion, the way the Spaniards conquered and ruled the Americas.[14]

Third, note that despite the separability of the moral principles from religion, religion is their best and most effective support. People, for whatever reason, are naturally religious and are affected in their actions and their convictions more or less by religion. Out and out atheism is rare among mankind and seldom an early or a natural development when it is. But non-religious men and atheists, or those who are so by persuasion and not by vice or passion, can have no grounds for complaint against the dominance of religious convictions in public life and education. Provided they accept and follow the associated moral principles that form the overlapping moral consensus (which they cannot fail to do except at the expense of what even they must concede to be reprehensible irrationality), and provided there is no state to force them to be educated in this way rather than that, they will suffer no inconvenience nor be forced to live in any way they do not wish.

Finally, note that even were the religious doctrines false, their utility could hardly be denied. While there are many motives for virtuous behavior, not least that virtue is good and the source of happiness, for most men nothing seems to be a more powerful deterrent from vice than the conviction that, even if they escape human judgment, there is a divine judge who they cannot escape. Such a conviction lacks in this form all disutility too because if true, it informs men of where lies their ultimate happiness, and if false, inflicts on them no harm or loss. No one suffers or is penalized by living, if only through fear, a life of virtue. True, it would be better to live a life of virtue through love of virtue. But the religious conviction, properly understood, cannot but be a most powerful support for this too. It teaches, and in a simple way accessible to all, that virtue could not be an object of love to the gods nor vice an object to them of hatred were virtue not, of its nature, surpassing fair and vice not, of its nature, surpassing foul.[15]

That is a doctrine whose utility, if not also whose truth, no one could rationally gainsay. It is my final proof of the thesis of this chapter: global religious education is the hope of the world.

NOTES

1. I say 'right' rather than merely 'possibility' because people are always able, even in religious societies, to believe what they want. What they are not able to do, even in liberal societies, is publicly challenge prevailing beliefs and practices without suffering adverse consequences, from social ostracism to imprisonment or even death.
2. Susan D. Collins, *Aristotle and the Recovery of Citizenship* (Cambridge: Cambridge University Press, 2006), 15, 31–35, 169; Robert B. Talisse, *Democracy After Liberalism* (New York: Routledge, 2005), 59–61.
3. H. H. Gerth and C. Wright Mills, trans., *Politics as a Vocation* (Philadelphia: Fortress Press, 1965), 2.
4. The sources are Hobbes' *Leviathan*, Locke's *Second Treatise of Government*, Rousseau's *Social Contract*, Kant's *Universal History* and *Perpetual Peace*, and Rawls' *Theory of Justice*.

5. Set forth in his letter *Duo Sunt* of 494 to the emperor Athanasius, although the phrase 'two swords' (from *Luke* 22 v. 38 "Behold, here are two swords") is first used for this purpose by Pope Boniface VIII in his bull *Unam Sanctam* of 1302.

6. Georg W.F. Hegel, *Philosophy of Right*, §258

7. Note that the state does not cease to have a monopoly of control just because the rulers are democratically elected. Elections determine who wields power not what power they wield.

8. A true definition of oppression depends on a true account of the human good and how it is to be achieved. Disputes about oppression are thus derivative from disputes about the good, and if liberalism is wrong about this, it will be wrong about oppression too.

9. The world wars were a function of mobilization, not of weaponry. They commandeered the whole society with all its material and mental resources for the effort of destroying the enemy. The sophisticated weaponry, and its availability in huge quantities, was made possible by this mobilization. Modern nuclear weapons have taken death and destruction to an extreme even beyond total war. But if anything can stop their use, it will not be the monopolistic state (which will use these weapons if it thinks it must, as the US did in 1945). Perhaps a renewed reverence for God might do it.

10. Hitler's views and intentions were put forward not only in *Mein Kampf* but also, and in some ways more clearly, in his so-called *Zweites Buch*. This book was written in 1928 but, for various reasons, Hitler decided not to publish it. A copy was discovered at the end of the war but was first published in 1961.

11. Hitler did, it is true, declare war on the US after Pearl Harbor, allegedly because of his alliance with Japan, but he did not attack the US. The US, on the contrary, had in effect declared war on Germany long before then by its war loans and arms shipments to Britain. Britain's own declaration of war on Germany in 1939 had come against Hitler's hopes if not entirely against his fears.

12. The commandments about not lying or stealing or killing or committing adultery are universally recognized within groups (even a gang of thieves needs a basic trust and honesty among its members if its thieving is to be successful). What is not so universal, but should be, is extending them to those outside the group.

13. Moral truths may ontologically depend on a supreme being, but they have a certain epistemological independence. Indeed, if there is a process of inference between the moral truths and a supreme being, it is from the former to the latter rather than the reverse.

14. Lewis Hanke, *Aristotle and the American Indians* (Chicago: H. Regnery, 1959).

15. I could also mention the works of charity, the involvement in community action, and the practical love of neighbor that religion also properly inculcates and inspires. These are implied in what I have already said about religion and the family and virtue, but an explicit discussion of them would figure in a full discussion of the values of religion and religious education. Here my focus has been on the first principles of religious belief and the moral commandments. I leave the fuller implications for social action to another occasion.

Contributors

Hanan Alexander is Richard and Rhoda Goldman Visiting Professor of Education and Israel Studies at the University of California, Berkeley and professor of philosophy of education at the University of Haifa where he heads the Center for Jewish Education. He is also a senior research fellow of the Van Leer Jerusalem Institute.

Harry Brighouse is Professor of Philosophy and Affiliate Professor of Educational Policy Studies at UW Madison. He is author of On Education (Routledge, 2006), and is currently working with Adam Swift on a book entitled Family Values, to be published by Princeton University Press.

Randall Curren is professor and chair of philosophy, and professor of education, at the University of Rochester in New York. He is the author of *Aristotle on the Necessity of Public Education* (2000) and many other works in philosophy of education, ethics, philosophy of law, and the history of philosophy. He is coeditor of the journal, *Theory and Research in Education,* and editor of *A Companion to the Philosophy of Education* (2003) and *Philosophy of Education: An Anthology* (2007), both published by Blackwell Publishing.

Dianne Gereluk is senior lecturer in the School of Education at Roehampton University, London, England. She is author of *Education and Community* and *Symbolic Clothing in Schools.*

Mark Halstead has an MA from Oxford in Oriental Studies (Arabic and Turkish) and a PhD from Cambridge for a thesis on the education of Muslim children in the UK. Early in his career he worked as a journalist in Lebanon and a lecturer in Saudi Arabia. He lived and worked for many years in Bradford, one of Britain's most multicultural cities. His most recent academic posts have been at Plymouth, Oxford, and Huddersfield Universities, and he is currently a research professor at Huddersfield. He has written widely on values in education, multicultural education, and Muslim schools and has served as a consultant to parliamentary committees on these topics. Recent publications include *Citizenship and Moral Education* (coauthored with Mark Pike, Routledge, 2006) and *The Common School and the Comprehensive Ideal* (coedited with Graham Haydon, Wiley-Blackwell, 2008).

Irfan Khawaja is assistant professor of philosophy at Felician College, an advisory editor for *Democratiya* (democratiya.com), and managing editor, with Carrie-Ann Biondi, of *Reason Papers: A Journal of Interdisciplinary Normative Studies*. He is the author most recently of "Lesser Evils and Dirty Hands," *Baltic Defence and Security Review*, vol. 10 (2008) and is at work on a book with the tentative title, *What Days Are For: Ethical Egoism and the Foundations of Ethics*.

Meira Levinson is an assistant professor at the Harvard Graduate School of Education, following eight years working as a middle school teacher in the Atlanta and Boston Public Schools. She is currently completing a book on the civic empowerment gap, focusing on civic and multicultural education in *de facto* segregated urban schools. Her previous publications include *The Demands of Liberal Education* (Oxford University Press, 1999), the coauthored *Democracy at Risk* (Brookings Press, 2005), and a number of articles and book chapters.

Paula McAvoy is a doctoral candidate in the department of Educational Policy Studies at the University of Wisconsin-Madison. Her area of study is the philosophy of education with specific interests in political theory, the aims of public schooling, and the ethics of teaching. Her dissertation is an argument for how public schools should respond to requests for cultural and religious accommodation.

Amy North is a research officer based at the Institute of Education, University of London. She is currently working with Elaine Unterhalter on the Gender, Education and Global Poverty Reduction Initiatives Project, which is concerned with global initiatives to advance gender equality in and through schooling in contexts of poverty, and the way in which these are interpreted and acted upon in different spaces at local, national, and international levels. Previously she was the policy officer for the Beyond Access Project and has worked with civil society networks on gender and education issues in Latin America, Tanzania, Kenya, and Bangladesh.

Gerhard Preyer is professor of sociology at the Goethe-University Frankfurt am Main, Frankfurt a. M., Germany, www.gesellschaftswissenschaften.

uni-frankfurt.de/gpreyer He is editor of *ProtoSociology an International Journal of Interdisciplinary Research* and Project www. protosociology.de

Yvonne Raley is associate professor of Philosophy Department, at Felician College in Lodi, NJ. Her areas of specialization are metaphysics and ethics.

Doret de Ruyter is professor in philosophy and history of education at the Department of Theory and Research at VU University Amsterdam. Before returning to her alma mater she worked as (senior) lecturer at the University of Glasgow. Her research interests include ideals in education, human flourishing, children's rights, and parental duties.

Harvey Siegel is professor of philosophy and chair of the department at the University of Miami. He specializes in epistemology, philosophy of science, and philosophy of education. He is the author of *Relativism Refuted: A Critique of Contemporary Epistemological Relativism* (D. Reidel, 1987), *Educating Reason: Rationality, Critical Thinking, and Education* (Routledge 1988), *Rationality Redeemed? Further Dialogues on an Educational Ideal* (Routledge 1997), and many articles on topics in philosophy and education. He is the editor of *Reason and Education: Essays in Honor of Israel Scheffler* (Kluwer 1997) and *The Oxford Handbook of Philosophy of Education* (Oxford University Press, forthcoming). He is past president of both the Philosophy of Education Society and the Association for Philosophy of Education.

Peter Simpson was born and educated in the UK but is now a naturalized US citizen living in New York. He is currently professor of philosophy and classics at the City University of New York. His main research interests are in ancient philosophy (chiefly Aristotle) and moral and political philosophy. A lesser, though related, interest is the phenomenological philosophy of Karol Wojtyla. He has written books on Aristotle, Moral and Political Philosophy, and Wojtyla and several articles ranging over the same areas.

Robert Talisse is associate professor of philosophy and political science at Vanderbilt University (Nashville, TN). His main area of research is political philosophy. He is the author of several articles and the books *Democracy After Liberalism* (Routledge 2005), *A Pragmatist Philosophy of Democracy* (Routledge 2007), and *Democracy and Moral Conflict* (Cambridge University Press, 2009).

Elaine Unterhalter is reader in Education and International Development at the Institute of Education, University of London. Her recent books include *Gender, Schooling and Global Social Justice* (Routledge) and the coedited volumes *Amartya Sen's Capability Approach and Social Justice in Education* (Palgrave, with Melanie Walker) and *Beyond Access* (Oxfam, with Sheila Aikman). She is currently coordinating a number of cross-country research studies on gender, education, and global social action.

Name Index

A

Aikman, S., 118, 121
Addis, A. 144
Adger, W. N., 73, 74
Ahlquist, R., 112
Ahsan, M. M., 182
Akhtar, S., 182
Albright, M., 139
Alexander, H., 32, 33, 41, 48
Ali, N., 187
Alilunas, L. J., 134, 153
Allen, C., 181, 186
Allen, W. F., 70, 71, 166,
Anderson, J. K., 144
Antrobus, P., 111
Appadurai, A., 111
Appiah, A., 60, 62, 79, 112
Archilochus, 36
Aristotle, 36, 37, 82, 92
Arnot, M., 112
Ashley, J., 187
Atkinson, D., 111
Atta, M., 91
Averett, J., 144
Axthelm, P., 142

B

Bacon, F., 41
Bailin S. and H. Siegel, 7, 8
Baldwin, T., 186.
Balzac, H. de, 36
Barry, B., 19, 193
Baylis, J., 110
Becker, L. C., 57
Benedict, R., 97
Benhabib, S., 11
Ben-Porath, S., 44
Bergman, L., 77
Berlin, I., 30, 32, 35, 36, 37, 38, 39,
    40, 44, 59

Bhabha, H. K., 112
Bin Laden, O., 91
Birdsall, H., 111
Black, R., 111
Bond, J., 129, 130, 155
Boni, A., 112
Boorstin, D., 131
Bourn, D., 112
Bowen, J., 198
Braidotti, R., 118
Brandeis, L., 139
Braun, M. C., 139
Brighouse, H., 3, 34, 38, 54, 72, 112,
    200, 210
Brock, G., 112
Bronfen, E., 118
Brown, G., 186
Browne, R. B., 142
Buber, M., 47
Buchanan, A., 24, 25, 72
Burchill, J., 187
Bush, G. W., 149, 151

C

Callan, E., 21, 33, 34, 39, 40, 207
Cameron, D., 187
Carmichael, W., 186
Carnegie, A., 137
Carlyle, T., 135
Carrim, N., 112
Carter, M., 138
Cavallaro, D., 144
Chan, J., 113
Chapman, S., 118
Chavez, C., 145
Churchill, W., 143, 156
Cicero, M. T., 33, 37
Clark, N. I., 133,
Clinton, B., 143
Cohen, R., 112

Columbus, C., 129
Connor, S., 67
Cooper, J., 81, 82
Cornwall, A., 118
Cowen, T., 143
Cromwell, O. 136
Curren, R., 3, 72, 74

D

Davis, J. E., 71, 112, 135, 139
Day, J., 167
Deci, E. L., 56
De Ruyter, 62
Descarte, R., 41,
Dewey, J., 78
Dhillon, P., 11, 193, 194
Diamond, J., 76, 77
Diener, E., 56
Dietz, 69
Dimond, S. E., 134
Dodds, W., 67, 68, 69, 70
Dostoevsky, J. M., 36
D'Souza, D., 193
Dyer, C., 194

E

Edelstein, A., 142
Edward, M., 112
Einstein, A., 205
Elliot, L., 111
Emerson, R. W., 140
Emmett, D., 59, 63
Erasmus, 36

F

Feinberg, J., 39, 57
Fishwick, M. W., 142, 143
Ford, G., 141, 143
Foucault, M., 34, 43
Franklin, B., 129, 133
Fraser, 113
Freire, P., 34, 35, 38, 47, 48
Freitas, D., 169, 170
Frost, R., 15, 16, 18, 19, 20, 21, 24
Frost, V., 21, 26, 27

G

Galston, W., 19
Gallup (G. H.), 129, 141, 144
Gates, B., 137
Gaventa, J., 112, 114, 120
Gereluk, D., 4, 182, 198, 199, 201, 203, 205, 208
Gibbon, P. H., 131, 140, 143, 144

Glaude, E. S., 156
Glencoe, 135, 153
Glicksberg, C. I., 131,
Goethe, J. W., 36
Goldman, A., 10
Gomes, P., 130,
Goodstein, D., 70
Gore, A., 112, 149
Graff, G., 91
Gray, J., 30, 32, 35, 38, 39, 40
Green, A., 110
Griffin, J., 55
Gur-Ze'ev, I., 34
Gutmann, A., 38, 39, 206

H

Halstead, J. M., 3, 11, 185, 188, 189, 191, 193, 194
Hansen, C., 70, 142
Hare, W., 55
Harrison, D., 187
Hartley, W. H., 135, 153
Hayek, F. A., 35
Hegel, G. W. F., 33, 36, 37, 38, 39, 42
Held, D., 111, 112
Herder, G, 33, 37, 38
Herodotus, 36
Herz, B., 114
Hickling-Hudson, A., 112
Higgins, I., 119
Hill, M., 115
Hitchens, C., 98, 99
Hobbes, T., 35, 215, 216
Hoekstra, T., 70, 71
Hook, S., 148
Hooks, B., 112
Holtzman, B., 4.
Honeyford, R., 185, 190
Hume, D., 35
Huq, S., 73
Hussein, S., 99

I

Ibsen, H., 36
Inglehart, R., 63, 64

J

Jackson, J., 133, 134
James, W., 139
Jefferson, T., 133, 134
Johnson, K., 77
Johnston, P., 186, 187, 188
Joseph, K., 185
Joyce, J., 36

Jung, A., 139

K

Kabeer, N., 114, 119, 120
Kahne, J., 152
Kammen, M. G., 134, 138
Kanner, E., 138
Kant, I., 33, 35, 38, 39, 73, 215
Kasser, T., 77
Kavka, M., 118
Kember, T. D., 144
Keller, H., 137
Kelly, C., 132, 133, 141, 146, 147
Kelly, R., 187
Kerry, J., 149
Khawaja, I., 3,
Kidwai, A. R., 182
King, E., 115
King, M. L., 129, 130, 131, 134, 138,
    145, 146, 151, 155
Klapp, O. E., 143
Kohl, H., 156
Kolbert, E., 70
Kraut, R., 55, 56
Kukathas, C., 17
Kunda, Z., 144
Kymlicka, W., 79, 80

L

Lather, P., 112
Lauder, H., 111
Lee, R. E., 133
Lewis and Clark, 137
Leland, M., 139
Levinson, M., 3, 42, 45, 46, 145
Levy, A., 169,
Lévy, B. H., 182
Lewinsky, M., 143
Lincoln, A., 133, 134, 138
Locke, J., 33, 35, 38, 39, 41, 81, 215
Lockwood, P., 144
Loewen, J. W., 148
Longwe, S. H., 119, 134
Lucas, R. E., 56
Lucretius, 36
Luke, C., 112
Lyons, L., 141

M

MacArther, D., 137
Mace, J., 73
Macedo, S., 17, 21, 22, 23, 24, 26, 27,
    39
Machiavelli, N., 33, 37,38

MacIntyre, A., 33, 38
Madison, J. 138, 139
Marr, A., 142, 146, 148, 149
Marshall, H., 112
Marshall, T., 139
McAvoy, P., 3, 202, 205
McCan, J., 149
McClenaghan, W. A., 134, 135, 153
McCowen, T., 112
McDorman, T. F., 142
McGraw-Hill, 135, 153
McKibben, B., 70
McLaren, P., 38
McLaughlin, T. H., 33, 34, 189, 191
Merry, M., 190, 191
Michelangelo, 57
Mill, J. S., 15, 33
Miske, 118
Modood, T., 181, 187
Mohanty, M., 118
Molière, 36
Molyneux, M., 119
Montaigne, 36
Monte-Sano, C., 129, 155
Moreau, J., 136
Mughal, S., 182
Mundy, K., 112, 121
Murphy, L., 112

N

Napoleon, 136
Newberger, E., 167
Newport, F., 130
Nietzsche, F., 36
Noddings, N., 45, 47
North, A., 3, 111, 115
Nozick, R., 32,
Ntuli, P. P., 112
Nussbaum, M. C., 72, 73, 112

O

Oakeshott, M., 30, 32, 35, 36,37, 40,
    41, 42, 43, 44
Obama, B., 131, 149, 150, 156
O'Hear, A., 189
Oishi, 56
Okin, S. M., 112, 187, 188, 190
Ostroushko, M., 138

P

Paavola, J., 73
Palin, S., 149
Pangle, L. S., 136
Parekh, B., 192

Park, R. 155, 156
Pascal, 36
Perlez, J., 77,
Perry, Michael, 26, 27
Pflieger, E. F., 134
Phillips, T., 186, 187
Plato, 34, 36, 37, 82
Plouffe, D., 156
Pomper, G. M., 144, 147, 148
Ponting, C. A., 82
Porpora, D. V., 131, 144
Powell, W. W., 111
Preyer, G., 4.
Proust, M., 36
Puschkin, A., 36

R
Rai, S., 112
Raley, Y., 4,
Rampal, 112, 119
Rao, N., 118
Rapport, 112
Rawls. J., 17, 18, 19, 20, 33, 35, 38,39,
    42, 54, 150, 168, 199, 204, 210
Raz, J., 38, 57, 62, 185
Redman, C., 76
Reich, R., 79
Rescher, N., 52
Richardson, R., 187
Rivlin, A., 139
Rizvi, F., 110
Robinson-Pant, A., 118
Robison, J., 144
Roosevelt, T., 133, 137, 143
Rose, P., 117
Rosenblum, N., 61
Rothko, 57
Rousseau. J. J., 80, 81, 140, 141, 215
Rushmore, M., 134
Ruyter, D. de, 2,
Rwanyange, R., 119
Ryan, R. M., 56

S
Sachs, J., 111
Sacks, J., 48
Said, E., 34, 112
Sandel, M., 33, 38
Sayr, W., 134, 153
Schlesinger, A. M., 136, 139, 147, 149,
    150
Schultz, T. P., 115
Schwartz, B., 138
Searle, J., 30

Sentamu, J., 187
Shrader-Frechette, K., 67, 75
Siegel, H., 2, 7, 8, 10, 12
Silverman, W. M., 142
Simpson, P., 4,
Singer, P., 77
Smiley, T., 156
Smith, H. L., 56
Smith, S., 110
Snellman, K., 111
Speizer, J. J., 144
Sperling, G., 114, 116
Spinoza, B. de, 105
Spivak, G. C., 112
Staid, E., 112
Steiner, G., 34
Stepp, L. S., 169
Stoetzler, M., 112
Stratton, A., 190, 191
Straw, J., 182
Suh, E. M., 56
Supp, F. 204
Sypnowich, C., 60

T
Tainter, J. 70, 71, 76
Talisse, R., 2
Tamir, Yael, 31, 32, 44, 45, 46
Taylor, C., 33, 38, 46, 47
Thompson, D., 38
Tolstoy, L., 37
Tomasi, J., 39
Truchard, J., 142
Truman, H., 137
Tyack, D., 42, 132,136, 137

U
Uleman, J., 12
Unterhalter, E., 3, 111, 113, 115, 119

V
Vaishnav, M., 111
Van Inwagen, P. 95
Vandemoortele, J., 110
Vavrus, F., 118
Vincent, W. S., 135, 153

W
Walker, M., 112
Walzer, M., 34
Washington, G., 132, 133, 137, 138,
    139
Watt, N., 187
Weber, M., 214, 216

Webster, N., 136
Wecter, D., 133, 134, 137, 138, 143
West, C., 156
Westheimer, J., 152
White, H., 111
Williams, B., 96
Williams, M., 82
Wineburg, S., 129, 155
Wolfson, S. C., 135, 153
Woll, P.

Woolas, P., 182
Wright, R., 76

Y
Yancy, A., 144
Yuval-Davis, N., 112, 118

Z
Zimmerman, J., 138, 139
Zinn, H. 156

Subject Index

A
Actions and events, 92
Agency assumption, 93

B
Bible, Christian 26

C
Capability approach, 72
Citizenship, 59
    and universal characteristics, 63
    Global, 59, 60, 67, 71
Civic value, 20, 22
Clothing
    Symbolic, 199, 200
Communitarians, 33
Compatibilism, 93
Concept of freedom
    Negative, 37
Conception of the good, 79, 80
Cosmopolitanisms, 51
Cultural difference, 9, 10

D
Danish cartoon affair, 183
Declaration of *jihad*, 101
Dilemma of democratic literacy, 31

E
Education
    Democratic public, 9
    Higher, 2, 166
    (Global) Religious, 212, 220

E
Environmental
    literacy, 76
    studies, 75
Evaluation
    Weak, 46

Extremism, 193

F
Frankfurt counterexample, 95
Freedom
    Negative concept of, 36

G
Gallup Organization, 140, 141, 144
Gender, 115
    quality, 110
Giraffe Heroes Project, 140
Global
    aspiration, 119
    Campaign for Education, 121
    citizenship, 51, 59, 67
    cooperation, 78
    cultural flows, 112
    interconnection, 119
    Lesson, 123
    obligation, 119
Globalization, 4, 51, 111
    Hyperglobalization, 111
Glocalization, 111

H
Hebrew culture, 31
Heroism, 136
Heroes, 140
Historical fatalism, 140

I
Ideals, 52
    Content ideals and, 54
    Educational (excellent/perfect values),
        53, 54
International contestation, 112

K
Kantian moral perspective, 73

Knowledge,
    Technical, 41
    Theoretical and practical, 41

L
Liberal (-s), 213
    democracy, 15
    institutions, 26
    nationalism (liberal communitarian
        view), 32, 45
    society, 16
Liberalism, 15, 16
    and democracy, 16, 18, 19
    Commitments of, 20
    Pluralistic, 39
    political, 20
    Two faces of, 35
    Universal (Comprehensive), 39,
        42
Liberty
    Positive and negative, 39

M
Methodological individualism, 94
Mozart case, 21
Mozart v. Hawkins, 20, 21
Multiculturalism, 99, 113, 183, 188, 191
    and essentialism, 191
    and extremism, 192
    Minimal (Tokenistic), 184
    Strong, 183
    Weak, 184

O
Objective goods, 57

P
Patriotism, 137
Pedagogical eclecticism, 122
Pedagogy of difference
    see Liberal nationalism
Perfectionism
    Weak, 46

Philosophical explanation, 32
Principle of capacity (Rawls), 204
Protestant revolt, 217
Protosociology, 4

R
Rationalism
    Critique of, 40, 41
Republicanism
    Critique of,
    National, 33
    Ideological (Ethical), 33
Role models, 144

S
Self-determination theory of psychol-
        ogy, 56
Singular affiliation, 191
Social epistemic liberalism, 24
Social theorists,
    Radical, 42
Society
    Ideal, 62
State of nature doctrine, 215
Subjective well-being theory, 56
Symbolic clothing, 204, 208

T
Terrorism, 91
    Islamic, 91
    Study of, 103
Toleration, 17

V
Value pluralism, 35

W
Ways of life
    Divergence and opposition, 16,
        17
Weak perfectionism, 45
Welfarist liberals, 18
Western political thought, 40